THE MIND AND THE MACHINE

WHAT IT MEANS TO BE HUMAN AND WHY IT MATTERS

MATTHEW DICKERSON

a division of Baker Publishing Group
Grand Rapids, Michigan

Published by Brazos Press
a division of Baker Publishing Group
P.O. Box 6287, Grand Rapids, MI 49516-6287
www.brazospress.com

Printed in the United States of America

Library of Congress Cataloging-in-Publication Data
Dickerson, Matthew T., 1963–
The mind and the machine : what it means to be human and why it matters / Matthew Dickerson.
p. cm.
Includes bibliographical references and index.
ISBN 978-1-58743-272-9 (pbk.)
1. Theological anthropology—Christianity. 2. Mind and body. 3. Spirit. I. Title.
BT702.D53 2011
233′.5—dc22 2010042053

11 12 13 14 15 16 17 7 6 5 4 3 2 1

For Peter Kreeft, Thomas Howard, and Dick Keyes,
who helped teach me to think and write carefully,
to pay attention to words, and to ask questions.

And for my wife, Deborah,
who steadfastly continues to sharpen my ideas (Prov. 27:17),
and who also challenges me to live out those ideas
(at least the good ones)
in my daily life as a father, husband, and fellow sojourner.

Contents

Acknowledgments

Profound thanks to Charles Taliaferro and Matthew Kimble for reading early drafts of this book and providing immensely helpful feedback (from your respective fields of expertise), as well as for occasional much-needed words of encouragement. Thanks to my editor Rodney Clapp for giving me the chance to write this book, for careful readings of both the preliminary and nearly final manuscripts, and for help making this a stronger book. Thanks to all my friends in the Chrysostom Society for your fellowship and for modeling such fine writing—and for letting me read from *poetry* and *fiction* at our annual gatherings, even while I was working on this book. And thanks finally to David O'Hara for your suggested readings as I prepared to write, and more so for your friendship over the past two decades; thanks also for occasional conversations explicitly and consciously philosophical, for many other conversations deeply philosophical but unconsciously so (especially ones about fishing), and also for many times of fishing when no conversations were necessary save the ones spoken with our reels, rods, fly lines, and flies.

Introduction

Why Any of This Matters

What does it mean to be human? More specifically, what does it mean to have a human *mind*? Is the human mind, in all its complexity, just a very complex machine? Can it be completely reduced to a *computational* model? Is the correct understanding of human persons that we are complex biochemical computers?

Until the past several decades, the vast majority of people would have answered those last three questions with a resounding no. They would have said that there is something more to the human person than the body, that we are something more than biochemical machines. To most people throughout history, humans were understood to be *spiritual* as well as *bodily* beings. For the past two centuries, however, a growing number of prominent, influential, and respected thinkers have answered the question differently.[1] They have said that the physical reality is *all* there is, that the human really is just a biochemical machine. Our minds, we are now told, are just very complex computers. If by the word *spiritual* one is referring to some sort of nonphysical reality, then no, we are told, humans are *not* spiritual.

This understanding had taken deep root by the middle of the twentieth century. In this first half of the twenty-first century, it is arguably the predominant understanding, at least in mainstream academic and scientific circles of the West. It is the view espoused in the teachings and writings of numerous influential figures over the past half century: scientists, philosophers, and mathematicians as well as artists, writers, and filmmakers. It is accepted in the university classroom and simply assumed to be true in countless newspaper articles and magazine stories, from the pages of *Popular Science* to those of *National Geographic*. And as this idea becomes more widely accepted, the implications are being explored. If humans are complex computers, then maybe we can get rid of our current biological mind (and body) altogether. Raymond Kurzweil is one of the chief proponents of this view. As a popular author and widely respected engineer and inventor, and as one of the PBS "sixteen revolutionaries who made America," as well as the winner of numerous awards for intellectual achievements, his views are highly influential. In his book *The Singularity Is Near: When Humans Transcend Biology*, Kurzweil predicts a rapidly approaching future "singularity": a "period during which the pace of technological change will be so rapid, its impact so deep, that human life will be irreversibly transformed." Eventually, he proclaims, the biological intelligence we now associate with human intelligence will be indistinguishably merged with computer intelligence. Our future will transcend biology.[2]

Kurzweil's ideas have been hailed by many other influential figures, such as Bill Gates (founder of Microsoft). There is now a regularly scheduled Singularity Summit, which has been held at prestigious institutions including Stanford University or in major cities, with high-profile speakers. As an example of how close to home these ideas can come, as I was completing this book I learned that Martine Rothblatt—the millionaire entrepreneur who founded both Sirius Satellite Radio and the multibillion dollar biotech firm United Therapeutics—had begun a nonprofit organization, Terasem Movement Foundation, Inc., and a related religious organization Terasem Movement Transreligion, in my own small hometown of Bristol, Vermont. Like Kurzweil, the fifty-five-year-old Rothblatt is predicting and working toward a future immortality through downloading our consciousness onto computers, and is using film and radio (and apparently a sizeable amount of money from her business ventures) to help promote her religious ideas.

The broad acceptance of these ideas is also evidenced by their transition from classrooms and philosophical treatises into popular media. In the culturally iconic *Matrix* trilogy of films (1999–2003), human consciousness has been connected to a computer, and the majority of humans live their entire lives in a virtual reality (without knowing it). Although humans still have biological brains and bodies (stored in vats and never used), the underlying assumption on which the Matrix is based seems to be that human *consciousness* is reducible to the bits and bytes that make up computer code and data. Indeed, in the much earlier film *Tron* (1982), the hero, Kevin Flynn, is captured by a computer when his *entire body* is scanned and downloaded into computer memory—again, with the assumption that a person is reducible to a pattern of data.

Of course, science fiction has us imagine the other direction as well: that of humanoid computers, or at least computers that think and act with human intelligence and apparent self-consciousness, even if lacking in humanoid bodies. Even as *The Matrix* shows humans whose consciousnesses exist in cyber reality, it also imagines computer programs (Agent Smith's and Sati's family of programs) behaving with human intelligence, and even human emotions. The list of examples goes on, including the films *Blade Runner* (1982), *A.I.* (2001), *I, Robot* (2004), and perhaps the most iconic example, the *Terminator* films and television series spinoff. The human imagination has seemingly long accepted the idea of the biological human and the silicon digital computer slowly merging and perhaps becoming indistinguishable—even when they are at war with each other, as in the more recent *Battlestar Galactica* television series and in both the *Matrix* and *Terminator* films.

The significance of such an assumption cannot be overstated. As Kurzweil's books illustrate, there are dramatic implications to our understanding of what it means to be human. Proponents of the view that humans are complex computers have argued the importance of accepting this understanding. To reject it, they argue, is to hamper scientific progress. To view the human as somehow spiritual is like imagining a ghost pushing buttons in a machine. It is superstitious and antiscientific. It prevents us from discovering, understanding, and ultimately making use of the real mechanisms of the computational human brain that controls our actions and determines who we are. Opponents of this view, by contrast—those who believe that there really is such a thing as human spirit that is not merely physical or reducible to a computational device—warn of the dangers of treating humans as though they were machines. They warn that it is dehumanizing and destructive to try to program, control, or tinker with them through conditioning, drugs, or genetic manipulation, as we might tinker with a car, computer, or DVD player. What if this new vision of human nature as computational really does lead to Kurzweil's prophecy of "irreversibly transformed" human life, they ask, but that transformation is based on something that is not true? What will we be transformed into?

These two different views of what it means to be human are mutually exclusive and profoundly at odds. What both sides agree on, however, is that the question is important: *Are we, or are we not, machines?*

The focus of this book is that one question. Are humans, in our totality, complex biochemical computers? Is the mind a machine? Hand in hand with that question, as the primary means of exploration, this book also asks the question, *What does it matter?*

Note that this is *not* the same as asking whether the human *brain*, with its immensely complex neural structure, is (or has the ability to function as) a powerful computer. As we will explore shortly, these questions are the same only if the *mind* and the *brain* are the same thing. The question of this book is whether the human *person* in her or his *completeness* is, and can be fully understood as, a computational device—a complex biological or biochemical machine. (I use the phrase *human person* above to distinguish from the *human body* in order to emphasize the possibility that the conscious person might be more than biological body. Hereafter I use the simpler *human* to mean the complete conscious *human person*, which may or may not be more than a biological human body.) As noted above, it is a widely held modern presupposition that the answer to this question is yes: that persons are nothing more than, or are fundamentally reducible to, complex computational devices.[3] Under the philosophical label of *physicalism* the assumption is that the *physical* human is the *complete* human, that all that exists of the human is the physical body.

Although the question is relatively simple to state, as I soon argue—and as the whole of this book repeatedly illustrates—it is vitally important in its significance and implications. Indeed, the broader underlying question is, what does it mean to be human? This is one of the most important and most interesting questions ever asked. It is a question of great philosophical interest. It is a question of anthropological, psychological, and historical interest. It is also a question of great practical interest, a question that matters as much to the present as to the past, as much to the common person on the streets as to professional philosophers, psychologists, and anthropologists. That is, it is one of the most important questions that *you* and *I* can try to answer today, tomorrow, and the next day.

What we believe it *means* to be human is vitally important to how we live our lives, day in and day out, at the most practical level. Professional philosophers (and books like this one) may help us understand what the question means and may provide useful tools for answering it, but ultimately, all of us ought to ponder the question for ourselves. We all live our lives based on some set of answers to this question, whether explicit or implicit, carefully thought out or not. And our answers matter. Our basic philosophical presuppositions, whether phrased in philosophical terms or not, impact our daily decisions and behaviors. That is to say, what we *think* about the world in which we live, and about our place in the cosmos, has a dramatic impact on how we *live* in the cosmos, and on how we interact with it and with our fellow creatures.

For many people, however, the idea of a *worldview*, or *weltanshauung*—one's fundamental outlook on life's major metaphysical questions—remains an abstract, academic, and esoteric concept with seemingly little practical significance to day-to-day life. Thus, it remains in the minds of many a topic interesting only in university classrooms (and perhaps not even there). When an academic defines the concept of worldview, his or her definition probably involves ontology, teleology, cosmology, epistemology, and, perhaps, cosmogony, cosmography, and even theology. All of these are important, but they can be difficult to translate from technical language to practical implications.

For example, we all have an implicit *epistemology*, a theory of knowledge, of what it means to know something, and how it is we *know* what we know. But our epistemology, though functional, may be subconscious. We may not even be aware of what it is, and we likely have a difficult time articulating it. We may know what we know, or think we know what we think we know, but we don't necessarily think about *how* or *why* we know it, and how or why we know that we know it, or just what it means to know it. In short, then, everybody has a worldview, but most people don't spend a whole lot of time thinking about what that worldview is, at least not in *philosophical* terms. And we don't think nearly enough about the implications of our worldview for how we live.

Sometimes the first important step is translation. Dick Keyes, the author of several excellent books, including *Beyond Identity*, and the director of a residential study center called L'Abri, suggests one helpful approach. He boils down one's worldview to three fundamental questions,[4] easy to state and to understand, but profoundly important:

1. What exists?
2. What is wrong?
3. What is the solution?

When phrased like this, it is easier to see why our answers will prove fundamental to how we live, whether we are consciously aware of our answers or not.

Consider, for example, the question, what exists? The question could lead in many directions. Do *I* exist? Do *other people* exist? Do *numbers* exist? Do *Platonic ideals* or forms exist? Does *God* exist? Do *objective morals* or ethics exist? None of these questions are trivial, and there is no universal agreement on any of them, except perhaps the first.[5] The focus of this book is what exists with respect to humans and human nature. What exists in the human individual? There are (at least) three different aspects of what it *might* mean to be a human, or three different parts of the human person that *may* or *may not* exist, and that have been explored, understood, affirmed, or denied by different philosophical traditions throughout history. These are *body*, *mind*, and *spirit*, sometimes collectively referred to as a tripartite soul.

Keeping in mind that there is no universal agreement on which, if any, of these three parts of the human person actually exist, here is one way they are traditionally understood. *Body* is the physical part of us—not only the skin, bones, heart, lungs, muscles, etc., but also the neurons in our brains that impact how we think and feel. *Spirit* is that part of us that might be said to be eternal or to transcend in some way the mortal body. If, as many religions and philosophies have taught, we as individuals have some sort of life after death—that is, a life after the death of our biological physical bodies—then since bodies obviously die, there must be some spiritual side of us that continues on after bodily death (perhaps, at some point, with a new and different body). The concept of *mind* (as distinct from the biological brain, which is just a part of the body) is often thought of as being in the middle, between body and spirit. The mind consists of our thoughts and identities as human persons, what we refer to or feel as our *consciousness* or *self-consciousness*. My mind—as in my memories, thoughts, beliefs, opinions, and emotional makeup—might remain largely unchanged even if my body were to undergo some dramatic transformation through illness, surgery, or accident, or simply over the course of time as my cells are continually replaced.

Of course, as noted, none of these three things *necessarily* exist. Different religions and worldviews have disagreed on what *is* and *is not* real. Those philosophers, poets, artists, and religious teachers through history who have spoken of any of these aspects of humanity *as though* they were real *might* be wrong. Some worldviews, for example, have denied the importance of, or even the reality of, the material body, or of material existence itself, saying that spirit is all that matters. Now, when one denies the philosophical reality or importance of the body, it is a natural step to next start denying the body itself—the bodies of others as well as the body of self. Extreme ascetic practices become common in the effort to free the spirit from the body or to deny the reality of the body altogether. We may abuse the body to free the spirit—scourging our own backs, or walking on hot coals, or simply denying ourselves any form of pleasure or even basic sustenance. Some worldviews are understood as denying the individual altogether, emphasizing only a grand collective unity or consciousness.

On the opposite side, the worldviews that have grown widely in acceptance in the modern and postmodern West have denied the reality of the spirit, claiming initially (for example, in some forms of Enlightenment rationalism) that mind and body are all that exist. However, if the material reality is the *only* reality—an assumption defining the worldviews known as *materialism* or *strict naturalism*—then it becomes more difficult (though not impossible) to understand mind as anything other than body.[6] And so this materialist worldview, in reducing the person to just a physical body, eventually also reduces the mind to just the biological *brain*. That is, it denies the traditional concept of the mind as being more than the brain, a mere physical collection of cells, and thus leaves us with the philosophy of physicalism. Not only does spirit not exist, according to this idea, but mind does not constitute a separate category from body, leaving the person as just body.

Modern Westerners might have difficulty seeing any important consequences of materialist presuppositions, precisely because it is such a common way of thinking that it is taken for granted. As I argue in the first chapter, naturalism (with its offspring of materialism and physicalism) is the dominant worldview today. Indeed, the noted mathematician and philosopher Bertrand Russell made the bold claim eighty years ago that "nobody believes" anymore that the human being could be anything more than a body composed entirely of matter, whose every movement is completely controlled by material laws.[7] That he would make such a claim shows how widespread the view was as early as 1930. Even if his use of the word *nobody* was an exaggeration, the philosophy of physicalism has, if anything, grown more popular in the century since Russell's comment. And seeing the implications of the worldview most common to your culture is a bit like hearing your own regional accent; we all think it is *other* people who speak with accents. So why would a denial of any spiritual nature in humans matter? Let's consider just one example of how it matters by looking at comparable states of body, mind, and spirit.

Goodness for the body, or a good *feeling* for the body, might be described with the word *pleasure*. Chocolate (for most people) and sex (for some) are prime examples of pleasure. For others it is coffee, backrubs, hot baths, fresh raspberries, or fine wine. By contrast, a good feeling for the mind we call *happiness*. Happiness of the mind and pleasure of the body are not the same, though they might (and often do) coincide. If my wife offers to bake one of her apple pies for me, I will start feeling happy well before the actual physical pleasure of eating that pie begins. Listening to my favorite music doesn't of necessity involve bodily pleasure, but it certainly impacts my happiness. Though it is certainly not easy to be happy in the presence of bodily pain, it is not impossible. At the end of one of my regular lunchtime basketball games (especially if I have been guarding one of the guys twenty years younger than I am), my body may be sore, tired, and uncomfortable. My knees and ankles can ache, I may have jammed a finger and be unable to move it, and I likely have a few bruises from collisions under the boards. In short, physical pleasure may be lacking. But if I played well, made some good passes, and kept the person I was defending from scoring at will on me (a task that grows harder with each passing year), I can feel quite happy despite the bodily discomfort.

Indeed, if we believe that mind is important as well as body, then we may pursue happiness as much as (or even more than) we pursue bodily pleasure. The serious professional or Olympic athlete, as well as the hardworking farmer or craftsperson, will often forgo bodily pleasure for extended periods of time, for the happiness that comes in the form of athletic prowess, or a well-tilled and skillfully farmed field, or a beautiful work of carpentry—something that comes only as a result of disciplined, difficult, and often physically unpleasant bodily labor. We might even deny our bodies feeling pleasure for the very purpose of making our bodies *look* pleasurable, which may help us feel happy.

Then there is what has traditionally been called the *spirit*. Many philosophers, theologians, and artists have claimed that analogous to a state of pleasure for the body, and happiness for the mind, is the state of *joy* for the spirit. And if these people are right that spirit is real, and joy is a spiritual state, then what applies to the relationship between happiness and pleasure may well also apply to the relationships between joy and happiness, and joy and pleasure. There are those who, even when there is no apparent reason for a mental state of happiness, and little or no bodily pleasure, still claim to experience spiritual joy. And they genuinely appear to exhibit *something* positive and transforming in how they live and act. The great twentieth-century Oxford University scholar and creative writer J. R. R. Tolkien, whose worldview affirmed the reality of spirit and mind as well as of body, gives a classic example of this in his famous story *The Lord of the Rings*. Approaching one of the darkest and most hopeless moments of the tale, when all seems almost lost and his mind is overcome with care and sorrow, the wise character

Gandalf is nonetheless able to experience and show joy. That joy is evident to the young hobbit Pippin, who is watching him. "Yet in the wizard's face he saw at first only lines of care and sorrow; though as he looked more intently he perceived that under all there was a great joy: a fountain of mirth enough to set a kingdom laughing, were it to gush forth."[8]

Many in our world have claimed to experience something similar. The joy that Pippin saw in Gandalf, others have seen in people like Mother Teresa, whose life afforded little in the way of physical pleasure, and who certainly was not "happy" about the circumstances of those she sought to help. Many others throughout history have been in the midst of circumstances that are by no means "happy"—the loss of a job, the death of a loved one, the failure of some important endeavor—and yet have exhibited some peculiar interior quality that defies their circumstances just as surely as my happiness at the end of a well-played basketball game may defy the physical pain in my aging body.

And on the flip side, there are plenty of examples of persons who have gained bodily pleasure but seem to have found no happiness or joy in those very things that provide that pleasure, just as there are persons who are doing fun things but finding no joy in them. The protagonist Jake, in Ernest Hemingway's *The Sun Also Rises*, has lost his ability to find joy or happiness in trout fishing or watching bullfighting, two pastimes he previously had greatly enjoyed.

Now, if we consider the spirit important, then we may also consider our spiritual *state* important, and we may be willing to forgo physical states of pleasure, or even happiness, for the sake of joy—perhaps by working toward something spiritually significant, such as Mother Teresa and Gandalf did, despite how difficult, frustrating, and painful those labors might be.

And here is where our worldview really comes to bear—where our answer to the question, *what exists*? becomes dramatically important, whether we realize it or not. If we believe only in the body, then joy *as a spiritual state* must be understood as an illusion. That doesn't mean that people don't experience what we call *joy*. It means only that the state of joy is not a spiritual state at all, but simply a bodily state: a chemical reaction in the brain that may have bodily or material significance, but not spiritual significance. After all, if only the body exists, and spirit is an illusion, then all of our states are bodily. This is what the philosophy of physicalism tells us. It denies the spirit, and by doing so inescapably also tells us that what we have called "joy"—what we had thought of as pleasure or happiness of the spirit—*must* be explainable in terms of body. Perhaps nerves in the brain trigger responses that we are conditioned to consider as pleasurable and that we associate, wrongly, with some spiritual reality that turns out not to exist.

If we really believe that spirit is not real, then whether we consciously decide to act on this or not, what ultimately becomes important to us is the state of our body. In particular, why bother to work toward a state that feels "good" for the *spirit* (that is, a state of joy) if we have no spirit? Once we realize that the body is all that exists, we should work instead toward a *bodily* state of feeling "good" (which is to say, a state of physical pleasure). Of course, as mentioned, if spirit is illusion, then mind (however complex) seems also to reduce to body, and so happiness as well as joy reduces to some physical sensation. Thus, finding joy or happiness reduces merely to finding bodily pleasure (perhaps pleasure of the brain). But if we realize that our spiritual sense is just an illusion, then we should no longer be willing to endure bodily pain for the sake of an illusory spiritual joy.

What is true of individuals is true of cultures as a whole. American culture and, more broadly, Western culture of the twentieth and twenty-first centuries—shaped by Enlightenment rationalism, Darwinism, the writings of Marx and Freud, and a host of other influences—has largely denied a spiritual reality and affirmed only a bodily reality. When a culture affirms only the body and denies the spirit, it naturally becomes a culture that pursues pleasure above all things. Life quickly becomes a mass pursuit of bodily fulfillment. This, it could be argued, is indeed a characteristic of our current culture. We are pleasure seekers. And though we may not often stop and explicitly connect this aspect of our cultural behavior to our cultural view of body, mind, and spirit, and though we might not recognize in our culture's pursuit of pleasure an obvious implication of an underlying philosopshy denying spirit, the correlation is there and it is strong.

It is also true that when a person or a culture denies mind and spirit, and believes only in body, then any perceived illness of spirit or mind must be reducible to an illness of body. We would expect such a culture to become deeply dependent on pharmaceuticals to heal all its ills. If every illness is bodily, then every cure is bodily—which, again, is an accurate depiction of our current society. As William Dembski has noted (in an article about the impossibility of material machines being spiritual): "In place of talking cures that address our beliefs, desires, and emotions, tomorrow's healers of the soul will manipulate brain states directly and ignore such outdated categories as beliefs, desires, and emotions."[9] We might argue that this is already true of today's healers; we needn't wait for tomorrow, for we are already a culture seeking pharmaceutical solutions to our problems. Indeed, like most aspects of culture, the pharmaceutical industry, in addition to *reflecting* our cultural worldview, has almost certainly helped to *shape* that worldview (through extensive marketing) and contributed to the prevalence of physicalism. Thus, the industry has helped shape how we as a culture *act* with respect to illnesses of the mind—thus also creating a very large market for itself.

In short, then, our philosophies do not remain abstract and irrelevant. They are real and are incarnate in how we live. Or, as the late songwriter Mark Heard wisely noted in one his songs, "We end up looking like what we believe."[10]

And this returns us to the basic question of this book: What does it mean to be human? As noted, there are four closely related and commonly held philosophies that all imply that persons are merely complex machines—highly evolved biochemical computers. These four philosophies are: *naturalism*, *materialism*, *physicalism*, and *determinism*. We will explore these in the first half of this book, and so we should now define them a little more formally and discuss their relationships with each other.

The first three of these terms have subtle differences in meaning but are almost interchangeable. *Naturalism*, in the strict form, is the philosophical claim or belief that the physical, natural world is all that exists: there is no *super*natural or *non*natural reality. *Materialism*, as already suggested, is the belief that everything can be adequately explained with reference only to matter. This is generally understood as a philosophy stemming from strict naturalism: if nature is all that exists, and nature is purely physical (or material), then ultimately all effects must have a material cause, and thus matter (material) is sufficient to explain everything. As a result, everything real can be studied by the natural sciences; all knowledge can be reduced to what can be learned by the methods of natural science. *Physicalism*, to borrow a phrase from philosopher David O'Hara, can be understood simply as "materialism applied to the question of the nature of the mind."[11] That is to say, physicalism is the philosophy that the human mind is fully explainable with reference only to the biological brain and the laws of physics and chemistry.

One of the central assumptions of these philosophies is *causal closure*. The philosophy of causal closure is that the material universe is a closed system; if there is anything other than material reality (for example, a spiritual or supernatural reality), it does not impact the material reality in any way at any time; all material events have material causes. As we will show later, this is a philosophical belief. It may be correct. It may be incorrect. In either case, however, the assertion of causal closure is not a scientific statement, although—as one of the cultural "accents" that our ears no longer hear—it is not always acknowledged as an explicit presupposition and thus is often mistakenly phrased as a scientific result rather than as a hidden assumption.

A broad version of what might be called *determinism* is another subject of this book. There are many types of determinism. Narrowly defined, determinism is the philosophy that everything that will ever happen has already been determined. Note that it is possible (though not necessary) for a physicalist to be a determinist, and it is also possible to be a determinist without adhering to any form of naturalism. There have been adherents of both combinations of philosophies. In the latter category, for example, one might believe in the existence of God or the gods, and even in some sort of human soul, but still deny ultimate free will or at least any important consequences of human free will. Under this belief, God or the gods completely determine the fates of the universe as well as the decisions and actions of individual humans. One who held this belief would be a *super*naturalist, and also a determinist—but not a physicalist determinist. This is not a philosophy we will explore in this book.

A narrow version of determinism, what I refer to as *strict determinism*, compatible with materialism and physicalism, is that the state of the universe and the laws of physics are what determine everything that will ever happen. If the human person is entirely physical, as physicalism claims, and if physical laws deterministically govern all physical behaviors, then of course determinism applies to humans as well as to the rest of the cosmos: every *thought* of the human mind and every subsequent *action* of the human body are already determined. This is a possible physicalist version of determinism, rooted in the belief that human mind reduces to biochemical brain, and the brain simply follows laws of physics. Thus, the human person is a determined device: a complex computer, biochemical rather than digital, but fully programmable and in fact already fully programmed. At its core, this form of strict determinism accepts the presupposition of causal closure and denies human free will. If the human mind is fully explainable entirely by its material properties, then there is no place for free will; our thoughts and behaviors all follow from the laws of physics.

Note that many, or perhaps even most, modern physicalists are *not* determinists in this strict sense. As a result of the modern theory of quantum physics, many strict naturalists and physicalists who accept causal closure still believe in the possibility of real random events and thus are not strict determinists. Specifically, as the twentieth-century development of the field of quantum physics has theorized and provided evidence for, there appear to be subatomic quantum particles that exist in the physical universe but do not follow any *currently known* laws of physics. These subatomic particles behave randomly, and their behavior is able to impact the behavior of particles at the atomic level. Some physicists believe that while these particles exist and *appear* to behave randomly, we will one day discover deterministic laws that govern their behavior, just as we have discovered laws of gravitation, electromagnetism, chemical reactions, etc., and thus the world really is determined in the strict sense. Other physicists believe that these quantum particles actually do behave randomly, and that there are *no* laws that govern their behavior—not only no *known* laws, but no laws at all that might later be discovered—and thus there is true randomness and not a strict form of determinism in the universe. Put another way, if modern theories of quantum physics are correct, these quantum particles do not behave strictly computationally, like instructions in a computer program.

Of course, if there are random purely physical effects and events, then one could deny any human spirit, or free will, or any supernatural reality at all, and yet still believe (as many indeed do) that the universe (including human behaviors) is not completely determined. That is to say, even physicalists can believe that neither all events in the future nor all thoughts and behaviors of human persons are already fully predetermined by laws of physics.

The exploration in this book includes this broader form of physicalism, physicalism that accepts random quantum effects. In that sense, the book—though it explores a computational view of humans—is really about physicalism and not about strict determinism. Note, however, that even if this sort of quantum randomness exists, it is not the same as free will. Under an assumption of physicalism that also affirms random quantum behavior, we would have to say that human behavior, though not determined solely by laws of physics, is still determined jointly by laws of physics *and* by physical randomness, and not by any *will* of the individual (free or otherwise). That is, under materialism and physicalism, the human person, and indeed the entire course of the universe, *is still determined entirely by physical processes*, even if some of those physical processes have inherent randomness and thus are not hypothetically predictable even with complete knowledge.

This might be viewed as a broader form of physical determinism. Whether or not we use the term *determinism*, however, with respect to the basic questions explored in this text, I believe that a physicalist belief in quantum randomness reduces in practice to the same position as the physicalist's version of strict determinism. So, for the first four chapters of this book, I will use the word *determinism* in this broader way as synonymous with *physicalism*. Where the distinction is critical, however, I will briefly return to the question of quantum reality and explain how the basic arguments of this book hold even under the assumption of random physical behavior.

And this leads, again, back to the fundamental question with which we began this book. This book explores two different answers to the question, one stemming from naturalism and physicalism, and one that might come out of a particular form of supernaturalism. The approach is not to argue for explicit evidence for or against naturalism, or evidence for or against the existence of God or some supernatural being, but to look instead at the *implications* of how we answer the question. The book will begin with the implications of strict naturalism with respect to the human person and will then contrast these with the implications of a theistic worldview that denies causal closure and affirms a supernatural reality.

After introducing some possibilities and alternatives, and defining some important terms in chapter 1, the book addresses this question in chapters 2 through 4 by looking at three sets of implications. In particular, we will explore the implications of physicalism to: human creativity and heroism (chap. 2), human ecological outlook and practice (chap. 3), and human reason and science (chap. 4). We will explore how these assumptions appear not only in philosophical discourse, but also in popular culture and in scientific discourse—or what is, in fact, philosophical discourse disguised as science. All along, we will be asking the question of what our philosophical assumptions and presuppositions mean to how we are able to live.

In the second half of the book, we will look at competing implications of one possible nonnaturalistic (and much older) alternative worldview: a theistic worldview that sees humans as both spiritual and bodily beings, and moreover as beings created in the image of a creator.

The basic argument of this book is that a physicalist worldview of what it means to be a human person—a philosophy that says humans are complex computing machines (perhaps with random number generators)—denies the importance not only of creativity and heroism, but also of healthy ecology and (most surprisingly) of reason and science. On the other side, we will present a dualist view of humans that is different from the dubious "ghost in the machine" and argue that this dualist view affirms the validity not only of creativity and heroism, but also of healthy ecology, reason, and science. That is, to live out this worldview will (or ought to) dramatically impact our artistic, ecological, and scientific practices.

PART 1

IMPLICATIONS OF A HUMAN MACHINE

1

Ghosts, Machines, and the Nature of Light

In the year 2000, inventor, author, and self-proclaimed "futurist" Ray Kurzweil published a book with the interesting title, *The Age of Spiritual Machines: When Computers Exceed Human Intelligence*. As noted in the introduction, Kurzweil's books have been praised by numerous critics, and his ideas have been lauded both by popular media (from the *Wall Street Journal* to the *New York Times*) and by many leading intellectuals. *The Singularity Is Near*, a 2005 sequel (or updated version) of *The Age of Spiritual Machines*, was a *New York Times* best seller and was also listed in the *Times* as the thirteenth most-blogged-about book of 2005. Kurzweil has been given thirteen honorary doctorates and has received awards from three US presidents.[1] Even the numerous critics who disagree with his ideas (a list that includes many respected thinkers and writers) have taken those ideas seriously enough to respond to them in print.

Although *The Age of Spiritual Machines* was ostensibly about the tremendous advances made in the field of computing in the twentieth century, with confident predictions about more advances to come in the twenty-first century, the book was also about humanness—what it *has* meant to be human, and what humanity *might* look like by the end of the new century.

Among the fundamental ideas behind Kurzweil's predictions is the philosophy of *physicalism*.He accepts the premise that human beings are really programmed devices consisting exclusively of physical matter.[2] We are computers, as it were, though admittedly complex biochemical ones. Indeed, we are astronomically more complex than any nineteenth-century mechanical device that we may associate with the word *machine*, and so old connotations of the word *machine* would do us injustice. We are profoundly more complex in our "circuitry" than even the most advanced computer of our own day. Still, Kurzweil believes, although our brains and bodies are made of biological matter rather than digital circuits (and so we don't *look* like the computers that sit on the top of your desk or lap, or in the palm of your hand), we are nonetheless automated machines, or simply *automata*. Since we are made of physical material only, we are fully explainable in terms of that physical stuff: molecules, atomic particles, and subatomic particles. Thus, just as the behavior of a computer is entirely *determined* by the set of computer programs it is running, so also are all the behaviors of humans determined by the "programs" loaded into the biochemical computers we call our brains. Although there may be disagreement among physicalists about how much of the *programming* is genetic and how much is societal conditioning, the assumption is that there is *some program* controlling or determining everything. In common parlance, we may debate whether we are programmed by our innate "nature" or by our societal "nurture," but we are understood to be programmed somehow. And this underlying assumption is not often even questioned.

This view expressed by Kurzweil is widespread,[3] evident not only in the writings of academics, but also in popular culture. We do not see this view primarily in a portrayal of humans as behaving like machines; we are not often represented as being like the old-fashioned robots in science fiction films of the 1950s and 1960s: "Robby the Robot" from the 1956 film *Forbidden Planet*, or B-9, "The Robot," from the 1965–1968 television series *Lost in Space*. (Although, ironically, both of these examples were actually played by humans inside robot suits.) After all, we know too well what human behavior is like, and so any dramatically different view of humanness that presents us as overly wooden and robotic would not be perceived by a popular audience as realistic. Rather, we see it in the portrayal of computers as behaving like, and even looking like, humans. As noted earlier, widely viewed and enjoyed films and television series include: *The Terminator* (and several sequel films and television spin-offs), with its humanoid robots from the future who come back to our present either to save or destroy humanity; *The Matrix* films depicting Agent Smith and other artificial intelligence agents of the computer system as capable of human intelligence, expression, will, and emotion; the recent *Battlestar Galactica* television series (2004–09) with its humanoid and "spiritual" Cylons (in contrast to the 1978 *Battlestar Galactica* series, whose Cylons looked more like B-9 from *Lost in Space*); the Harrison Ford film *Blade Runner*, inspired by the Philip K. Dick novel with the telling title *Do Androids Dream of Electric Sheep?* and the film *AI*, based on Isaac Asimov's writings. Even the recent *Transformers* films starring Shia LaBeouf, based on the animated television series of the 1980s, portrays robotic beings called Autobots (programmed machines) who display emotions, have a moral universe of good and evil, and develop friendships with humans—though, unlike the previous examples, the transformers are not humanoid in form or (when they are not in the form of automobiles) are only vaguely humanoid, with torso, head, eyes, and four limbs. These and a host of other examples have made popular and brought into our day-to-day lives the notion that computers can behave just like humans. And if a programmable computing device can be indistinguishable from a human, it stands to reason that humans can also be understood as programmable computing devices.

Now, the behavior of any computer-controlled device in response to its input could, in theory, be known and predicted by somebody who knew and understood all the computer's code. That's what a computer program is: it is a set of rules and instructions specifying exactly what steps to take based on its data. So what if humans were also fully determined by our "programs"? Then the same thing that is true of computers would be true of us: every response we make to the sensory input of our surroundings could be fully determined and known in advance if we had a complete knowledge and understanding of all the neural connections in our brains—what is often called the "wiring" of our brain. This would be true not only of our actual surroundings, but of any hypothetical surroundings we might invent. With enough study of the brain, we could know exactly how any given person would react under any circumstance, real *or* imagined.

Another way of stating the premise of physicalism is that *mind* = *brain*. It is the belief that the human mind ultimately reduces to the biological brain, with its physical set of neurons and their connections that reside as a complex collection of living cells inside our hard, protective skulls.

For many who accept, along with Kurzweil, this notion of what it means to be human, it is not difficult to have a great faith in the future of computer technology or to accept the popular science fiction examples mentioned earlier as somehow realistic. Think of all the incredible tasks we humans do with our minds, including not only the elaborate muscle control used by the concert pianist to play a great concerto, but also the memory employed to learn the concerto by heart. And, of course, these tasks would also include the human creativity to write that symphony in the first place. If our human minds are merely complex computers—if human *mind* is nothing more than human *brain*—then why couldn't computers do the same things? The answer is that there is no reason at all why they eventually could not. Kurzweil's book makes reference to computers that are already composing music and producing paintings, and we know that the best computers can play certain strategy games, such as chess, better than humans. If the physicalist assumption is correct, then once our understanding of the brain becomes more advanced and computers become complex and fast enough, computers should be able to do, think, and feel all the things humans do. And they eventually will, we are often told (even if it doesn't happen quite as soon as Kurzweil optimistically predicts).

Indeed, since computers are getting faster and more powerful with each passing year, and also smaller and more portable, we should expect not only that computers will do the same tasks, but that they will eventually do them *better* and *faster* than humans. Take as witness the remarkable 1997 chess victory of the IBM chess-playing computer Deep Blue over the best human chess player in the world at that time, Garry Kasparov.

One of Kurzweil's predictions in *The Age of Spiritual Machines* is that by the end of the present century, we humans will have the ability to download our consciousness into a computer and thus live forever. Our thinking will even be improved by the addition of more and faster circuits. Our consciousness will continue in perpetuity, steadily evolving as data and as instructions in a computer. The computer will be conscious *with our consciousness*! Of course, the notions both of immortality and of better brains are widely appealing, and so Kurzweil's ideas have moved beyond his books and into our popular imagination—including previously mentioned well-funded efforts by organizations like the Terasem Movement Foundation to bring this vision to pass. Though some people today are appalled by this vision of immortality, others are enthralled. It is the new eternal life—as long as the computer memory storing our consciousness doesn't get erased and our backups don't fail.

A moment's thought about Kurzweil's basic premise shows that his book is actually *mis*titled. Kurzweil doesn't believe in human spirituality in any traditional sense of the word *spiritual*. He believes that humans are entirely physical beings. This is precisely why he believes that physical devices such as computers have the potential to eventually equal and surpass humans as computing machines, and why he believes human consciousness may someday be fully portable to computer memory. Computers will be *spiritual* only in the same sense that humans are spiritual under a presupposition of physicalism. But the very assumption of physicalism denies the reality of *spirit*, and so this physical human is not *spiritual* at all in any meaningful sense of the word; the human has body, but not spirit.[4] What Kurzweil really means by *spirituality* is simply *consciousness*. He is promising an age of *conscious* machines. But the central idea of consciousness, in human terms, is generally *self*-consciousness, or self-awareness. Humans are self-aware. And, according to Kurzweil, someday computers will be programmed to be self-aware also, or human self-awareness will be transferred to computational devices. Thus, the subtitle of Kurzweil's later book, *The Singularity Is Near: When Humans Transcend Biology*, is a more accurate representation of his ideas.

Now Kurzweil, though he may be among a small number of people willing to predict the porting of human consciousness to computers in the twenty-first century, is far from alone in his beliefs about the human mind being a computational machine. As early as the seventeenth century, both Thomas Hobbes and Baruch Spinoza, though lacking the depth of our modern knowledge of the brain, believed that humans were deterministic machines, with our consciousness fully explainable in naturalistic terms. By the twentieth century, there was no shortage of well-known philosophers, scientists, and psychologists putting forth the same opinion. B. F. Skinner argued for much the same thing in various essays and lectures, including his famous work *Beyond Freedom and Dignity*. The idea had taken full root well before the start of the twenty-first century. Thus, in the opening section of his 1994 book, J. Allan Hobson gets to the punch line that fundamentally motivates his work: "I can no longer make any meaningful distinction between the state of my brain and the state of my mind."[5] Hobson, like Skinner and many other well-known writers and thinkers of the past century, has taken the philosophical step (sometimes couched in scientific terms) of reducing human thought and consciousness to a biochemical phenomenon (complex though that biochemical process may be). Hobson's work has been praised by such Harvard colleagues as E. O. Wilson. If the material world really is a closed system, as so many suppose, then human consciousness and mind must (almost by definition, some would argue) be reducible to biological brain. And our brains (as both science and experience have shown) do possess very complex biochemical information-processing abilities.

Three Views of Mind and Consciousness

The wording used by many of these writers shows that they have no doubt about their underlying physicalist presuppositions. They assume without question that humans are a form of automata—deterministic and determined, at least in the broader sense; if not fully determined by known laws of physics, we are determined by physical properties, including both quantum physics (with its random or unpredictable behavior) and deterministic laws. Their ideas about human nature and human consciousness then follow from this assumption.

However, this physicalist assumption, that everything—including human nature and the human mind—is ultimately explainable with reference only to the material, is by no means the only view, though it has become a predominant and even religiously accepted view in Western academia. A competing worldview is that humans have both a spiritual and a physical nature; we are material beings made of the stuff of the earth, but not *merely* material beings. This nonmaterial part of our makeup might be called our *spirit*, or our spiritual side. And here the word *spiritual* means something different from Kurzweil's diminutive use of the word in the title of his book. It means something more than just consciousness as Kurzweil understands consciousness—the ability to carry out instructions, respond to stimuli, and have some memory or knowledge about the self. It means even more than indefinite perpetuity. It is an affirmation of something more than or in addition to the physical reality, not subject to material laws of physics, but which coexists with the physical world. And the affirmation of any spiritual reality that has any connection to the physical reality is a denial of causal closure, and thus of naturalism, materialism, and physicalism.

Traditional nonmaterialist views have associated the spirit with one's fundamental existence and identity, with something eternal that might continue its existence even if the material body were to die, or possibly even in the absence of *any* material body at all. The spiritual self is able to sense the presence or nature of other spiritual beings (including the divine being or other human spiritual beings), not through material means or material bodily sensations of sight, sound, touch, taste, or scent. Again, at the core of this idea of what it means to be human is that the spiritual part of the human being exists as something other than or more than (and possibly separate from) a material body, though possibly in intimate relationship with the body. That is what is meant by the words *spirit* and *spiritual* (which is why the very phrase "spiritual machine" is an oxymoron). If some form of this worldview is true, then while the human *brain* may be a complex biochemical computer, the human *mind*—the eternal human identity and consciousness—cannot be reduced to the biochemical brain (as Hobson claims); could not be ported to a computer (as Kurzweil hopes); and could not ever be fully mimicked by a computer, no matter how fast the computer and how powerful its circuitry.

It is worth considering briefly just what such an alternative model to materialistic humanity might look like. Broadly speaking, this philosophy is often known as *dualism*, although this term is problematic because it has two different meanings. The term *dualism* is sometimes used to refer to a religious understanding of the nature of good and evil, attributed to the teaching of the third-century Persian prophet Mani. Roughly summarized, Manichaean dualism is the view that there are two equal and opposite powers in the world, one good and light and spiritual, and one evil and dark and physical. These forces are perpetually balanced and perpetually in conflict with each other, and this conflict is worked out in human history. In this book I am *not* using the term *dualism* in this Manichaean sense, though the distinction between spiritual and material is not altogether unrelated.

Rather, I use the term *dualism* as a description of human nature, to indicate both a bodily and a spiritual aspect of that nature. Stewart Goetz and Charles Taliaferro, in their book *Naturalism*, define it as follows: "Dualism is the view that manifests itself in the ordinary belief that persons are substantial, individual beings who persist self-identical through time. It is our souls that endure across time, notwithstanding the radical changes in our bodies."[6] Even in this second sense, the term is broad and has several variations and associations that we will not seek to explore or defend. This definition includes any religions and philosophies that attribute something like a spirit or soul to humans or that deny that the material body is all that exists. It includes, for example, Platonism, Cartesian dualism, and Gnosticism (including Manichaean forms), as well as Christian and Jewish theism. Because of this broad meaning, many theists who affirm a spiritual reality avoid the term *dualism*. (Gnosticism and Manichaeanism, for example, have been viewed by the Christian church as heresies and as incompatible with a Christian understanding of reality.)

In this book, I use the term *dualism* in this second way, as a contrast to physicalism, to represent a worldview in which persons are understood to be bodily as well as spiritual beings and which takes both the body and the spirit seriously. In the final chapter, I explore in more detail the particular type of dualism referred to by Taliaferro as *integrative dualism*:

> Integrative dualism affirms that the embodied person thinks, sees, looks, glimpses, smells, tastes, touches, and so on, as truly embodied.

> It fully recognizes the united character of personal life, and does not leave the body and person dangling in scandalous disarray, picturing the person as inhabiting the brain or delivering commands to the brain from some remote, mental theatre.[7]

Because of the broad array of meanings of the word, however, it is worth a few more words about forms of dualism that I do not seek to explain or defend in this book. One common association of this "spiritual human" is with Cartesian dualism, or with Platonic forms of dualism, which view the *spirit* (or alternately the *soul*, or in some versions the *mind*) as distinct and independent from the body, but inhabiting and governing the body. Now, some acknowledgment of both spirit/soul and body, and of the difference between the two, is fundamental to all forms of dualism, and indeed may be considered as the definition of dualism broadly understood. But the form of dualism associated with René Descartes's Enlightenment rationalism suggests a very strict separation (a rational separation, as it were) between the two, in which, as philosopher Peter Kreeft summarizes, they have "nothing in common. Matter takes up space and does not think; mind thinks and does not take up space."[8] The very idea of the body as being located in space—being *spatially extended*—is an important part of the philosophy of Descartes, from whom we learned to think of space, and to locate objects in space, in terms of three-dimensional Cartesian coordinates (x, y, z).

The British philosopher Gilbert Ryle, in his book *The Concept of Mind*, rejected and critiqued dualism, and in particular this Cartesian dualism between mind and matter. He coined the phrase "the ghost in the machine" to describe what he considered an old-fashioned idea of a nonmaterial spirit inhabiting a material body, and doing all the thinking while just giving instructions to the body. "If my argument is successful," he writes, "there will follow some interesting consequences. First, the hallowed contrast between Mind and Matter will be dissipated."[9] Though later thinkers, even those with a materialist philosophy, would reject many aspects of Ryle's philosophy, the phrase he coined persists. Thus, the alternative to a materialist view of humanity is usually reduced to a ghost-in-the-machine view (as though it were the only dualist alternative to materialism), and then summarily ridiculed and dismissed. Indeed, the very step of reducing a nonmaterialist view to Ryle's ghost in the machine is often the most important rhetorical step in defending the materialist view and attacking a nonmaterialist view.

But for many who hold to an understanding that humans cannot be reduced to material existence, and that the human mind is more than just the biochemical computer known as a brain, physicalism and ghost-in-the-machine Cartesian dualism are not the only two views. Another possibility acknowledges that there is truth to both the spiritual and material views of reality. It affirms that humans are undeniably physical biological beings, with brains that really do think and possess memory, but that we are also spiritual beings with some sort of eternal soul or identity, and something that transcends the deterministic material composition. In this view, spirit and body both exist, yet they are not so distinct and unrelated as Ryle's reduction or as Descartes's dualism.

Interestingly, this other view may perhaps be illustrated by metaphors from science. Consider the nature of light. Or, rather, consider the *dual* nature of light. There was, for a long time, a debate about whether light was best understood as a particle or as a wave. Some, like Isaac Newton, presented and held to a particle theory of light. In the nineteenth century, however, most scientists had swung to a wave theory of light. These two theories were understood as being mutually exclusive and irreconcilable with each other, and for many years scientists continued to debate the subject with an either-or approach. Early in the twentieth century, however, many ideas, theories, and experiments came together to suggest the modern theory of light. This modern theory—a theory widely accepted today—affirms that light is both wave and particle. That is, it is both wavelike and particlelike. Light is a wave, but it is not *only* a wave; it consists of particles, but not *only* particles. Light has a dual nature. Indeed, this is understood to be true not only of light, but of all matter and energy.

The point of this analogy is twofold. The first point is that the simple reductionism of either the particle view or the wave view is false or incomplete. Light is *both* particle *and* wave, and reduction to one or the other is inadequate. But there is another sort of reduction that also misses the complexity of the dual nature, and this is our second point: it would also be inaccurate to say that the relation between particle and wave is simply that of a "ghost in a machine." That is, one could affirm both particle nature and wave nature but miss the complexity of the dual nature. Particle and wave are intimately related and linked; one doesn't merely reside in the other like a visitor giving orders.

Yet another illustration comes from the intimate relationship between electricity and magnetism. Both exist. And they can be measured with *different* tools or techniques. I may test whether something is magnetic by putting it near steel shavings and observing whether it attracts them, or perhaps just by attempting to stick it to my refrigerator. I use a magnet to find studs in my wall when I want to hang a new picture. I couldn't directly use a battery or electricity from a wall outlet for either of these tasks. But I could use a battery to light a flashlight bulb, which I could not do directly with a magnet off my refrigerator. Electricity and magnetism can be studied, explored, and made use of separately. Yet despite these differences, there is no Cartesian dualism between the two; they are not independent entities. Indeed, they are best understood—some would argue *only* understood—in conjunction with each other.

Changes in a magnetic field induce an electric field. This is how the gas-powered backup generator at my house works. The gas-powered combustion engine rotates wires in relation to a magnet so that the changing magnetic field causes an electric current through those wires, powering electricity through my house when a snowstorm knocks out our power line. Likewise, a changing electric field creates a magnetic field, as some of us may remember from high school science experiments when we wrapped a wire around a steel spike, then attached the ends of the wire to a battery, and found that the spike had become a magnet. Magnetism is no more a ghost in the machine of electricity than electricity is a ghost in the machine of magnetism. (As a side note, if we assume *a priori*[10] that magnetism is all there is, and if we had no tools for measuring electricity and did not believe in electricity, then we would assume also that all magnetic effects were understandable merely in terms of magnetic forces. And we would be wrong.) In any case, the point of these analogies is that, even from a viewpoint of natural science, we can see that there may be forms of dualism that are far more complex than mere ghost-in-the-machine reductions.

These analogies break down, however, as most analogies eventually do, in that both the particle and wave properties of light obey material laws of physics; both are open to the tools of scientific inquiry from the natural sciences (which is how the two natures were discovered in the first place). Spirit, however, is not material at all. Even if spirit and body have a relationship to each other that may be metaphorically more like matter and energy, or particle and wave, or electricity and magnetism, than they are like a ghost in a machine—at least in terms of interconnectedness, intimacy, and complexity—we cannot *measure* the relationship with different scientific tools; we cannot reduce the immaterial spirit to matter. While there are direct causal relationships between magnetism and electricity—that is, there are material *laws* that tell us *exactly* how a change in magnetic field will impact electrical current and vice versa—the relationship between spirit and body does not follow any *natural* laws or *physical* laws.

In that way, the relationship between spirit and body may be more like how we have long understood the relationship between mental happiness and bodily health than it is like electricity and magnetism. There is certainly some connection between happiness and pleasure, or mental health and bodily health. It is easier to be happy when our bodies are feeling good. And in the other direction, many studies have indicated that our bodies are healthier when our minds are happier; laughter really is good medicine, even for purely physical or physiological things like heart disease. But as noted in the introduction to this book, the relationship, while real, is not a direct causal one; it is possible to be happy even when our bodies are ailing or in pain, and it is possible to be unhappy and even miserable when our bodies are healthy or are experiencing pleasurable sensations. Indeed, many people turn to bodily pleasure (chocolate, potato chips, sex, or alcohol) precisely because they are feeling unhappy, and unfortunately they often find that the bodily pleasure does not drive away the mental misery.

In short, then, scientific inquiry, while being very useful for studying the material *body*, provides no tools for studying the nonmaterial *spirit*. It provides tools to understand the *brain*, but if the mind is more than the brain, then science cannot fully understand the *mind*. Spirit is not physical. It is not subject to physical laws. It does not occupy three-dimensional space in the same way a body does; it has no Cartesian coordinates. It cannot be weighed or measured. We may, at times, be able to observe the effects of the spiritual on the physical reality. (Historically, we may call these effects *miracles*.) Likewise, we may observe the effects on the human body of the human spirit or of the dual nature of body–spirit. But we cannot control these. We cannot carry out experiments on the spirit by performing physical experiments on the body, as though the spirit followed material laws. To claim that we could carry out physical experiments using the tools of natural science to somehow perceive or study spiritual reality is to assume that the spiritual was merely an extension of the physical, which is essentially a denial of the spirit *as spirit*. Even if our physical experiments on the body had effects on the spirit, and those spiritual effects in turn caused bodily effects, we would be able to observe only that the bodily causes had bodily effects. Indeed, the very nature of such an experiment would assume that the spirit was subject to physical laws, which is to assume that the spirit is not spirit but *matter*.

One further analogy that does not come from science might help illustrate a concept about human nature that cannot be reduced either to the merely material or to the ghost in a machine. Consider the relationship between characters and plot in a story. Think, for example, of your favorite novel. A plot is empty without characters. But neither is a plot simply a box into which to place a character; a writer does not create a plot independent of the character as a mere vehicle for the character to ride around in and then discard. (At least a *good* writer working with a *good* story does not do this.) Plot and character are intimately related. A complete story needs both. It is true that a character may have some existence that goes beyond the plot; the plot of a particular book can end, but its characters may eventually go on to inhabit another plot. Think, for example, of Arthur Conan Doyle's nineteenth-century sleuth Sherlock Holmes, who appears in some sixty stories, or of the numerous Dorothy Sayers novels involving her detective Lord Peter Wimsey, or of the more recent seven books by J. K. Rowling about the adventures of Harry Potter and his friends and adversaries. The plot and the characters are different entities, but in each story both plot and character are necessary for each other, they complete each other, and they are intimately linked.

Couldn't it be that spirit and body, though not the same thing, and not reducible to each other, are also related in a way far more intimate than is suggested by Ryle's metaphor, that the natural body—the biological body—is made for the spirit, and the spirit for the body, in a much deeper way than an apartment is made for a tenant, or a farm tractor for a farmer?

The Debate: Experiments of Thought and of Science

Let us return, then, to the question of whether humans are simply material beings, complex biological machines—whether the human mind is reducible to the biological brain. This debate has continued now over several decades and even, at some level, through centuries. Though heated at times, it has also often been enjoyable and enlightening, with contributions (on both sides) from many gifted thinkers and writers.

One relatively recent and fascinating entry into the debate is the Chinese room thought experiment posed by John Searle in 1980.[11] Searle himself is a philosophical naturalist and argues against dualism. "It is assumed," he writes in his 1992 book *The Rediscovery of the Mind*, "that the only alternative to the view that the brain is a digital computer is some form of dualism." He then firmly denies that notion. "Rhetorically speaking, the idea is to bully the reader into thinking that unless he accepts the idea that the brain is some kind of computer, he is committed to some weird antiscientific views."[12] In short, then, Searle denies that humans are spiritual beings and refers to a spiritual understanding as a "weird antiscientific view," and yet he still argues that human consciousness is more than computation—which is to say that the human mind is more than a biological brain following a program. In his 2004 book *Freedom and Neurobiology: Reflections on Free Will, Language, and Political Power*, he explains his own view further.

> The consciousness of the brain can have effects at the neuronal level even though there is nothing in the brain except neurons (with glial cells, neurotransmitters, blood flow, and all the rest). And just as the behavior of the molecules is causally constitutive of solidity, so the behavior of neurons is causally constitutive of consciousness.

> When we say that consciousness can move my body, what we are saying is that the neuronal structures move my body, but they move my body in the way they do because of the conscious state they are in. Consciousness is a feature of the brain in a way that solidity is a feature of the wheel.[13]

No matter how far artificial intelligence progresses, Searle argues, a computer cannot have a mind. Or, perhaps more accurately, he is claiming that a computer cannot *be* a mind, or that the mind cannot be reduced to a computational device manipulating symbols. (Thus, Searle is proposing and defending a view of human consciousness that is compatible with a dualist worldview, even though he himself does not believe in spirit.) One part of Searle's approach is a thought experiment of the following form.

Suppose in one room is a computer. It takes as input a sequence of Chinese characters provided by some person outside the room, who does not know she is writing these symbols for a computer but thinks she is communicating with a Chinese-speaking person. The computer then follows an algorithm: a computer program, which is a sequence of deterministic instructions. The program transforms the input into another sequence of Chinese characters that get sent back as a response to the person outside the room. Now, suppose the computer performs this task so convincingly that a native Chinese-speaker believes she is having a conversation with a human who understands Chinese. Does this mean that the computer really does understand Chinese?

To answer this, Searle posits another room in which there is a human who does not speak Chinese, but only English. The English speaker receives the same input (handed in through a slot in the door), follows the exact same algorithm as the computer (except written out in English instead of in a computer language), and produces the same output of Chinese characters (which he slides back through a slot in the door). Because the human was following the same program, the results are identical to that of the computer. Again, the Chinese-speaker would also be fooled into thinking that the human spoke Chinese. But it is clear now, to the observer who knows what is going on, that the human person in the room does *not* really understand a word of Chinese. If you asked him what the exchange was about, he would have no idea. The human doesn't understand what was written on the paper that was passed in to him, and he doesn't understand what he wrote on the paper that was passed back out of the room. He is simply very good at following directions written in English.

And that is the point of the thought experiment. Searle's conclusion is that the computer in the one room doesn't understand Chinese any more than does the human in the other. More broadly speaking, the computer doesn't understand *anything* it does; it simply follows instructions. There is no real *mind* at work in the computer, only mindless manipulation of symbols. There are real minds involved. They are the minds of the persons who designed the complex computer and also the minds of the persons who wrote the translation program and who certainly must have a very good understanding of Chinese. But the computer itself is not a mind.

Is Searle's argument—his thought experiment—convincing? For some it is. For many it is not. Most published responses to the article have been attempts to refute it. One reply or counterargument is that while the computer itself does not *understand* Chinese, the room *as a whole* could be said to have an understanding of Chinese. That is, the entire system comprised of the English-speaking human (or the computer) and her rules and dictionaries combine to form a *collective understanding*.

Another argument that has been used as a response to Searle (though it has taken many forms, and in its earliest form predates Searle's Chinese room) poses a different thought experiment. Suppose that we could create a nanocomputer that perfectly simulates a single neuron in the brain. We then choose a human and begin to replace his neurons one at a time. Initially, he has all human neurons. At the end of the process, his brain is entirely composed of tiny computers. That is, the brain has literally become a digital computer—in particular, a digital computer simulating a brain. But the process is gradual, one neuron at a time. The question is whether that human's consciousness ever disappears. Critics argue that if Searle is right, and if the conscious mind cannot be reduced to a computational device, then consciousness would have to disappear at some point during this process; the process ends with a fully digital computer and no remnant of the original human brain, and by Searle's assumption this digital computer cannot be conscious. The critics then go on to argue that it doesn't make sense for there to be any *unique* point in the process when conscious awareness would end. Would a person who has just one neuron replaced suddenly cease to be human and cease to be conscious? How about two neurons? Or three? It is hard to argue that a person who has lost or had replaced some small number of neurons would cease to be conscious, and it is likewise hard to argue that a person who had lost some number of neurons and was still conscious would suddenly cease to be conscious after the loss of just one more neuron. For these critics of Searle, it follows that the entirely digital synthetic brain at the end of the process must be the same as the human mind at the start of the process, and thus a computational device can be as fully conscious as a human.[14]

Searle, in reply, discounts the notion that the consciousness is either all or nothing, and suggests that it might actually disappear gradually rather than instantaneously. As you go through the brain prosthesis, he explains,

> you find, to your total amazement, that you are indeed losing control of your external behavior. You find, for example, that when doctors test your vision, you hear them say, "We are holding up a red object in front of you; please tell us what you see." You want to cry out, "I can't see anything. I'm going totally blind." But you hear your voice saying in a way that is completely out of your control, "I see a red object in front of me." . . . Your conscious experience slowly shrinks to nothing, while your externally observable behavior remains the same.[15]

In short, the subject of the gradual brain transplant would gradually cease to be self-conscious and would *become* a computational device—though he might still *appear* to be conscious.

There are many other replies, or attempted refutations, from a variety of disciplines and approaches. And there are (from Searle and others) replies to the replies, and so on, illustrating just how intriguing this discussion is, and how potentially important is the conclusion. The debate directly relates to the question of whether humans are just complex computers. Are we, like computers, completely governed by some sort of programming? Are our minds the same as our brains, and could our brains theoretically be replaced by computer circuitry without loss of human consciousness? The conclusions also relate, at least indirectly, to our basic worldview questions. What exists? Does the human person have a mind that is more than a brain? Does a human have a spirit? Or is a human simply a body? As suggested in the introduction, and as explored through the next six chapters, this has dramatic implications for how we live. A thorough summary of Searle's original argument, his more recent variations, the arguments against it, and the long ensuing dialogue of replies, would require a book-length treatment—as would a dialogue about Searle's concept of mind that denies spirit and yet still claims that there is a consciousness not explainable by computation.

What is interesting to consider, however, is the usual methodology of this particular debate, including both thought experiments and scientific experiments. The so-called thought experiments, such as Searle's Chinese room or the brain prosthesis, are more philosophical than scientific in nature. Thought experiments do not fit the framework of an experiment in the sense of the natural sciences. Their usefulness has been, and continues to be, debated. They have been used by both naturalists and nonnaturalists, by dualists and physicalists. In defense of thought experiments, Charles Taliaferro notes, "Thought experiments make explicit our conception of the nature of properties and objects, testing the adequacy of our conception schemes and enabling us to consider in what direction such schemes need to be enlarged, restricted, or abandoned altogether."[16] I would also argue that they are helpful vehicles for philosophical exploration and discussion. They help one, or even force one, to clarify ideas by exploring how those ideas might be worked out in various imagined situations, which may be possible but not actual scenarios or merely hypothetical (and perhaps impossible). They can reveal inconsistencies in ideas. Thought experiments also may avoid certain materialist assumptions present in scientific experiments, as we will see in a moment. And thought experiments engage our imagination, which is a vitally important aspect of human reasoning and learning.

Nevertheless, my own perception of philosophical thought experiments is that—while having the benefits mentioned above and being useful tools in helping us to think—they serve more often to reveal one's *existing* presuppositions regarding human nature than they do to answer the question of what the *correct* understanding is. What usually happens in discussions centered on these thought experiments is that persons in different philosophical camps think about the experiment and then explain the imagined scenario and answer the question posed based on the presuppositions they already hold. Furthermore, careful thinkers on both sides may do so in a way that is consistent with their existing presuppositions, and therefore each thinks that his or her answer makes the most sense, and that the other possible answers make less sense or no sense at all.

It is interesting, for example, that both Searle (who is a naturalist) and those who put forward the prosthesis arguments (who are also naturalists), still seem to think about the mind and consciousness in terms of physicalism; they both discount the possibility of a real spirit. This is subtly evident in their assumptions about the conclusion of the experiment after each neuron has been replaced. Both sides agree that if consciousness remained in the prosthetic brain, it would be an indication that consciousness could be explained computationally. Thus, Searle denies that consciousness would remain, and his opponents argue that consciousness would remain and is thus computational.

But what if spirit is real? More specifically, what if the human person whose brain was slowly being replaced was a spiritual as well as a physical being? It seems that while Searle's suggestion—the slow loss of consciousness—is one *possible* outcome consistent with this belief, it is not the *only* one. Consider this from a viewpoint of dualism or supernaturalism. Isn't it also *possible* that the human spirit, which together with the human brain gives us our consciousness, would continue on in relationship with the new prosthetic brain? Using a reasoning similar to that of Searle's opponents, but also a different underlying assumption, suppose a spiritual human had an accident or illness resulting in a leg amputation and replacement prosthetic leg (or arm, or hip, or heart valve, or all of the above). We would not expect that person to cease being spiritual—to have their spirit die or to desert what remained of the body—simply because of that prosthesis (or those prostheses). It seems possible, then (though I would not want to submit my own brain to the experiment), that the same might hold with a brain: that the spirit could continue to dwell in and with the body, despite the changes to that body and even to the brain—although if this happened, it is important to note, it would also be the case that the resulting digital brain implanted in the body would cease to be a mere computational device but would now be a part of a spiritual being. It is not so much the case that the spirit would dwell in a computer (as a ghost), but rather that each nanocomputer would be incorporated into the spiritual and bodily human person as a prosthesis (as would the artificial heart valve or prosthetic leg).

And this is where the thinking of Searle's opponents is faulty, or rather is restricted by their presuppositions against the possibility of spirit. In the same way that physical neurons in a brain (though composed of physical matter) may be *more* than physical matter when they are part of a human body inhabited by spirit, so each small prosthesis, though itself a small computer, would become *more* than a computer once it became a part of the human. In short, the new brain, because it would be inhabited by spirit, or would be part of a spiritual being, would no longer be a mere computational device.

Now, the point here isn't to argue that this is the correct answer to the hypothetical question of what would happen if the brain prosthesis experiment were actually carried out. We don't know what would happen. If we really are spiritual beings, then it might be the case that there is no *law* that specifies how it *always* happens, because the spiritual human is not subject to physical laws. The point is in part to reveal the underlying assumptions of the proponents of various views.

Perhaps even more importantly, we need to question the entire experimental methodology with respect to this question. Modern science, and in particular its experimental approach, has proven extremely effective in discovering properties and answering questions about the physical world. Its discoveries have been effective in driving new technologies. So we have come to place great trust in scientific experiments. Advertisers know this. We are told that their claims about everything from shampoo to breakfast cereal are backed by scientific experiments. While thought experiments are not intended as scientific experiments, they may draw some of their popularity from the popularity of scientific experiments. Consider that at least some of the proposed thought experiments could be carried out as actual experiments, at least in theory.

Indeed, some of the modern history of the discussion of whether the human mind is a computational device can be traced to yet another famous experiment—an experiment that has been carried out numerous times and continues to be repeated in different formats and versions on a regular basis. The experiment is called the Turing test, named after Alan Turing. The Turing test is a proposal for determining a machine's ability to demonstrate intelligence. Suggested by Alan Turing in 1950, in his paper "Computing Machinery and Intelligence," it is based on the premise that the use of natural language, and especially the ability to carry on a conversation, is one of the most complex tasks demonstrating intelligence. It is a test of what we call natural language *processing*—though even that phrase presupposes that the use of language can be reduced to a *process*.

The Turing test pits a human against a computing device in a competition of natural language use and conversation. The judge is another human. The judge carries on a text-based conversation with both the human and the computer, without knowing which is which. As with the Chinese room thought experiment, the judge is in a different room from both the human and the computer. But here, the experiment is a real experiment and not just a thought experiment; it is meant to be carried out as a real test. If the judge (or, in a repeatable experiment, a collection of judges) is (are) unable to distinguish between the human and the computer based on their use of language, then the computer passes the test, and we conclude that the computer is displaying human intelligence.

Daniel Dennett, one of the central figures of the debate arguing for a physicalist understanding of mind, in his article "Can Machines Think?" summarizes Turing's purpose in designing his test. "Turing proposed that any computer that can regularly or often fool a discerning judge in this game would be intelligent—would be a computer that thinks—*beyond any reasonable doubt*."[17] Dennett himself states his own complete agreement with Turing's premise about how we should view this test. "The Turing test," he writes early in his paper, "conceived as [Turing] conceived it, is (as he thought) plenty strong enough as a test of thinking."[18] And in his conclusion he states even more strongly, "My philosophical conclusion in this paper is that any computer that actually passes the Turing test would be a thinking thing in every theoretically interesting sense."[19]

Contrary to Dennett's hypothesis, however, a careful look at what we are really asking suggests that when we move from thought experiments to actual scientific experiments to try to determine whether human nature is best described by physicalism or dualism, the experimental approach (at least in the scientific sense) ought to be completely discarded. The Turing test may be interesting for many other reasons. Indeed, as a computer scientist I have often been fascinated by various incarnations. If we define "thinking" in a limited enough way, I suppose it might even be a reasonable test of whether a computer thinks. But as a test of whether the mind is reducible to a brain, it cannot answer the question.

The Debate and Its Physicalists' Presuppositions

Consider the fundamental assumption of these last two experiments, the Turing test and the brain prosthesis. They presuppose that the intelligence and consciousness of computers is testable by science, and in particular that the question of *whether* computers are intelligent ("in every theoretically interesting sense") or conscious is answerable by the scientific method. Dennett, for example, refers to the Turing test as a scientific test, "no worse than any well-established *scientific* test," and as such "we can set *skepticism aside*."[20] So is there a problem with putting complete faith in the ability of science to determine the intelligence of computers? Should we be willing to cast aside all our skepticism about the nature of intelligence, because science is involved? What about the nature of consciousness?

The answer depends, in part, on how we define intelligence and consciousness. If we define intelligence as the ability to carry out a certain task (or set of tasks), then—assuming the tasks are well enough defined—of course we can test intelligence by testing whether that task (or those tasks) can be carried out by the entity in question. The test is just an application of the definition. But most of the time, as is the case with all of the previous examples, the underlying definition of intelligence is the ability to *think like a human*. In fact, one of the underlying questions is what human consciousness is, and whether computers can be conscious *like humans*. Intelligence and consciousness become intimately related. Thus, Dennett and Kurzweil both talk about computers in terms of human consciousness and try to explain human consciousness computationally. Consider the claim of Kurzweil mentioned earlier: the prediction that we will one day download human consciousness into computers. Or consider the goal of one of Dennett's most famous books, *Consciousness Explained*, which claims to explain "the phenomena of human consciousness . . . in terms of the operations of a 'virtual machine,' a sort of evolved (and evolving) computer program that shapes the activities of the brain."[21] The Chinese room and brain prosthesis thought experiments, and the Turing test, all explore intelligence and consciousness in this sense, defining them in terms of what humans do. Moreover, the question of whether computers can think and be conscious like humans is seen explicitly as equivalent to asking whether human thought is computational: whether the intelligent human mind is reducible to the biological brain.

So what these tests are attempting to do is understand *human* consciousness and *human* intelligence through the scientific method.[22] Thus, the intelligent tasks are *not* the definition, but simply one proposed approach to get at something deeper: whether human consciousness and intelligence can be understood computationally. But there is a serious philosophical problem with approaching this question as though it were answerable within a framework of science. The scientific method presupposes the conclusion that the phenomena in question are explainable in materialist terms—in this case, that the mind is explainable in physicalist terms. Put another way, Dennett has put faith in natural science to prove the absence of the *nonmaterial* aspect of human nature. He claims that these scientific tests can conclude that dualism was false and physicalism was true.

Let us consider this further, because it is a pervasive problem. Science itself is an experimental method that assumes a set of natural laws.[23] This brings us back to a subject we began to explore in the previous section, with respect to our various analogies for dualism. The scientific method is an extremely effective tool for determining material causes and for understanding the material universe, precisely because it ignores, by definition, anything that is not material. If we presuppose that the *only* reality is the material reality, then of course science might be taken as an effective tool—perhaps the *only* effective tool—for *all* endeavors toward knowledge. Dennett, toward the end of his article "Can Machines Think?" moves from the topic of intelligence to the more emotionally charged topic of consciousness and makes that materialist presupposition clear.

> But, of course, most people have something more in mind when they speak of self-consciousness. It is that special inner light, that private way that is with you that nobody else can share, something that is forever outside the bounds of computer science. How could a computer ever be conscious in this sense?
>
> That belief, that very gripping, powerful intuition is, I think, in the end simply an illusion of common sense. It is as gripping as the common-sense illusion that the earth stands still and the sun goes around the earth. . . .
>
> If you look at a computer—I don't care whether it's a giant Cray [supercomputer] or a personal computer—if you open up the box and look inside and see those chips, you say, "No way could that be conscious. No way could that be self-conscious." But the same thing is true if you take the top off somebody's skull and look at the gray matter pulsing way in there. You think, "That is conscious? No way could that lump of stuff be conscious." Of course, it makes no difference whether you look at it with a microscope or with a macroscope: At no level of inspection does a brain look like the seat of consciousness.[24]

Dennett has already assumed that the mind is the same as the brain—that to look at the physical cells that compose the brain is the same as to look at the mind. The mind is the collection of cells *and no more*. This is clear from what he proposes.

But if there is some reality—say, a *spiritual* reality—that is not material and is thus not bound by the *natural* laws of the universe, then for all of the tremendous abilities of science, there are going to be truths that science is not capable of discovering or uncovering or experimenting upon. This is a point we noted in the previous section as well with respect to the possible relationship between body and spirit. It is an important point that bears repeating. Consider Richard Dawkins's book *The God Delusion*, which makes the same mistake as Dennett, but even more bluntly. Dawkins repeatedly makes the strange assertion that claims about the spirit *are*, in fact, accessible to the tools of natural science. "I hope chapter 2 will change your mind," he writes at the start of his book, "by persuading you that 'the God Hypothesis' is a scientific hypothesis about the universe, which should be analysed as skeptically as any other."[25] That claims about the spiritual nature of humans, or about spiritual reality, ought to be analyzed skeptically is not what is in question; I would also agree that these claims ought to be questioned and considered with care and reason (which is the point of *this* book). What is in question is whether tools of natural science alone are adequate for that inquiry. Or, put another way, it is whether by definition every *reasonable* hypothesis is also a *scientific* hypothesis.

Dawkins claims that they are, and this claim is central to his book and is thus repeated throughout. "Contrary to Huxley," he writes a little later, "I shall suggest that the existence of God is a scientific hypothesis like any other. Even if hard to test in practice, it belongs in the same . . . box as the controversies over the Permian and Cretaceous extinctions."[26] And again later he adds, "I am arguing that . . . the God question is not in principle and forever outside the remit of science."[27] Dawkins's claim makes sense only if spirit were either somehow composed of matter or were reducible to matter, or if the interaction of spirit and body followed fixed rules of nature. Both of these assumptions are essentially equivalent to a materialist assumption about the universe. Of course, Dawkins is free to hold that assumption a priori, but he then tries to use that assumption to argue that there is no spiritual reality. That is, in assuming that we can scientifically experiment on the spiritual, he must assume that the spiritual is reducible to the material, which is equivalent to saying that the spiritual reality doesn't actually exist. He then uses that assumption to argue that belief in spirit is ridiculous. By claiming that natural science can answer the question of God (Dawkins's so-called God Hypothesis), he has a hidden assumption that somehow the supernatural is reducible to the natural, functions under natural laws, and is thus testable. Without that assumption, nothing he says makes sense. He then argues a conclusion that science does not discover the supernatural; therefore, only the natural exists. But he had to assume that only the natural exists in the first place, before he could put all his faith in natural science to discover reality.

The circularity of Dawkins's reasoning is even clearer in some of his other statements. For example, he writes, "I suspect that alleged miracles provide the strongest reason many believers have for their faith; and miracles, by definition, violate the principles of science."[28] Dawkins begins with a usual understanding of science, that *science deals only with the natural world*. By this definition, science cannot explore the spiritual, or nonmaterial, or miraculous. This is a valid and important point, but Dawkins doesn't seem to understand exactly its implications. To say that science doesn't have tools to explore a miracle is different from saying that a miracle is a "violation" of science. The tools of literary criticism are inadequate to determine certain natural properties, such as the speed of light or acceleration of gravity, but that doesn't mean that the speed of light *violates* literary criticism. For that matter, scales for weighing mass, no matter how accurate, also cannot measure the speed of light, but this does not suggest that the speed of light violates laws of gravity, mass, or weight. Ironically, Dawkins is claiming that miracles violate science, without recognizing that miracles are not testable by science.

Another related and repeated assumption that comes out again here is that anything not scientific is therefore also unreasonable, or even impossible. That is, by assuming that miracles violate science, and that science can discover all truth, he assumes a priori that miracles cannot be true, and thus no evidence could possibly exist to support a miracle. In short, then, Dawkins is claiming as his starting *assumption* that miracles cannot happen, and therefore that miracles as evidence for a faith in a spiritual reality should be dismissed. So he is *assuming* that there is no spiritual reality, and from that assumption draws the *conclusion* that we should not believe in a spiritual reality. Of course, if his assumption is correct, then so is his conclusion, and thus we are tempted to accept it without realizing the circularity of the reasoning. But why should we accept his assumption in the first place?

That Dawkins's claim is seen somehow as a scientific statement rather than as a philosophical statement about science illustrates that this sort of strict naturalism or materialism has become deeply ingrained in our modern consciousness. To return to our earlier analogy, it is the accent with which we speak. Even the naturalist John Searle acknowledges, "There is a sense in which materialism is the religion of our time, at least among most of the professional experts in the fields of philosophy, psychology, cognitive science, and other disciplines that study the mind. Like more traditional religions, it is accepted without question and it provides the framework within which other questions can be posed, addressed and answered."[29]

In fact, Dawkins's book is full of statements, such as the one about miracles, giving testimony to Searle's assertion that materialism is a new religion. In another place, Dawkins writes, "Creative intelligences, being evolved, necessarily arrive late in the universe, and therefore cannot be responsible for designing it."[30] Dawkins may be correct in his assertion that creative intelligences are evolved; he may be right that there is no supernatural reality. But this assertion is an assumption, not something provable. Dawkins then once again reasons from that in circles. If we assume that creative intelligences are evolved, then because evolution is a slow process, we might also agree with the next *necessity*: that they arrive late. And if they arrive late, then of course they cannot be responsible for designing the universe. So if we begin with the assumption that creative intelligence was not there at the beginning to design the universe, then not surprisingly we arrive at the inescapable conclusion: creative intelligence was not there at the beginning to design the universe. Mysteriously, however, Dawkins writes as though he were drawing some sort of new conclusion from evidence, when in fact he simply assumes what he wants to prove and then shows how the conclusion follows from itself.

In short, Dawkins's reasoning is circular and flawed at many levels. As we discussed earlier, it is also a fundamental flaw to use a scientific experiment to attempt to prove the nonexistence of a nonmaterial reality. Natural science, by its very nature and definition, has no tools for this. As we see from the previous example, when the naturalist *claims* to give an argument for naturalism from science, it is an argument where we need to assume the conclusion before we reach it. One is free to take as an a priori assumption that there is nothing other than the material reality. Again, if this is the case, then we might also assume that scientific experiments are the only valid way to discover the nature of mind. But this is a statement of faith, and not a scientific statement. It is another statement *about* science rather than a statement *from* science. (The very statement "Science is the only way to know truth," if it were true, could not be known to be true, because it is a philosophical or metaphysical statement and not a scientific one, and thus by definition would be unknowable. And the statement "scientific truth is the only truth" is self-contradictory and thus couldn't be true.) One cannot, then, use this assumption to prove its truth. If human consciousness is somehow both natural and spiritual, if it cannot be reduced to a mere biochemical machine, then science has no means to discover this, because something in the very nature of that consciousness would not be open to the tools of science.

Richard Dawkins is not the only naturalist to make this sort of circular argument or to base philosophical conclusions on naturalistic assumptions without acknowledging the assumptions. Examples abound. Daniel Dennett, who in general writes more carefully than Dawkins, falls into the trap. His presuppositions are clear, for example, in the earlier passage when he claims that our view of consciousness is an "illusion" to be corrected. One wonders how he knows this.

Or consider an example from another of his essays titled, "In Darwin's Wake, Where Am I?" appearing in *The Cambridge Companion to Darwin* in 2003.[31] In this article, Dennett argues for a physicalist explanation of creativity. (We will return to the question of creativity in the next chapter; for now, we are interested not in creativity itself but in exposing the presuppositions with which many begin this discussion.) One illustration in Dennett's argument is the chess victory of the Deep Blue computer system over Garry Kasparov, and the comparison between the computer's approach and the human's. A physicalist who believes that the human brain is an automaton must understand a human chess player's supposed creativity in playing chess as an advanced computer program. A dualist would say that the human's creativity is not completely reducible to computation but has some component—the human as a spiritual as well as a material being—that is fundamentally different from a computer's. In response to the idea that Deep Blue's "search methods are *entirely* unlike the exploratory process that Kasparov uses," Dennett says unequivocally, "But that is simply not so—or at least it is not so in the only way that could make a difference in this debate." He goes on to explain, "Kasparov's brain is made of organic materials, and has an architecture importantly unlike that of Deep Blue, but it is still, so far as we know, a massively parallel search engine." In other words, Dennett is operating under the assumption of physicalism, reducing Kasparov's mind to his organic brain, and claiming that this brain is a computational device: an engine. Dennett hedges his statement slightly with the preface, "as far as we know," paying lip service to the possibility that there might be *something* else. Yet he continues to repeat the same sort of claim that the approaches of Kasparov and the computer are similarly reducible to computation: "Both presumably do massive amounts of 'brute force' computation on their very different architectures. After all, what do neurons know about chess? Any work *they* do must be brute force work of one sort or another." Dennett has reduced the mind to a collection of neurons and assumed that there is nothing else—no spirit, for example. His use of the word *presumably* is, perhaps, telling. It is his expectation that this is the correct explanation, though despite his use of the word he doesn't seem to acknowledge that any alternate explanation is possible.

This leads Dennett to the following paragraph, in which he presents the conclusion he draws from the Kasparov example.

> It may seem that I am begging the question in favour of a computational, AI approach [to explaining apparent creativity] by describing the work done by Kasparov's brain in this way, but the work has to be done somehow, and no *other* way of getting the work done has ever been articulated. It won't do to say that Kasparov uses "insight" or "intuition" since that just means that Kasparov himself has no privileged access, no insight, into how the good results come to him. So, since nobody knows how Kasparov's brain does it—least of all Kasparov—there is not yet any evidence at all to support the claim that Kasparov's means are "entirely unlike" the means exploited by Deep Blue. One should remember this when tempted to insist that "of course" Kasparov's methods are hugely different. What on earth could provoke one to go out on a limb like that? Wishful thinking? Fear?[32]

Consider carefully Dennett's arguments—or lack of arguments—and his terminology. He simply *claims* that "it won't do" to give any form of *non*computational creativity as an explanation for Kasparov's chess playing. Why won't it "do"? His only reason for that claim is that no explanation has ever been "articulated." But of course an explanation has been articulated, many times and in many places:

one explanation is that *mind*, as something both *spiritual* and *material*, is more than brain, and thus the mind is not fully explained by physicalism and computation; creativity really might be a (partly) supernatural phenomenon. Dennett, with his hidden presuppositions, has simply discounted that possibility, and he assumes that we must discount it also. He assumes that intuition and insight are illusions to be dismissed—that they are ultimately computational processes. But he doesn't argue why; the only argument is the circular one, that we have already assumed strict naturalism and causal closure to be true.

His use of the word *evidence* is also telling. He claims that there is no evidence of anything other than computation. Yet Dennett excludes (by assumptions of physicalism) any evidence not from natural science; he excludes by assumption both "intuition" and "insight," and thus his assumptions preclude him from accepting *any* evidence to the contrary. He has assumed that creativity (or what we call creativity) can be reduced to "work," and he has also assumed flatly that there is "no other way" that this work can be done other than computationally. (Again, one might well ask, "Why not?") Even his continued use of the word *brain* carefully discounts, as an a priori assumption, the possibility of mind as more than biological brain. At the end, though he has not provided any actual argument why we must *assume* Kasparov's brain is working like a computer, or why we ought to discount any alternate possibility, he ridicules any opposing view as "wishful thinking" or "fear." So, despite Dennett's claim to the contrary, begging the question is precisely what he is doing.

A comment Dennett makes in *Consciousness Explained* on the topic of human consciousness may give the clearest insight into what his presuppositions are, and that they need to be understood as a priori assumptions and not conclusions. Specifically, the passage helps us understand how his assumptions determine his conclusions on this topic and often lead to circularity in his reasoning.

> This fundamentally antiscientific stance of dualism is, to my mind, its most disqualifying feature and is the reason why in this book I adopt the apparently dogmatic rule that dualism is to be avoided *at all costs*. It is not that I think I can give a knock-down proof that

> dualism, in all its forms, is false or incoherent, but that, given the way dualism wallows in mystery, *accepting dualism is giving up*.[33]

What Dennett acknowledges here is that he dogmatically rules out a dualist explanation of consciousness, and *not* because of any fundamentally convincing argument that it is false. Here and elsewhere he then draws all of his conclusions based on this personal philosophical choice: his own subjective preference to avoid what he refers to as "wallowing in mystery" and hence "giving up." (One might argue that refusing to engage in something that is mysterious is as much "giving up" as it is to accept that something might be mysterious.) So when Dennett concludes, in both "In Darwin's Wake, Where Am I?" and "Can Machines Think?" that a computational understanding of consciousness is the only possible understanding, the conclusion only makes sense because he has already dogmatically ruled out any other understanding as antiscientific because of his own unscientific a priori commitment to naturalism.

I argue in chapter 7 of this book that some forms of dualism such as Christian Theism actually provide a stronger basis than naturalism for trusting scientific inquiry. Integrative dualism in particular is not in any real sense antiscientific; it does not deny the value or effectiveness of science in general. It does, however, deny that science provides a tool for answering whether there is a spiritual reality. If the a priori assumption of naturalism is not correct, but rather some sort of dualistic assumption is closer to the truth, then science does not provide an adequate tool for determining whether human consciousness and intelligence are fully explained only with respect to the physical. A faith in science to be able to fully understand human consciousness is a faith that human consciousness is purely physical, which begs the question. So Dennett chooses naturalism and disqualifies dualism because he has put his faith in science as the only way to answer the question, and he must have put his faith in science as the only approach because he has already disqualified dualism and chosen naturalism, which again is circular. Why Dennett calls a dualist explanation "giving up" is also a mystery. Presumably, he means that accepting a dualistic explanation is "giving up" on a physicalist explanation, which he has already committed to. But in this passage he commits to a physicalist explanation and calls his audience to do the same because he doesn't want to accept dualism.

Another approach used by both Dennett and Dawkins is also telling. Both writers repeatedly return to the distinction between what they call *skyhooks* and *cranes*. Both devices can lift something up, but while a skyhook just comes down from nowhere, a crane is rooted in the ground. They give this example to distinguish between naturalistic and supernatural explanations of phenomena like human creativity. A crane is a naturalistic explanation, because it is placed on the ground and is able to lift something up higher than its own base. Darwinian evolution is proposed as the ultimate crane, because it understands human intelligence as evolving from nonintelligent sources. A skyhook, by contrast, metaphorically represents a supernatural explanation, because it suggests something from above that pulls an earthborn object skyward: a divine reasoning being creates human reasoning creatures. Note what Daniel Dennett says about skyhooks and cranes. "Skyhooks, like manna from heaven, would be miracles," he notes early in his article, "and if we posit a skyhook anywhere in 'explanation' of creativity, we have in fact conceded defeat."[34] One thing is very clear here. Once again, Dennett is not making any scientific or even a philosophical argument against the possibility that human creativity is supernatural (or miraculous) or that humans could be spiritual beings. He has no reasoned argument that supernaturally caused events do not or cannot happen. He is stating that his audience must—blindly as it were—simply *refuse* to accept miracles, skyhooks, supernatural events, or spiritual humans as possibilities, even if there is evidence to support them, because if they allow for the possibility, then they have "conceded defeat." But, we ask, on what grounds have they been "defeated"? Only on philosophical grounds of their presupposition of naturalism. Allowing for supernaturally caused events doesn't suddenly invalidate science or the possibility of naturalistic causes. The possibility of skyhooks doesn't even invalidate the existence of cranes. There is no reason to consider this a defeat unless one is committed to strict philosophical naturalism, but this commitment must then be understood as a philosophical one and not a scientific one. It is a philosophical starting point to be taken before looking at evidence, rather than a conclusion drawn from evidence.

Dennett comes back to this point toward the end of the essay. "The renunciation of skyhooks is, I think, the deepest and most important legacy of Darwin in philosophy, and it has a huge domain of influence, extending far beyond the skirmishes of evolutionary epistemology and evolutionary ethics. If we commit ourselves to Darwin's 'strange inversion of reasoning,' we turn our backs on compelling ideas that have been central to the philosophic tradition for centuries."[35] Dennett (unlike Dawkins) is at least able to understand and acknowledge (as he does here) that this is fundamentally a philosophical point (and not a scientific one), that it is a battle (or "skirmish") of assumptions (and not of evidence), and also that (as a philosophical assumption) naturalism has had a pervasive influence that can be hard to escape. Here and earlier he is charging his audience to make a philosophical commitment to strict naturalism and to cling to that commitment on purely philosophical grounds, rejecting all prior competing philosophies no matter how compelling they are.

Now, the previous sections, in arguing that science does not provide tools for exploring the human as a spiritual being, in no way imply or are intended to imply that science can tell us nothing about the brain. Science is a great tool for exploring the brain, and decades of study in psychology, neurology, and brain physiology have provided invaluable knowledge. Indeed, even most modern adherents of forms of dualism, including theistic dualism, would likely see some of Kasparov's chess-playing ability as explainable in terms of brain physiology. But if the mind is not merely the brain, then at some point there will be questions that science cannot answer.

To see unacknowledged assumptions of physicalism at work impacting conclusions, consider one final example. One type of experiment that has been conducted in numerous ways at numerous times is to connect sensors to a human brain and study brainwaves during various activities. In one variation I read about in a major newspaper a few years ago, a neurophysiologist collected brainwave data from a subject during the practice of meditation. When the experiment was done, the scientist carrying out the experiment observed that there were altered brainwave patterns during meditation, and he excitedly reported that he had discovered the changes in the part of the brain that *caused feelings* of meditation. The conclusion illustrates a fundamental fallacy that in almost any other context would have been pointed out and criticized immediately and sharply. Why can the scientist assume that the change in brainwaves *caused* the spiritual feelings of meditation, rather than the other way around: that the spiritual act of meditation *caused* the change in brainwave patterns? That the brainwaves change during meditation is an observation. That the changes in the brainwaves are the cause of the meditative experience is an assumption, not a conclusion. In making that assumption, the scientist also makes an even deeper assumption that meditation is just a *feeling*, rather than a real spiritual event such as a real spiritual state of a person, or a discourse between two (or more) spiritual beings. In short, both of the conclusions assume that there is no spiritual reality.

To put it another way, isn't it possible that the spiritual–bodily human person used the brain to meditate? Humans who believe in a divine being often kneel to pray to their God. Though they understand praying to be, at least in part, a spiritual act of communion with a spiritual being, as bodily creatures they use their knees to kneel. If we observed someone in the act of praying, we might also observe her kneeling, but her bent knees do not *cause* her to pray. In the same way, a spiritual and bodily human would also use her brain for the act of prayer and meditation. So, of course the activities of prayer or meditation would have an impact on the physical body: the knees perhaps, and the brain certainly. Why should we start with a physicalist assumption, then? Shouldn't the scientist, if he is honest, excitedly report on a great discovery of what happens to the brain when a person meditates, without the assumption that the change in brainwaves *causes* the feeling of meditation?

Consider, for example, if scientists were studying a turbine propeller in a wind tunnel. They observe in repeated experiments that the propeller always spins at the same time the wind is blowing. This observation alone would not be enough to conclude the direction of cause and effect. Did the spinning of the propeller cause the wind, or did the wind cause the spinning of the propeller? Some other observation, and perhaps another experiment, would be necessary before a conclusion could be drawn. The unquestioned conclusion of the neurophysiologist that brainwaves *cause* spiritual feelings of meditation shows just how pervasive is the a priori assumption of physicalism. Only if one begins with the assumption that there is no spiritual reality can one discount spiritual reality as an explanation or cause of physical effects—as the authors of the previous experiments apparently do.

Of course, that assumption may be correct, but it should be acknowledged as the underlying assumption. And it cannot be used as *evidence* that one's feelings of meditation are caused by certain brainwaves; that meditation is caused by changes in brainwaves is the assumption rather than the conclusion. More broadly, if one begins with these assumptions of strict naturalism, causal closure, materialism, and physicalism, then those assumptions should be acknowledged honestly as presuppositions. In particular the assumption should not be hidden and then used in a conclusion that materialism is true.

In a like manner, the proposed scientific experiments to determine whether the mind is a computing device also (without acknowledging it) often confuse the a priori assumptions with the conclusions. If the mind is more than the brain, if the human consciousness is not reducible to something material—in short, if humans are more than complex biochemical computing devices—then science is inadequate to answer the question. And if the reality of the world transcends the material reality, if there are spiritual as well as physical *truths*, then we also say that it is fully possible to be *reasonable* without being *scientific*—and also without being *anti*scientific.

Again note that the many discoveries of science is still just as interesting and valid even if there exists some spiritual, nonmaterial reality on which science cannot operate. The discovery about the ways that *physical* brain activity changes during meditation, for example, is still a fascinating discovery even if meditation is a real *spiritual* event that involves a mind that is more than a brain. The difference, in the understanding of the integrative dualist, is that the discovery tells us something about the way that we, as spiritual and biological beings, use our biological brains in the act of meditation, or even as a way that we can bodily feel our meditative state. The discovery confirms what many spiritual people have said frequently—that meditation changes our body. What it does not tell us is what *causes* meditation.

Where Do We Go?

So where do we go from here? By no means do we abandon science and all it has offered and promises to offer. But if science is inadequate to answer the question of whether humans are spiritual as well as bodily creatures, then we should have some idea where we might turn. Are there other *reasonable* ways we might seek the truth?

I think there are. This book, in particular, is not trying to present a *scientific* approach to determining whether the worldview of determinism and physicalism is correct, but it does hope to present a *reasonable* approach. The basic premise is that if the human mind, the human consciousness, the human *person*, really transcends physical reality, then something besides the natural sciences as a study of the physical world may be a good guide. If there is a spiritual as well as a physical reality, and if we as humans are spiritual as well as bodily beings, then we might expect to have some sort of spiritual sense (or senses) in addition to our physical ones. This sense might relate to what is sometimes described with terms such as *intuition*, *insight*, *conscience*, or even *creativity*. If something about the universe makes sense, if it connects with how we *feel* the universe *ought* to be, if it comes to us by insight, or if it speaks to our consciences, or with what we intuitively believe about our own natures, then maybe that is a guide to what is true and should not simply be discounted.

The philosopher Charles Taliaferro suggests something like this.

> I propose that we approach the philosophy of human nature by taking appearances seriously, trusting them until we have reason to distrust them. When we do take appearances seriously, we take up what may variously be described as the first-person or subjective point of view, according to which there is a discernible feel or awareness we have as conscious beings of our own states and activities.[36]

This response seems very reasonable. Science cannot tell us whether we are spiritual beings. If we are spiritual beings, we need and should expect some sort of spiritual sense. We should somehow feel as Sting does when he sings the repeated chorus of the classic Police song "Spirits in the Material World."[37] If we are spiritual beings, perhaps we should feel a spiritual hunger for spiritual nourishment, akin to our bodily hungers. We should wonder, as Emmylou Harris does in her song "The Pearl" (on the album of the same name), why we would have a hunger for heaven unless there really was a heaven.

In other words, where Daniel Dennett invites you to reject that "very gripping, powerful intuition" as "simply an illusion of common sense," this book suggests that we pay attention to that intuition, and that we listen to some other *sense* that seems to have been *common* throughout nearly all human history and culture. It may be the wisdom that comes to us as beings who are both bodily creatures endowed with brains as well as spiritual beings endowed with minds. In any case, it is a blind-faith assumption of naturalists to reject this approach altogether, just as some of the spiritual or religious views rejected by naturalists require their own assumptions of faith.

We might return also to another comment by Richard Dawkins in *The God Delusion*, similar to that of Dennett. Dawkins, in explaining away the apparent references to spirituality from many famous scientists, writes, "A quasi-mystical response to nature and the universe is common among scientists and rationalists. It has no connection with supernatural belief."[38] Our response is, "Why not?" Why should we *assume* that there is no connection to supernatural belief? *If* there is a supernatural reality—a spiritual nonmaterial reality—then just because it cannot be explored by natural science doesn't mean that it does not exist or that it is not reasonable to believe in it. If the dualist hypothesis that humans are spiritual as well as physical beings is true, then perhaps as humans we have tools other than scientific ones for exploring it. Perhaps the very mystical sense that Dawkins speaks of, and then dismisses, or even the mystery that Dennett is afraid to "wallow" in, could point us in the right direction.

Or perhaps, more simply, we really do have some spiritual sense or intuition akin to our physical senses. This doesn't mean our spiritual senses would always point us in the correct spiritual direction, or toward spiritual truth. Our physical senses do not always lead us toward truth either. Sight, sound, taste, and touch may all be deceiving. Optical illusions can be powerful, as even Dawkins admits. There are poisonous foods that look, feel, smell, and taste good. But our physical senses do provide some true reflection of reality. If there is a spiritual reality, then we should expect some other sense—even if that sense is not fully accurate or is readily deceivable—that would tell us about it or at least suggest its reality. Rather than blindly accepting the presuppositions of naturalism, this path seems to be worth at least some exploration.

To consider this path, the first half of this book explores several implications of accepting a materialist view and asks us whether the implications make sense in the universe we live in—whether they are tenable and livable to what our spirits seem to be telling us is true. We will explore the implications of physicalism to human creativity and heroism; the implications to ecology and human care for the rest of nature and the nonhuman world; and lastly (and perhaps most surprisingly), the implications of physicalism to the validity of reason and science itself. In the second half of the book, we explore an alternative view that affirms both spirit and body (a dualist view, but one that is more complete than the ghost-in-a-machine dualism). I hope to show that this other and much older view of humanity affirms creativity, heroism, ecology, reason, and even science itself in a way that physicalism cannot—in particular, that to hold to a traditional Judeo-Christian theistic view of humanness ought to lead one to a much healthier way of living in relationship with others, with ourselves, and with nature.

This is not an exercise only in pragmatic philosophy (though it certainly has some relationship to pragmatism); I am not saying that one *ought* to accept a spiritual understanding of the universe *merely* because it seems to work or to be satisfying—though neither do I dismiss the importance of these practical considerations. After all, one of the great reasons for the tremendous modern faith in science is not any philosophical arguments for materialism, but simply that the scientific approach has yielded practical results; ignoring the historical dimension of spirituality and final causes, and focusing instead on the material world, has resulted in technological advances. We trust science because it seems to work. It provides explanations. And it feeds technology; using science, we can build bridges that don't fall down. This faith in science is also rooted in the pragmatic.

Rather, I am arguing that *if* we really are spiritual as well as bodily beings, then our spiritual wisdom ought to provide some sort of guide to reality; if an idea rings profoundly true to our inner ear, to our consciousness as well as to our conscience, then it may be evidence that this idea is true or holds some important truth. Rather than assuming this spiritual understanding is false, let's ask what we might expect *if* it were true. Our intuitive side should have something to tell us. Dawkins himself frequently defends naturalistic assumptions on the grounds that they can explain things ("Like nothing else, evolution really does provide an explanation for the existence of entities whose improbability would otherwise, for practical purposes, rule them out. And the conclusion to the argument, as I shall show in chapter 4, is close to being terminally fatal to the God Hypothesis"),[39] but then oddly he turns right around and says we must *not* accept supernatural explanations simply because *they* can explain things. This seems inconsistent to me. Why not ask whether the nonnaturalist explanation makes sense of what our consciousness, or intuition, suggests is true of the world? (Or we might ask whether a nonnaturalist explanation makes good sense of consciousness and intuition themselves.) Put another way, can we really accept all the implications of naturalism when taken seriously? Or does something else ring more true?

2

Physicalism, Creativity, and Heroism

What is creativity? When we speak of being "creative," different people mean different things at different times. An attempt to explain the source of human creativity, or to help someone to become more creative, is far beyond the scope of this book—or, indeed, the scope of many books. So is the topic of heroism. But in a chapter on the implications of physicalism to creativity and heroism, it is important to explain just what we mean by the word *creative* and also what defines a *hero*.

In this book, I mean by *creativity* the *ability* to bring into being something new, which does not proceed entirely from what has gone before or what already exists. According to this definition, creativity might not actually even exist. But before we pursue that question, let's consider this traditional meaning of the word. This is not a manufactured definition, intended only to serve my purposes; I claim it is a natural and accepted definition, etymologically accurate, and also in line with the understanding of creativity that is the goal of some of the naturalists whose ideas I explore in this chapter. To create something is to *cause* it to *exist*. Certainly there is nothing ever made by human minds and hands that is *completely* new. Every work of art ever made has been made in the context of some culture and with reference to or influence of prior works of art or of the world itself. It could not be created otherwise, and if something entirely new with no context or connection to the past were created, it almost certainly would not and could not be understood by those who heard it, read it, or viewed it. Yet (though we may be wrong in doing so) we *do* speak not only of painters and poets being creative, but also of the creativity of carpenters and chefs, of filmmakers, gardeners, teachers, and parents. We even speak of the artistry of athletes, such as that of a pitcher throwing a perfect game. Somehow, something new at least *seems* to be flowing out of our creativity. Though made in part with the materials of countless prior creators, and of the world itself, the creation also comes in part from its creator, in a way that does not wholly proceed from anything that has ever been.

Perhaps the best synonym for creativity is *originality*. To be creative is to be original. *To be original is to be the origin of something*. When we are creative, even though we make use of or reference to something outside of ourselves, something also originates *in* us. Note that this implies also something of *intent* or *purpose*.

That, at least, is what is commonly or historically understood as creativity. Whether such creativity exists is what is in question.

What is also in question is heroism. This is a more complex concept to define, since different ages have had not only different heroes, but different *types* of heroes. It is also difficult because the word has been overused and diminished. Sports announcers speak almost nightly about "heroics" of various players, as if scoring a winning basket or a winning goal at the last moment of a game were somehow comparable to risking one's life to save somebody else. In doing so we diminish the meaning of the word *hero*. In light of that, Dick Keyes in his book *True Heroes in a World of Celebrity Counterfeits*, makes a valuable distinction between real heroism and mere talent or celebrity—two things often confused with heroism. He centers heroism in moral character, and he notes:

> That means human greatness is not *in its deepest essence* tied either to talent or fame, although it may coexist with either. Heroism becomes less a question of a person's ability to lead a talented or dramatic life, and more a question of virtue as a whole human being. By "virtue" we mean not just a single morally good act but the habit, tendency, or disposition to do good in some important aspect of life.[1]

Thus, heroism, in this understanding, is linked to one's actions, and in particular to making virtuous choices. Keyes goes on to add, in defense of this view, "Some will disagree with the idea of linking heroism to moral character. But it is worth noting that the only people who are almost universally accepted as heroic are seen as much not for their high performance skills or renown but for their moral qualities."[2] This is the concept of hero I address in this book.

The concept of heroism is also a concept central to perhaps the best-known author of heroic literature of the twentieth century: J. R. R. Tolkien. In Tolkien's Middle-earth writings, *The Lord of the Rings* and *The Hobbit*, as well as in his posthumously published material, most notably *The Silmarillion*, a hero is defined by his or her choices. A hero is one whose choices are rooted in moral virtue—one who acts in a way that is virtuous even when those actions come at great personal cost or risk. This, at least, is the definition of heroism given within Tolkien's books by his wise characters. In *The Lord of the Rings*, when Frodo accepts the central role in the heroic quest of the Ring, the wise Elven king Elrond tells him, "But it is a heavy burden. So heavy that none could lay it on another. I do not lay it on you. But if you take it *freely*, I will say that *your choice is right*; and though all the mighty elf-friends of old, Hador, and Húrin, and Túrin, and Beren himself were assembled together, your seat would be among them."[3] Frodo's place in the pantheon of great heroes, according to Elrond, is not based on his strength or stature. Indeed, as every reader of the book realizes almost at once, Frodo the Hobbit has little of either. He cannot begin to compare in physical strength to the least of Men or Elves, and even among his own people he never gains the fame of his companions Sam, Merry, or Pippin. His heroism is not even dependent on the success of his quest. It is defined by his choice: his willingness to take a heavy burden for the sake of others. Because of that choice, he is compared with Beren, the greatest hero in all of Tolkien's tales. Speaking of the great heroes of old like Beren, who set out on quests that define them as heroes, Frodo's companion Sam Gamgee also observes, "I expect they had lots of chances, like us, of turning back, only they didn't. And if they had, we shouldn't know, because they'd have been forgotten. We hear about those as just went on."[4] Again, the definition of the hero is the *choice* to go on, even when offered a much easer choice to turn back.

Does it make sense, then, to talk about somebody being heroic? Or to speak of humans as creative? Or are creativity and heroism only illusions?

A Materialist View

In many ways, this chapter is the easiest of the book to write. Its central premise is very simple and can be stated up front: a physicalist view of humanity that we are complex biochemical computers not only denies free will but, by denying human free will, also denies any real possibility of human creativity or human heroism.

This is an easy chapter to write because most of the central proponents of the physicalist worldview agree with this statement. This may be why somebody like Richard Dawkins expresses hostility toward creative endeavors of the church: "Religion devours resources, sometimes on a massive scale. A medieval cathedral could consume a hundred man-centuries in its construction, yet was never used as a dwelling, or for any recognizably *useful purpose*."[5] That there may have been injustices involved in the making of some medieval cathedrals is not the question. The question is whether art and creativity have possible value in and of themselves, perhaps as expressions of beauty, or whether their only value comes from some "useful purpose." The Dawkins view expressed here is the latter. His criticism of the medieval cathedrals, which are tremendous works of architectural art, is their lack of usefulness. That view is consistent with his denial of human creativity. How can one appreciate the beauty of a creative endeavor if creativity itself is illusion? Dawkins is glad to have the world rid of the sort of creative expressions that consume resources with no utilitarian value. Indeed, many like Dawkins not only admit that denying free will also denies creativity and heroism, but they applaud the denial and add to it, "Good riddance. We are happy to be done with the old-fashioned illusions."

At least they would say as much in *words*. What I will also suggest in this chapter is that while such a philosophy is easy to state and impossible to refute—and also impossible to prove for that matter, as Dennett concedes—this philosophy turns out to be very difficult to actually practice, even for its most adamant and vocal defenders.

The philosophy of human free will is a belief that humans can behave in ways independent of any controlling force; it is a belief that we actually make decisions and act of our own choice. As a religious doctrine, it states that every action of every human person need not be under the direct control of God or the gods. More generally, it is a belief that our actions are not determined solely by causes outside ourselves, whether by gods or any other force such as physical forces; it is the view that at any given moment, we are free to choose how we will act at that moment. The English word *freedom* survives from two Old English words: *freo*, meaning "free," and *dóm*, meaning "judgment" or sometimes "choice." From the Old English *dóm* we get the modern English *doom*; freedom means that we are free to choose our own doom.

The philosophy of determinism, in a broad sense, is essentially the opposite of free will. It is a belief that humans are not free (from the gods in a religious determinism, or from the laws of physics in a naturalistic determinism). It is the belief that all of our actions are completely controlled by something outside ourselves. In the physicalist version of determinism (in a strict or broad form), is the philosophy that impersonal physical forces (atomic or subatomic) are responsible for everything that happens. It is the philosophy that even our thoughts, which seemingly control our decisions and actions, are themselves completely controlled by purposeless motions of physical particles.

As noted in the introduction, a strict determinism denies even random physical effects, and claims that all actions of all humans through all history—and, indeed, every movement of every particle in the entire universe—have been preprogrammed, and we are not free to change them. In this view we cannot change any of our actions in the future any more than we can change our actions in the past. Everything that has ever happened and will ever happen was determined from the inception of the universe. But physicalism, even if not leading to this strict form of determinism, still insists on a broader form. And this broader form, though it allows for possible random movements of subatomic particles—which may in time affect the positions and actions of atoms, and thus of molecules, and eventually of human bodies—still denies free will. It allows that the future would remain hypothetically unknown even could we compute the position of every particle in the universe, but it still holds to the idea of thoughts as things that have nothing other than physical components. According to physicalism, our actions may be controlled by our thoughts, but our thoughts are physical things that are determined by atoms following laws of physics or by quantum behavior. That is, the behaviors of particles may be predictable or unpredictable, but they still completely control us. Hence, University College neuroscientist Chris Frith can say, "I think in the next few years we will have quite a good understanding of the brain mechanisms that underlie our feeling of being in control of our actions."[6] Being in control of our actions is a *feeling*, but not a *reality*; it is an illusion that, if Frith is correct, will soon be explained away.

Kurzweil, for example, in his prologue to *The Age of Spiritual Machines*, speaks of computers in the twenty-first century "increasingly appear[ing] to have their own personalities," and he goes on to say that "they will appear to have their own free will."[7] His use of the word *appear* here suggests that computers won't *really* have any free will. But, he makes it clear, neither do humans, and so we are in the same boat as computers. Computers will be *as free as humans*, which turns out not to be free at all. Later in the book, he explores the question of free will in more detail, connecting his reflections with those of the philosopher Plato. After raising the question, "Will machines make their own decisions, or will they just follow a program?" Kurzweil suggests that there is here no distinction between computers and humans. "On the one hand," he writes, "human beings partake of the natural world and are subject to its laws. Our brains are natural phenomena and thus must follow the cause-and-effect laws manifest in machines and other lifeless creatures of our own species."[8] This is the philosophy of physicalism in a nutshell—an affirmation of strict naturalism and causal closure. Here, Kurzweil simply assumes it to be true, without any argument or even an acknowledgment that it is an assumption open for discussion. This philosophical position is repeated throughout his book as though it were fact. He also explains implications of this view to the subject of free will, namely, that free will does not exist. "Free will is purposeful behavior and decision making," he gives as a definition, and then he comments, "but if human decision making is based on such predictable interactions of basic particles, our decisions must also be predetermined. That would contradict human freedom to choose."[9] In the glossary of his book, along with his definition of free will, he also makes the point explicit: "A primary philosophical issue is how free will is possible if events are the result of the predictable—or unpredictable—interaction of particles."[10] What Kurzweil doesn't mention here is that if human actions are *not* always the result of the interaction of material particles, then we don't have this philosophical problem of the impossibility of free will (though we may have several other philosophical concerns to wrestle with).[11] He would rather have the trouble disappear in another way: by simply getting rid of the notion of soul or spirit, and claiming a priori that we are just bodies, and thus that free will is only an illusion.

A final note about Kurzweil's presentation of the free-will debate returns us to the discussion in the previous chapter of our blind faith in the scientific process as the only valid way of discovering truth. Kurzweil presents and then argues against (or simply dismisses) several competing views of the nature of human consciousness that affirm free will. The fourth one he summarily dismisses is a view he refers to as "The 'Consciousness Is a Different Kind of Stuff' School." This view includes any "mystical" view of consciousness that suggests a dual body–spirit nature, including not only a Cartesian dualism or a ghost-in-a-machine view, but also presumably the sort of more complex view I suggested in the first chapter (and return to in the second half of the book, especially in chap. 8). His basic argument against this view is that it would be unverifiable by science and therefore eventually rejected as false. "To the extent that this school implies an interference by consciousness in the physical world that runs afoul of scientific experiment, science is bound to win because of its ability to verify its insights."[12] It is not clear what Kurzweil means by "bound to win." If he is predicting only that there will be widespread cultural disbelief in the idea of a "mystical" soul, because it cannot be verified by science, there is nothing to argue with; such disbelief has been widespread for a century already (though it is by no means universally accepted).

However, Kurzweil's allusion to a body–soul view "run[ning] afoul of scientific experiments" implies a much stronger meaning to the phrase "science is bound to win." It implies a meaning equivalent to "the denial of soul is *bound to be the correct or true view*." It should be clear that this is circular reasoning, and the reasoning must be rejected as an argument, just like the arguments of Dawkins mentioned in the previous chapter. Kurzweil has essentially hidden his conclusion in his assumptions. His *assumption* is that anything *not* verifiable by science *cannot* be true, and thus that we should reject any nonscientific verification. But his *conclusion* is that one particular effect not verifiable by science (the so-called interference of the soul in the physical world) is therefore not true. It is worth repeating here that scientific experiments can measure cause and effect only in the *material* world. Kurzweil understands this point, though Dawkins apparently does not. If there is a soul that is not merely body, and a mind that is not merely brain, and this soul or mind is a part of our consciousness, then it cannot be experimented on as a physical object by the tools of science. Unfortunately, Kurzweil doesn't seem to understand the implications of the point.

Where Kurzweil is helpful, though, is in expressing some of the implications of physicalism, including a denial of free will and many of the further implications that go along with that denial. Many gifted thinkers—philosophers, scientists, mathematicians, theologians—of the past century have made the same sorts of points. One of the clearest writers on this issue is the twentieth-century mathematician-philosopher Bertrand Russell, who notes the following in his essay "Has Religion Made Useful Contributions to Civilization?"

> Materialists used the laws of physics to show, or attempt to show, that the movements of human bodies are mechanically determined, and that consequently everything we say and every change of position that we effect fall *outside* the sphere of any possible free will. . . . If, when a man writes a poem or commits a murder, the bodily movements involved in his act result solely from physical causes, it would seem absurd to put up a statue to him in the one case and to hang him in the other.
>
> . . . My own belief is that . . . the physicists will in time discover [these] laws governing minute phenomenon, although these laws may differ very considerably from those of traditional physics.
>
> . . . Whatever may be thought about it as a matter of ultimate metaphysics, it is quite clear that nobody believes in [free will] anymore.[13]

Russell here (like Kurzweil) is arguing explicitly that there is no such thing as free will. And while he is obviously wrong that *nobody* believes in free will anymore, his conclusions about *possible* free will are consistent with his presuppositions about the movements of bodies and causal closure. He begins with the hypothesis that "the movements of human bodies are mechanically determined." (By *mechanically*, he means "according to mechanistic laws, or laws of physics" and not the narrower sense "by the use of mechanical gears and levers." Today we might say "biochemically determined," or something like that.) But our bodies are controlled by our muscles, which are in turn controlled by nerve impulses generated in our brains. So our actions, including the sounds generated by our vocal cords resulting in what we call *speech*, are controlled by our minds—which if Russell is right is the same as saying "our brains." So Russell's real hypothesis is that "the *thoughts* of our *brains* that control our actions are mechanically determined." *If* that hypothesis is true, *then* Russell's conclusion is immediate and is the same as Kurzweil's: there is no such thing as free will.

The Abolition of Creativity and Heroism

But Russell goes on to take the next step, which many naturalist philosophers leave out, perhaps in embarrassment or because it is so bleak; he explicitly considers the implications of denying free will. Human creativity, and also the possibility of human heroism, both disappear with the denial of free will. Russell is reasoning consistently and in a valid way when he writes, "*If*, when a man writes a poem or commits a murder, the bodily movements involved in his act result solely from physical causes, it would seem absurd to put up a statue to him in the one case and to hang him in the other."[14] It is somewhat shocking to link the writing of a poem with the committing of a murder. But why should it be? If the whole world is just one big machine, and we are cogs in it, then whatever happens has long ago been determined to happen, and we have no say in the matter. If I write a poem, it is only because the big computer program that is the universe, without any purpose, produced a poem through me, by blind chance. If I commit a murder, it is because the gears of the program committed a murder through me, again by blind chance and without any purpose. In both cases, we say it was the universe that did it, and not us. We may be awed by the *universe's* ability to produce surprising things, but we should not be awed by the creativity (or illusion of creativity) in the *individual*. Put another way, according to Russell *nothing* originates with the individual, and hence there is no such thing as originality or creativity—or at least there is no creativity in any sense that we defined it above. So why treat the individual, the human person, as though he or she had any role in it? Indeed, why treat the individual as an *individual* at all? It is more accurate to consider the entire universe as one cohesive closed system, since, according to Russell and the philosophies of strict naturalism and causal closure, there exists no individual within the system with any freedom apart from the system. (The only possible individual that might behave independently from the system as a whole seems to be the subatomic quantum.)

Thus, Russell goes on to add, again drawing conclusions consistent with his denial of free will:

> The one effect that the free-will doctrine has in practice is to prevent people from following such common-sense knowledge to its rational conclusion. When a man acts in ways that annoy us we wish to think him wicked, and we refuse to face the fact that his annoying behavior is a result of antecedent clauses which, if you follow them long enough, will take you beyond the moment of his birth and therefore to events for which he cannot be held responsible by any stretch of the imagination.[15]

Again, where does this leave creativity? Everything we do and say is determined by antecedent clauses—by events that happened outside of us and before us, governed solely by physical laws. That is what Russell repeatedly and explicitly points out: *nothing* originates with us. Not our poems. Not our murders. Anything resembling the sort of creativity we described at the start of the chapter is impossible. We cannot be responsible for originating *anything*. Everything we do proceeds *entirely* from what has gone before.

This means that heroism also is impossible. We cannot make morally virtuous choices, because we do not make choices at all.

So the good news, if the materialists are right, is that we cannot be responsible for any of our wickedness or "annoying behavior." The bad news is that neither can we be heroic. That is, we may behave in a way that somebody would call "heroic" based on traditional concepts, just as we may act in a way that is "moral" (based again on traditional concepts). Readers at the end of Tolkien's *The Lord of the Rings* may be saddened that Frodo never receives the honor he deserves for his heroic quest to destroy the ring and save Middle-earth, but Russell's point is that this is how it should be; Frodo did not make *choices* to do right any more than his nemeses in the Shire, Lotho Sackville-Baggins or Ted Sandyman, or even the greater villains of Middle-earth like Sauron or Saruman, made *choices* to do wrong. Nor, according to Russell, did any of the New York City firefighters who bravely risked and gave their lives on September 11, 2001. We do not make any real heroic choices or any moral choices. There aren't really any choices being made at all. Poems and murders are one and the same. We are not responsible.

B. F. Skinner, the famous behavioral psychologist of the twentieth century, makes similar arguments. The very title of his book *Beyond Freedom and Dignity* suggests his main arguments. Our modern scientific knowledge, he argues, has brought us *beyond* the old-fashioned belief in *freedom* by showing us that we live in a determined universe, and that we ourselves are determined beings. "Personal exemption from a complete determinism is revoked as scientific analysis progresses, particularly in accounting for the behavior of the individual."[16] If we ignore the fact that scientific analysis cannot possibly *prove* this (it can only *assume* it), it immediately follows that this "progress" has also brought us beyond outdated notions of human dignity, such as a belief in the creativity of the artist or the virtuous choices of the hero. "The individual does not initiate anything," Skinner explained in a speech at Westmont College in Santa Barbara after the publication of his book.[17] In the terminology of this book, he would say, "The individual does not *originate* anything." We are not the source of anything original. We are not creative.

And here is why this part of the chapter is easy. Skinner does not try to preserve notions of heroism and creativity after arguing for a physicalism. He is far more consistent with his assumptions. Rather, he proclaims a death of the notion of heroism and then rejoices in that death. He writes:

> What is being abolished is autonomous man—the inner man, the homunculus man, the possessing demon, the man defended by the literatures of freedom and dignity.
>
> His abolition has long been overdue. Autonomous man is a device used to explain what we cannot explain in any other way. He has been constructed from our ignorance, and as our understanding increases, the very stuff of which he is composed vanishes. . . . To man qua man we readily say good riddance. Only by dispossessing him can we turn to the real causes of human behavior. Only then can we turn from the inferred to the observed, from the miraculous to the natural, from the inaccessible to the manipulable.[18]

Skinner here takes the extra step of not only denying free will—the notion of an "autonomous man"—but of criticizing the "literatures of freedom and dignity" that suggest the existence of free will.

In fact, the above passage is in response to C. S. Lewis in general, and especially to his book *The Abolition of Man*. Of equal or perhaps greater importance to the topic of heroism, Lewis also wrote several works of heroic literature, most famously the seven books of *The Chronicles of Narnia*. In his fiction as well as his essays he expresses the same concept of heroism as J. R. R. Tolkien and Dick Keyes. Thus Lewis both wrote and defended what B. F. Skinner refers to as "literatures of freedom and dignity." Skinner responds to Lewis's fear of "the abolition of man," saying "good riddance" to these heroic notions. Skinner's use of the word *abolition* with respect to *man* is almost certainly in reference to Lewis's book title, and is explicitly in opposition to Lewis's ideas. Where Lewis warned of our impending abolition, Skinner thought that concept of humans (as moral free will beings capable of heroism) ought to be abolished. Skinner believed these ideas stood in the way of scientific progress, and especially in the way of his agenda for psychological conditioning of human behavior. Any heroic literature that depends upon a human's responsibility for his or her actions falls under this attack. Skinner's phrase "possessing demon" chimes the same bell as the "ghost in the machine." He is critiquing the worldview that humanity and the universe have a miraculous or supernatural reality as well as a natural reality—that there may be some effects that do not fall within the control of natural laws and thus cannot be explained by science. It is a view, Skinner argues, that must be rejected. Since humans are machines, let us abolish notions of creativity and heroism, dispossess the machine from its ghost, and focus instead on how to program or manipulate the machine that is the human.

An Attempted Physicalist Recovery of Creativity

Before concluding the chapter on implications of physicalism, and asking whether it is possible or even consistent, we need to return once more to the ideas of Raymond Kurzweil. He, unlike Bertrand Russell, while dismissing real free will does *not* dismiss artistic creativity in computational devices. Indeed, he takes pains to praise the sorts of creative work already being done by computer programs and argues that this creativity will be far more impressive in the future. He gives examples from music, fiction, poetry, visual arts, and even the making of jokes.

> The age of the cybernetic artist has begun, although it is at an early stage. *As with human artists*, you never know what these *creative* systems are going to do next. To date, however, none of them has cut off an ear or run naked through the streets. They don't yet have bodies to demonstrate that sort of creativity.
>
> The strength of these systems is reflected by an often *startling originality* in a turn of phrase, shape, or musical line. . . . The frequent *originality* of these systems makes them great collaborators with human artists, and in this manner, computers have already had a transforming effect on the arts.[19]

Note what he says. He refers not only to human artists, but also to computer systems, as "creative." At the heart of his description of creativity—what he calls the "strength of these systems"—is originality, both "frequent" and even "startling." Thus, Kurzweil is attempting to draw on the same understanding of creativity as we do in this book: real creativity is defined by *originality*.

But, from what Kurzweil says elsewhere, he can't possibly mean that computers are truly original, or even that humans are original, despite his convenient use of that word. He makes it clear that computers and humans both are purely physical machines, whose every action is the result of antecedent causes. We are automata, Kurzweil tells us. We are beings determined by physical causes (predictable or unpredictable), and our actions are determined actions. As we have noted throughout this chapter, a determined action is always, by definition, the result of other actions, and never truly the *origin* of any action. Any art that is produced by the "system" originates entirely in some combination of the hardware and programming code of the programmers who designed the system, and in the data that have been entered into the system. Even if the program acquires data "on its own," it is acquiring data only by following a computer program for data acquisition that originated elsewhere, and the acquired data are also something already existing that originated elsewhere. This is true of everything a computer does, whether creating art or tallying spreadsheets. (For those who believe that humans are not computers, this explains why these systems work well primarily as "collaborators with human artists," because the human artists can provide a means not only of evaluating what art is pleasing or meaningful to humans, but also of inserting some sort of real creativity—or originality—into the system.)

Perhaps this lack of ultimate originality is clear from one of Kurzweil's own descriptions of a creative system. Referring to a visual art–creating program called Aaron, programmed by Harold Cohen, Kurzweil notes, "While Cohen wrote the program, the pictures created are nonetheless always a surprise to him. Cohen is frequently asked who should be given credit for the results of his enterprise, which have been displayed in museums around the world. Cohen is happy to take the credit, and Aaron has not been programmed to complain."[20] Why does Cohen take the credit? Because he designed the system. Everything Aaron does is in complete obedience to its code, written by Cohen. Kurzweil's final comment that Aaron does not complain about the lack of credit given to it seems tongue-in-cheek, but in fact it is important and carries many implications. The system is complex enough that even its creator may be surprised by the results; nonetheless, the results contain nothing that was not entered into the system from outside the system. Everything, ultimately, originates elsewhere than in the program that is supposedly creating. *Even the possibility of complaining must be programmed into the computer!*

So what does this mean? The human Cohen, and not the computer system Aaron, is the originator of the instructions that produce the art. Unless of course Cohen himself is also a computer (of the biochemical kind), in which case you push back the credit for everything onto the causally closed universe itself and acknowledge that there is no true creativity or originality in the computer *or in the human*. For Kurzweil, Aaron's inherent determinism is not a problem to his use of the word *creative*, because he would argue that humans are also determined—which, in fact, is the point of this chapter. All he can really mean is that computers have the same *illusion* of originality, and thus of creativity, as do humans. That is, according to Kurzweil, human creativity is also an illusion. Or, rather, he needs to weaken the meaning of the words *creative* and *original* just as he did the word *spiritual* (in the title of his book). The whole universe is a machine, and the physical particles in our body are parts of that machine, following laws of physics. Our mind as a whole has no more possibility of originality than does an individual physical atom of carbon, or hydrogen, or oxygen that is part of our body.

The same assumptions and conclusions are evident in how Daniel Dennett explains the work of another of these cybernetic artists: the music composition software called EMI, created by David Cope.

> When EMI is fed music by Bach, it responds by generating musical compositions in the style of Bach. When given Mozart, or Schubert, or Puccini, or Scott Joplin, it readily analyzes their styles and composes new music in their styles. . . . When fed music by two composers, it can promptly compose pieces that eerily unite their styles, and when fed, all at once . . . all these styles at once, it proceeds to write music based on the totality of its musical experience.[21]

There is no question that Cope's creation is a brilliant work of programming—that Cope is a gifted programmer and probably also a musical genius, expressing his creativity in writing his EMI program and coming up with the algorithms that EMI follows to output music in very good imitation of its input. However, the description of what EMI produces—that is, the description of its output—seems to me at least to be not so much a creative process as a carefully controlled *imitation* of the creativity of others. (Does EMI even understand that both its input and output are "music"?) Even Dennett comments that what really moves him is how much the EMI *imitation* of Puccini sounds *like* Puccini. EMI must be fed music—note the passive voice of the verb *fed*—which it then manipulates to produce a different output, but one in imitation of its input. It follows an algorithm that involves data entry, and the data that get entered are the creative work of past composers. Its analysis of those data is completely determined by its program, designed by Cope. *All* of its work comes to it through the programming and the data entry. Dennett might claim that human composers such as Bach are doing the same thing—that Bach was merely taking as input all the music he had heard, synthesizing it, and spitting it out based on some programming that was inherent in his brain. But that assumes a priori that Bach, and the other composers whose work EMI manipulates to produce its output, and indeed all members of the human race, were (and are) also automata. Whether that is true is what is at question. If he assumes it is true to begin with (which he does), then he should not draw that as a conclusion (which he also does).

Again, the purpose of this example is not to point out the lack of real originality in EMI, but the lack of originality in humans if Dennett's physicalism is correct. Dennett and Kurzweil are essentially arguing that under their assumption of physicalism, programmed digital computers have the potential to be every bit *as creative* as us programmed humans. But this is really the same as arguing that humans can be *no more* creative than computers; our creativity is just as much an illusion as that of Aaron or EMI. Perhaps this explains why Kurzweil is so eager to defend some notion of creativity in computers. He needs to believe that human creativity is still real and valuable even under his physicalist assumptions: "In my view," he writes, "relying on the patterns of matter and energy in the human body and brain to explain its behavior and proficiencies need not diminish our wonderment at its remarkable qualities."[22]

We return, then, to Kurzweil's efforts to defend the creativity of computers. To the extent that creativity is defined in terms of originality, as I argue above, his concepts cannot be consistently defended; physical automata, whether of the digital computer variety or of the biochemical human variety, are not capable of originating anything. Now Kurzweil actually seems to be aware of this deficiency, and so in the end—perhaps hoping to salvage some notion of creativity that does not require originality—in both *The Age of Spiritual Machines* and in his defense of that book in his essay response to Dembski, he finally falls back on the idea of *unpredictability* as his defense of creativity: "You never know what [they] are going to do next."[23] Now unpredictability can give an *illusion* of creativity, yet ultimately unpredictability is a different and far weaker thing.

It is worth taking a little bit of time to understand this. As Kurzweil illustrates, there are two basic ways that a computer program—say, a cybernetic artist—could be unpredictable. Unpredictability can come from a lack of knowledge on the part of the human viewing or using the system. Or something can be unpredictable because of inherent randomness in the system itself. Of course, if physicalism is true and humans are automata, then the same thing is true of human artists. If the automata view of humanity is true, we can understand the human artist by exact analogy to the computer artist (assuming our computers have the potential now or in the future to grow in complexity). So let us consider first unpredictability of behavior (of humans or computers) from lack of knowledge. Kurzweil wants to call something creative if it does something we don't expect. This seems to me a bit like watching a six-year-old learning to play tic-tac-toe three-in-a-row. Every reasonably intelligent adult who has taken more than a few minutes to think about the game knows there are only a small number of possible tic-tac-toe games that can be played, and knows how every game (between two intelligent adults who are both trying to win) will be played to one of the same small handful of draws every time, depending on how the first two moves are made.[24] To the six-year-old child, however, the course and outcome of a game may be unpredicted and surprising, and in particular the play of another person (especially an adult who knows how to win consistently) will appear creative. Predictability, here, comes from knowledge, and unpredictability from lack of knowledge. What is unpredictable to some people may be predictable to others. This is an important point. Creativity, if the word is to have a significant objective meaning, must be a property of an artist. Unpredictability based on lack of knowledge, unlike creativity, is ultimately a property *not* of the artist, but of the viewer of that art, or the observer of the artist. Unpredictability thus cannot be the same thing as creativity.

Now one of Kurzweil's points—a thoughtful point based on an accurate assessment—is that modern computer systems are so vastly complex that even their designers cannot know how they will behave under all circumstances. A more accurate analogy in this view would be the ancient game of Go. There are 129,960 possible combinations of moves for just the *first round* of Go—a single move for each of the two players—in contrast to a mere seventy-two for tic-tac-toe. There are over sixteen billion possible combinations of moves for just two rounds, and more than 2×10^{15} moves for the first three rounds. After only about sixteen rounds of the game, the number of possible moves exceeds the number of estimated atoms in the entire observable universe.[25] And a game could last over a hundred rounds. There are still only a finite number of possible Go games that can be played, and hypothetically for two players who knew all the possible games, the best move of another player with complete knowledge would cease to be unpredictable. However, the number of possible games is so astronomically large that it is inconceivable that there could ever be a human or even the most powerful supercomputer imaginable capable of searching through all possible moves to determine a winning strategy. (Interestingly enough, computers are also not very good at the game of Go, which some people would argue really does seem to require intuition and creativity and not just fast computation. The best computer programs play at not much better than a good amateur level.)

In the same way, a complete knowledge of a computer system (such as a cybernetic artist) and its state hypothetically would make all of its behavior fully predictable, as would complete knowledge of the state of a human's physical brain (if physicalism is true). And, if we had that thorough knowledge, the computer (or human) artist would thus cease to be unpredictable and so would also cease to appear creative. But nobody has such a full knowledge of such a complex system as a cybernetic artist (or any modern computer), and certainly not of the human mind of an artist, and so it is unpredictable based on our limited knowledge. So we might try to argue that unpredictability really is inherent in the complexity *of the system*, and not of the viewer or user of the system. This would still not make *unpredictability* the same as *creativity* rooted in *originality*, but at least it would make it a stronger imitation.

Note, however, that this is a practical, not a theoretical or philosophical, distinction. Practically, the complexity of the cybernetic artist makes it unpredictable *to us*, and thus it *appears* creative. In reality, its behavior *would* be predictable *if* we took the time and had the knowledge to study the system. The same is true of the complex brain if physicalism is true. The designers of the chess system Deep Blue, for example, would not have been able to predict what move Deep Blue would make next in a game against Kasparov (at least not in the amount of time it took to actually make the move), because they could not process that large amount of information quickly enough. (That's why they needed the computer to beat Kasparov.) But they did understand exactly how the algorithm works that determines that move. As for human complexity, Kurzweil himself argues that by the end of this century we will finally understand the human biochemical computer that we call a brain well enough to download our consciousness into computers. Our lack of knowledge, Kurzweil argues, is steadily disappearing. To be honest, then, what we must do is call the system *unpredictable* based on our limited knowledge, but not *creative*.

A second, stronger type of unpredictability comes not from a lack of knowledge but from randomness. If a computer can be programmed to behave randomly, then it could in theory be unpredictable even to the person with complete knowledge. Now, the idea of being *programmed* to behave *randomly* may seem oxymoronic to some people, since the very notion of a program is based on deterministic instructions. A programming language such as Java, or Lisp, or Fortran, or C on a modern computer can make use of what are often *called* random numbers, but they are more accurately named *pseudorandom* numbers because they are deterministically generated. Pseudorandom numbers *appear* random to the user only because the algorithm that generates them is complex, and it uses input data that are considered irrelevant to the program and unknown to the user (such as the number of milliseconds that have passed since the start of 1970), and so the pseudorandom numbers are *unpredictable* only in the previous sense of that word: we would need a lot of knowledge to predict them. Thus, this sort of pseudorandom number reverts to the type of unpredictability described above.

However, some scientists believe in the possibility of *real* random numbers based on the randomness of quantum physics (which, as mentioned at the start of this book, may or may not be truly random). At some level, we might be tempted to argue for something like originality—something that did not come from the computer's explicit design and its data entry—if it were based on these random numbers. This is what Kurzweil himself notes in his response to Dembski (despite the fact that these truly random quantum numbers, even if they do exist, are not available in normal computer systems and almost certainly are not currently in use by most or even any of the cybernetic artists described).

> Even today's computer programs routinely use simulated randomness [pseudorandom numbers]. If one needs truly random events in a process, there are devices that can provide this as well. Fundamentally, everything we perceive in the material world is the result of many trillions of quantum events, each of which displays profound and irreducible quantum randomness at the core of physical reality. The material world—at both the macro and micro levels—is anything but predictable.[26]

Accepting Kurzweil's assumption of quantum randomness, and even his predictions of dramatically greater complexity of future computer systems in comparison with the already complex systems of today, there are still several problems with referring to the results of randomness as *creativity* (with respect to either humans or computers). A small point that is easy to see with respect to computer programs (though more difficult to visualize with the human mind) is that, even if a program uses random numbers, the use of those numbers is deterministic. In other words, the computer programmer still specifies to the computer *exactly* what to do with the random numbers. At a simple level, we may say that *if* a random number is odd, *then* we perform one action (use blue paint), *else* we perform another action (use red paint). At a more complex level, we may choose an action (selecting a color, for example) not from among two choices using a simple *if-then-else* structure, but from a vast array of possible choices. But the behavior of the system based on that random number must still be described in complete detail by the programmer. The random numbers may be used to determine the output, but at some basic level they do not determine the behavior.

Another, more serious problem, getting closer to our twofold definition of creativity, is that the results of this potential randomness cannot ultimately be attributed to the creativity of either human or computer, but only to some quantum behavior somewhere in the universe. Put another way, randomness in the view of the physicalist who holds to quantum theory is still not a property of a mind as a *mind*, or of any will or intent, but rather it is a property of purposeless elementary subatomic particles. The human person, or the computer, is still a physically determined device under assumptions of quantum physics—all of the causes still lie outside the person or the computer in the strictly physical universe—but it is an *un*predictably determined device. Kurzweil himself acknowledges this in his description of "events" as being "the result of the predictable—or unpredictable—interaction of particles."[27] The idea of intent, or purpose, however, is also an important part of our understanding of creativity. Ocean waves may make beautiful random patterns in the sand as the tide comes in and goes out, but we know these patterns to be without purpose. We don't call the ocean *creative* for this endeavor, even if we call the patterns beautiful. Randomness, by its very nature, has no purpose or intent; a subatomic particle has no purpose or intent, and "many trillions of quantum events" collectively have no purpose or intent. We may not be able to predict the results of a dice roll or coin flip, but we don't call those results creative. We might even create an interesting pattern from the results of hundreds or thousands or even trillions upon trillions of such dice rolls, and that pattern would be unpredictable but not creative. Randomness is not a property of creativity that comes from an individual. To confuse random quantum behavior with design and creativity is the same mistake as confusing purely naturalistic evolution based on random chance with design.

So what is going on? Kurzweil would have to be recognized as a creative person—tremendously creative, in fact, as evidenced by his many accolades, accomplishments, and inventions. Reading his books, one gets the sense that he is very aware of his own giftedness and creativity. It must be difficult, then, for him to really believe that all that creativity and originality, including his own creativity, is just an illusion. So, he continues to use the words *creative* and *original*. But as the previous paragraphs have shown, he does so in a way that is inconsistent or at least a very loose use of language. The systems Kurzweil describes are like a beautifully designed house, or even like one of the elaborate Lego constructions made by one of my sons. I may be surprised by the special features of their Lego construction, which I might not have predicted even looking at the construction closely. I certainly would not have constructed them even with my knowledge of the myriad types of Lego pieces available. And I would say to my child, with full sincerity, "That is really a creative Lego space station you have built."

Or at a more profound level I might look in awe at the incredible work of architecture—a Frank Lloyd Wright house, or a medieval European cathedral—and marvel at how "creative" and "original" it is. If by my use of these words I mean that my child, or the building's architect, exercised great creativity in its design and construction, and the result is original, my observation would make sense. But if I meant, by calling a building creative, that it was itself capable of creating something new, or of originating something other than itself, then my statement ought to be met with skepticism. A building may be the result of creativity, but it cannot be creative. But in the same way neither can any of the art-creating programs (or artist programming systems) described by Kurzweil. They are the result of brilliant creativity by computer programmers (such as Kurzweil himself), but they do nothing original that was not somehow coded into them (even if in unpredictable ways because of their complexity).

Of course, if the physicalists are right about humans, then not even the system designers are creative. We simply have a digital computer program written by a biochemical computer program written by the program of the universe itself without any purpose, and hence—even by Kurzweil's definition of free will, which involves purpose—by a universal program that has no freedom or creativity. So Dennett eventually concludes that, "on close inspection, even on close *intro*-spection, a genius dissolves into a pack rat, which dissolves in turn into a collection of trial-and-error processes over which nobody has ultimate control."[28]

Living without "Freedom and Dignity"

A final question we ask in this chapter, then, is whether we can really believe the view of humans that comes from strict naturalism and causal closure. Neither computers nor Kurzweil's physicalist model of humans have free will, and thus they cannot originate anything. There is no creativity, not if Kurzweil, Dennett, Dawkins, and Skinner are right.

Still, although Kurzweil understands this, he cannot escape the language of creativity. It is deeply embedded in us. If it is an illusion, it is a powerful one. Might this inescapable sense of the reality of our creativity, or the importance of real heroism, be some pointer to the truth that science might not be able to give us?

Or, to ask in another way, if creativity and heroism, both of which depend on free choice, are illusory and not pointers to something true about ourselves, should we not be able to expect at least the most well-educated and ardent defenders of the philosophy of physicalism to be consistent in defending and living out that view? Yet a closer look at the writings of these brilliant minds committed to naturalism suggests that even the most ardent and hostile deniers of a spiritual reality cannot actually live, speak, and write consistently as though free will, creativity, and true heroism were false.

Consider, for example, another of Skinner's comments. In denying the existence of any objective moral values—the sort of moral values that might, for example, define heroic behavior—he notes, "The problem is to induce people not to be good but to behave well."[29] In other words, the moral goodness of an individual is not a real category, because morality itself is not a category; we should be concerned only with one's behavior. This raises several questions, at least one of which presents some real inconsistency with his thinking.

The first question is, what is meant by "behaving well"? The word *well* implies some sort of end, or *telos*—a purpose or goal toward which the behavior is aimed. Skinner seems to want simultaneously both to deny and to affirm the existence of objective standards. But if there are no objective criteria defining a person's "goodness," then what objective criteria could define what behaving "well" means? Does Skinner mean behavior that is most acceptable or convenient for the most number of people? If so, wouldn't we have to say that defending the minority against an oppressive majority—behavior that has often been called "heroic"—would be *not* behaving well? Now this first line of questioning leads to old debates about the definition of good behavior in the absence of objective standards. For some this is not a troublesome issue. While I believe it leads to inconsistencies in Skinner, with respect to the central point of this book it is not the main problem.

The next concern, and a more important one, is what he means by "induce." Skinner probably chose this word carefully. Remember that he denies free will, including by necessity free will with respect to what we think, since what we think controls what we do. If we were free to change our thinking, we would be free to change our actions. But our thinking, according to Skinner, is just as explainable in physical terms as our actions (at least in theory). So he would not want to say we should *convince* people to behave well, or help people to *choose* to behave well, because the notion of *convincing* just as much as the notion of *choosing* would imply that we are free to change our thinking, which (according to him) we are not. Rather, his careful use of the word *induce* implies something more like behavioral conditioning, which does assume—consistent with his other claims and arguments—that those whose behavior is being *induced* are automata to be programmed.

But who is doing the programming? That's the question that trips Skinner up time and again. He seems to view the *masses* as people who can be—and, indeed, *must* be—conditioned to behave well for the good of society (assuming that there is some objective standard of what is "good" for society). But at the same time, he is inferring the existence of, and indeed depending upon the existence of, some elite group of people who are *not* completely programmed, who can be *convinced* to make the *choice* to program the others. This is perhaps the most significant point of *Beyond Freedom and Dignity* and the Westmont College speech. There is a "problem" to be solved regarding the human race, and he is suggesting that a certain group of people take hold of the reins, as it were, and bring about the solution. Some groups of people have free will and initiative and can make choices, and these are the ones who will induce the behavior of the others.

This idea continues to emerge in Skinner's writing. "It is the environment," he notes, "which is 'responsible' for the objectionable behavior, and it is the environment, not some attribute of the individual, which must be changed."[30] Once again, the first part of this quote is consistent with his other writing. He doesn't blame individual human free will for objectionable behavior, but rather he blames environmental factors that condition or program us humans. There is neither heroism nor villainy, because we are not responsible for our behavior at all; the environment is. And this leads to his argument that we *must* change the environment, since it is responsible for all our problems. But who will change it? Doesn't his solution presuppose some group of people who are actually capable of transcending their environmental programming and acting—a group of people who *do* have free will? Even the word *must* implies that it is moral obligation rather than something already determined to happen, and that there is some *telos* or end toward which we need to strive.

He presented the same argument in a BBC interview with even stronger words. "If the power of a technology of behavior does indeed fall into the hands of despots, it will be because it has been rejected by men and women of good will."[31] The "technology of behavior" of which he speaks is the knowledge to program human beings. Skinner's explicit message is that such a technology exists because humans are, after all, determined and programmable. But notice what follows. For all his denial of heroes, he falls right into the language of heroism, speaking not only of evil "despots," but also of "men and women of good will." His language, here, might have come right from the heroic literature he condemns; people who have the "will" to do "good" is the essential definition we had of heroes. The definition implies both the existence of will (freedom) and some definition of good.

Again, this repeated reference to good, which implies some moral measure of goodness, though inconsistent with his denial of objective values elsewhere, is not even his biggest inconsistency. We get back again to this underlying notion that Skinner cannot shake free of, even in his boldest denials of human free will or of anything other than physical properties of the human: there are, in fact, people completely free of this physical determinism, who can choose what to do to make society better. These hypothetical future men and women of whom he speaks apparently have the freedom to either accept or reject the power to control others, and they may choose to reject it.

Not only does the use of the word *will* imply human freedom, but so also does his speaking of what will happen "because" those of good will "reject" his political agenda: things will happen in the world, he tells us, *because* of human choice to *reject* an idea. He is thus calling for heroes who will make virtuous choices. Put another way, Skinner writes as though the future were *not* already determined, and that certain things *ought* to be done, and that we could actually, by our choices, do these things and determine the future. But if the determinism he argues for in his books were actually true, this would be impossible; the future would never be hypothetical but always certain.

It is as if Skinner, for all of his arguments against the existence of free will, knows deep down that he himself has free will to choose and to act. So whatever he says and argues for, he still acts personally on the assumption that we (or at least he) make(s) choices. And not only that, he writes as though our choices have some meaning based on a fixed moral definition of right and wrong.

B. F. Skinner is not alone. Richard Dawkins repeats the same sorts of inconsistencies. Consider a typical comment by Dawkins, where he rants against theists.

> Of course, dyed-in-the-wool faith-heads are immune to argument, their resistance built up over years of childhood indoctrination using methods that took centuries to mature (whether by evolution or design). . . . But I believe there are plenty of open-minded people out there: people whose childhood indoctrination was not too insidious, or for other reasons didn't "take," or whose native intelligence is strong enough to overcome it. Such free spirits should need only a little encouragement to break free of the vice of religion altogether.[32]

We will return to this quote in chapter 4 in another context, but for now it is worth observing a couple points. Dawkins implies two categories of people. Those who are not free to think ("dyed-in-the-wool faith-heads"), because they have been indoctrinated since childhood, and those who have broken free of their indoctrination through native intelligence. So are we, as humans, physically determined or not? If we are, then *nobody* is free from the complete control of physicalism—neither Dawkins, nor those who agree with him, nor those who disagree with him. If Dawkins's claim of physicalism is correct, then there is no such thing as a "free spirit" and nobody can "break free" of any vice. We are all programmed beings, or "dyed-in-the-wool faith-heads"; the only question is what color of dye has gone into our wool. But of course, for all of Dawkins's preaching, he can't actually act as if his own nature were fully programmed, physical, or determined; he can see others as being programmed—*insidiously*, he claims, which is an interesting word, because it implies some sort of moral judgment, while Dawkins, like Skinner, also denies any objective grounds for morality—but he can't actually see himself as (or live himself as) one who is programmed and devoid of freedom.

And this is the main point of this chapter. Physicalism may be correct. Strict naturalists like Russell, Skinner, Kurzweil, Dennett, and Dawkins may all be right. But even if they are, they can't live as though they were. They might argue that this is only because they themselves have been too deeply programmed by cultural thinking. The worldview of Kurzweil denies free will and the possibility of creativity and makes it out to be an illusion, but Kurzweil's writings cannot escape from his own deep-down sense of creativity, and his attraction to that which is creative. Our argument here is that maybe this is evidence that the worldview of physicalism that denies spiritual reality is missing something. Is our own intuition, and the way we are able to live, in line with what B. F. Skinner explicitly argues for? Or is it more in line with his inconsistencies and with how he actually lives—with the view that we can and do make choices, and moreover, that we can make choices that are morally good or evil, that we can be creative, that we can be heroic?

Should we believe the physicalists that creativity and heroism are illusions? At least one answer is that we should not, because our deeply seated and universal intuition—what we might attribute to our spiritual insights or wisdom if we are indeed spiritual beings—tells us that creativity and heroism are not only both real, but also that they are to be valued. The second reason to doubt the assumptions of physicalism is that the physicalists themselves don't fully seem to believe the assumptions.

3

Naturalism and Nature

The Ecology of Physicalism

We explored, in the previous chapter, the implications of physicalism and determinism for our view of ourselves as humans, and specifically for the concepts of heroism and creativity. We now turn our attention outward. What are the implications of physicalism to our view of the *world outside us*? In particular, what sort of ecological behaviors naturally follow from a philosophy of physicalism? We will begin by looking at implications of a very narrow sort of belief espoused by Raymond Kurzweil—ideas that may not (yet) be broadly accepted even among the most ardent physicalists or strictest adherents of naturalism. Then we will turn to two more implications that follow from more general forms of physicalism.

Virtual Reality and the Disembodied Human

"We don't always need real bodies. If we happen to be in a virtual environment, then a virtual body will do just fine."[1] This may sound like a statement from a science fiction film such as *The Matrix*, where the human race has (unknowingly) ceased to use their bodies and exists entirely in a virtual world. But it is the voice, once again, of Ray Kurzweil, from *The Age of Spiritual Machines*. He makes the startling prediction that by the end of *this* century humans will no longer need bodies at all but will be able to download our consciousness into computer memory and lead eternal virtual lives—lives much better than the ones we currently lead.

Ideas such as this have drastic ecological implications. At first glance it may seem that a worldview affirming only the bodily and physical reality, and denying any spiritual reality, would place a *higher* value on the physical world—that is, on what we usually call *nature*—and as such could provide a better basis for healthy environmental practices. But passages like the above, from intelligent and creative thinkers like Kurzweil, should make it clear: this is not the case at all. In fact, physicalism, at least in the vein of Raymond Kurzweil, in many ways eliminates some of the most important underlying principles and motivations for healthy ecology.

Let us begin by exploring Kurzweil's idea further. The previous chapter in his book explains how humans, in the same way that we have replaced bad knees and hips with synthetic ones, and replaced parts of our hearts with artificial valve and pumps, will also eventually replace our brains with nanotechnology. This, he argues, will be a much better form of intelligence than our current biochemical brains. If you begin with Kurzweil's assumptions about our mind being no more than our brain, and our consciousness no more than a physical reality, then what he promises makes sense. The difficulties of building synthetic human brains have to do only with the complexity of the brain, and not with any fundamental philosophical difference in kind between human minds and silicon-based "intelligence." Having reduced our minds to automata, not only will it eventually be possible, in theory, to build a computer and write a program to *do* anything our human brains can *do*—that is, to *think* any thoughts we can *think*—there will be nothing to prevent us from replacing our brains with computers. The prosthesis experiment discussed in chapter 1 ceases to be a *thought experiment* and becomes a real world goal.

But once we have replaced our brains, why do we need our bodies at all? If we go through all the work of loading our consciousness into a computer, and thus replacing our biochemical brains as computing devices with modern nanotechnological computing devices, why should we then bother to take that computer and hook it back into our frail bodies? Our bodies, after all, are susceptible to disease and aging, with all their many limitations. If our brains are just computers, we might as well carry out our entire existence as part of a computer, where virtual reality could eliminate those limitations. We could all be like Neo in *The Matrix*, unbound by the physical limitations of mortal flesh.

This, indeed, is Kurzweil's thinking, as he himself goes on to suggest. "There is no obvious place to stop this progression until the human race has largely replaced the brains and bodies that evolution first provided."[2] In short, he promises, since consciousness is nothing more than advanced computation, we will be able to download our consciousness into a computer.

> Actually there won't be mortality by the end of the twenty-first century. Not in the sense that we have known it. Not if you take advantage of the twenty-first century's brain-porting technology. Up until now, our mortality was tied to the longevity of our *hardware*. When the hardware crashed, that was it. For many of our forebears, the hardware gradually deteriorated before it disintegrated. Yeats lamented our dependence on a physical self that was "but a paltry thing, a tattered coat upon a stick." As we cross the divide to instantiate ourselves into our computational technology, our identity will be based on our evolving mind file. *We will be software, not hardware.*[3]

As I noted, this is a rather stunning idea. It is *this* century he is speaking of. That last sentence is not even stated as a *remote* possibility of what *might* happen, but as a *prophecy* of what *will* be: we will cease to be bodily creatures altogether and will become just disembodied brains, or brains with only virtual bodies—though brains that are far more powerful than our current ones. "Today, our software cannot grow," he writes. "It is stuck in a brain of a mere 100 trillion connections and synapses. But when the hardware is trillions of times more capable, there is no reason for our minds to stay so small. They can and will grow."[4] And a little later, he adds that "our twenty-first-century physical technology will also greatly exceed the capabilities of the amino acid–based nanotechnology of the natural world."[5] For some the idea is terrifying. For some it holds wonderful promise. For some, it is perhaps both.

Again, lest we have any misunderstanding of this vision, or doubts that Kurzweil could really be making this promise, two sections (of chap. 7) suggestively titled "Virtual Bodies" and "The Sensual Machine" go on to explain what will follow from his promises. For example, there are powerful implications for romantic and sexual human relationships. "In addition to direct sensual and sexual contact, virtual reality will be a great place for romance in general," Kurzweil envisions. "Stroll with your lover along a virtual Champs-Élysées, take a walk along a virtual Cancún beach. . . . Your whole relationship can be in Cyberland."[6] What will make all this possible? Kurzweil explains his predictions.

> By the fourth decade [of this century], we will move to an era of virtual experience through internal neural implants. With this technology, you will be able to have almost any kind of experience with just about anyone, real or imagined, at any time. It's just like today's online chat rooms, except that you don't need any equipment that's not already in your head, and you can do a lot more than just chat. You won't be restricted by the limitations of your natural body as you and your partners can take on any virtual physical form. Many new types of experiences will become possible.[7]

Indeed, Kurzweil goes on to say, our experiences will not be limited to simulating physical experiences; we will be able to directly control our emotions, ideas, and spiritual experiences as well, since these are all—he claims and tries to justify—just biochemical sensations of the brain.[8] "Regardless of the nature and derivation of a mental experience, spiritual or otherwise, once we have access to the computational processes that give rise to it, we have the opportunity to understand its neurological correlates." What follows, he then claims, is this: "With the understanding of our mental processes will come the opportunity to capture our intellectual, emotional, and spiritual experiences, to call them up at will, and to enhance them."[9]

I could continue giving more examples of this thinking, about which Kurzweil himself elaborates at length, but at this point it is worth turning from the ideas to their implications. At the heart of this is the promise that we will be free of our physical bodies (including our biological brains); we "won't be restricted by the limitations of [our] natural body." This is what it means to live in a *virtual* (as opposed to material) reality. Our physical bodies are no longer important. Indeed, they are hindrances. Now *ridding ourselves* of the material body may seem like a strange end to reach when we begin at the starting place of affirming *only* the material body, but Kurzweil does a convincing job of showing how his goals flow naturally from his assumptions. It is very reasonable—perhaps nearly unavoidable—for one who holds the basic assumption that humans are complex biochemical computers to be drawn at some level to Kurzweil's goals of enhancing our computational powers and freeing ourselves from our bodies.

And yet these goals may be deadly to healthy human interaction with the natural world in which we live. Put another way, the ecological practices that will emerge—and indeed have already emerged and taken shape—from the presuppositions shared by Kurzweil and others, have a high and terrible cost.

In short, when you devalue the body, as happens with Kurzweil's brand of physicalism, you devalue the entire physical (or natural) world. For the body is the very means by which we interact with this world of *nature*. It is with our hands that we work the soil and bring forth fruit. It is with our mouths that we taste the goodness of that fruit, and with our bodies we receive its nutrition. If we can create virtual tastes, then why cultivate real, healthy food? If we can live with virtual bodies, then why care for the world that in turn cares for our bodies? Why worry at all about the health and beauty of the world, when we can live in virtual worlds of our own imaginings? And, on the other side, it is our bodies that will grow sick—and, indeed, already grow sick—as the air, soil, and water around us get progressively more toxic. But if our bodies don't matter anymore, who cares?

Norman Wirzba explains this well in his essay "Placing the Soul: An Agrarian Philosophical Principle."

> To put the point more practically, can we *properly* engage the world if we despise the bodies in terms of which such engagement occurs, or despise the natural bodies upon which our own lives so clearly depend? One of the lasting contributions of [Wendell Berry's collec-

> tion of essays] *The Unsettling of America* was to show that on both counts the answer is a resounding *No!* Though we might dream of ourselves as disembodied, immortal souls, or as complex computers that will finally shed all biological and physiological limitations, the fact remains that we live necessarily through our bodies.[10]

The answer to Wirzba's initial question, "Can we *properly* engage the world if we despise . . . the natural bodies upon which our own lives so clearly depend?" is, I believe, "No. We cannot." If we despise our natural bodies (as Kurzweil apparently does), then we will not properly engage the world. Our only engagement with the *natural, material* world will be to extract energy necessary to fuel our *virtual* worlds—and perhaps, for a short time only, to extract resources to sustain our physical bodies until we can be rid of them.

Now, it is fair to ask whether I am taking Kurzweil's ideas too far. The answer, I think, is that I am taking them no further than Kurzweil himself has taken them. He explicitly envisions for us a new world, and he claims his new world is not only good, but better than our current one. With respect to the destruction of the world that results from this type of thinking, and the subsequent destruction of all the good and healthy benefits our bodies enjoy from a healthy ecology, Kurzweil seems to say, *So what? Soon we won't need it.* In fact, he promises something like this explicitly. "Food, clothing, diamond rings, buildings," he writes, "could all assemble themselves molecule by molecule." But what about fruit and vegetables and the produce of the soil? In his envisioned new virtual world, he tells, us, "Any sort of product could be instantly created when and where we need it. Indeed, the world could continually reassemble itself to meet our changing needs, desires, and fantasies."[11] The underlying assumption here is that the world exists only to meet our needs, desires, and fantasies. His most frightening comment comes two pages later. "If we're going to enter a new world, we had better get rid of traces of the old."[12]

Though made in the context of making virtual reality experiences more realistic, this comment is very suggestive of the underlying agenda. Anybody who cares about the healthy ecology of this world, who cares about the cleanliness of our water and air, or the ability of our soils to continue to sustain diverse life—who cares about anything in the natural world beyond the production of energy—should be terrified by Kurzweil's vision. It is a vision that calls for getting rid of any remaining traces of our old, physical, ecological world. The consequences of this materialist thinking—in particular, of viewing the brain as a mere complex computational device—is devastating to the health of the physical earth on which we live. And this ought to lead us also to ask whether this sort of thinking really rings true. If we live it out, and practice it, does it satisfy the soul or spirit?

A final thought is in order in this section. I began this chapter by suggesting that the first set of implications explored is particular to Kurzweil's brand of physicalism. Many physicalists would distance themselves considerably from this vision. Ideas that Kurzweil puts forth as promising, others would see as disastrous. So we must ask, are these extremes, which envision humankind moving toward virtual reality, truly a logical conclusion to physicalism, as Kurzweil makes them out to be? There are thoughtful philosophers who share Kurzweil's basic presuppositions of physicalism but deny his conclusions, enough so that I won't argue that these conclusions follow *inevitability* from the underlying philosophy. And yet I cannot help but notice that many in our current Western culture—a culture strongly influenced by physicalism—show frightening signs of moving wholeheartedly toward living virtual lives.

Consider, for example, not merely the popularity of spectator sports (which have been around since the ancient Greeks), but of so-called fantasy sports. These virtual leagues are growing at a phenomenal rate and now exist not only for baseball and football, but also for basketball, hockey, and even fishing. Not only would we rather watch sports on television than play the sports ourselves with our own bodies—not only do we root passionately for carefully managed personae we have never met, following the ongoing crises and attention ploys of star players as carefully as anybody follows soap operas or tabloids—but with the rise of fantasy teams, we no longer even care about the actual regional teams we watch. We may be more interested in our fantasy team than in the "real" teams, and thus more interested in statistics of players independent of actual outcomes of games than we are in who wins the game.

And this is only the mildest of examples. We could speak about the meteoric rise of video game cultures over the past two decades.

Most video games are set in virtual worlds, where players spend hundreds or even thousands of hours playing the parts of virtual characters with virtual bodies (enhanced by imaginary powers) fighting virtual battles for virtual rewards. One could argue that we are already living virtual lives.

Ken Myers, director of the *Mars Hill Audio Journal*, gives another poignant illustration of how virtual our lives are by addressing the popularity of the television series and character *Hannah Montana.*

> Miley Cyrus plays the lead character on Hannah Montana, a character named Miley Stewart. Stewart has migrated west from her humble Tennessee origins to live in Malibu, to pursue her dreams as a superstar singer known to the public as Hannah Montana. Hannah Montana is thus a persona, an alternate identity assumed by Miley Stewart. Miley Stewart is also a character, performed by Miley Cyrus. What makes it even more reflexive is that Miley Cyrus performs in concert as Hannah Montana, bypassing Ms. Stewart entirely. One might ask if Miley Cyrus is really a celebrity pop sensation, or whether she just pretends to be a pop sensation when she's in character.[13]

Now Myers was not specifically addressing the concern of living in an increasingly virtual world, but rather the "disorders encouraged by celebrity culture." He is wondering if our "six- and seven-year-old daughters really benefit from having as a guide to growing up a performer playing a performer playing a performer."[14] But the topics are related, and his final comment is very revealing. It is already an abstraction—a move toward virtual reality—when we are more absorbed by celebrity performers than by real people who live next door. But now we are absorbed by "a performer playing a performer playing a performer." We are three levels of abstraction away from reality. We are living a virtual reality inside a virtual reality inside a virtual reality.[15] Have we already entered Kurzweil's vision?

Wendell Berry, one of the most important writers of the past fifty years to focus on environmental and agrarian concerns, also addresses the impact of this way of thinking about the mind and body. The topic is important enough that he touches upon it in several of his essays, but perhaps his clearest comments on this topic can be found in his essay "The Body and the Earth."

> And it is clear to anyone who looks carefully at any crowd that we are wasting our bodies exactly as we are wasting our land. . . . Our bodies have become marginal; they are growing useless like our "marginal" land because we have less and less use for them. After the games and idle flourishes of modern youth, we use them only as shipping cartons to transport our brains and our few employable muscles back and forth to work.[16]

Berry's observations are profound. We are already acting like a society that has denied the importance of body and thinks only of mind.

Nothing Unnatural

The devaluing of the body may be peculiar only to Kurzweil's vision of the human as a complex computing machine—though cultural evidence suggests that it is more widespread. However, there are other ecological implications of physicalism that are worth exploring, because they are potentially of great consequence. One inescapable conclusion of physicalism is that everything humans do is, *by definition*, natural. Moreover, everything we do is not only natural, but also out of our control. It is even inevitable, in a certain sense, though perhaps unpredictable.

Pulitzer Prize winner Gary Snyder is one of today's best-known American nature writers. It is altogether likely that Snyder would cringe in revulsion at the futuristic vision of Raymond Kurzweil and would warn readers of its dangers much as I did in the previous section. However, in at least one essay Snyder also defends a worldview of naturalism. His definition of "nature," from his essay "The Etiquette of Freedom," includes "'the material world or its collective objects and phenomena,' including the products of human action and intention." In other words, humans are fully a part of nature. Not just human bodies, but human action *and intention* are part of nature. This means that *all* our thoughts have naturalistic explanations. This is almost a definition of physicalism. It is certainly a denial of any sort of dualistic nature that sees humans as both spiritual and bodily beings. Or, rather, philosophically speaking, the implication works in the other direction: if we assume that humans are physical beings only, and not beings with any spiritual or supernatural nature, then it follows immediately that everything we do is not only *explainable* by nature (materialistic causes only), but is actually a *part* of nature. That means *everything* we do is natural. Thus, Snyder goes on, bringing us to the consistent conclusion: "Science and some sorts of mysticism rightly propose that *everything* is natural.[17] By these lights there is nothing unnatural about New York City, or toxic wastes, or atomic energy, and nothing—by definition—that we do or experience in life is 'unnatural.'"[18]

This bears repeating. If physicalism is true, then everything done by humans, including fouling the rivers, depleting the ozone, toxifying or plowing under our soil, razing Amazonian rain forests, causing the extinctions of species, or carrying on war with one another, is completely natural *by definition*. To reference a famous old question, "Does a bear poop in the woods?" we answer, "Yes, that is the natural thing for a bear to do." And likewise if we ask, "Does a human dump sewage into the river?" our answer to this question also *must* be, "Yes, that is the natural thing for humans to do." If humans have done it, and if humans are entirely part of nature, then it is a natural thing for humans to do, and therefore also a natural thing to be done. Humans dumping sewage, or spilling unimaginable quantities of oil into the Gulf of Mexico, under the philosophy of naturalism, is as natural as grass growing, bees collecting pollen, and water flowing downhill. Sewage in rivers as well as oil in the Gulf *must* be viewed as *the natural state of things*.

Not only that, but if physicalist determinism is true, then it is also *inevitable*. That is, not only has the fouling of our air, water, and soil been *natural*, but it has been the *only* possible outcome since the beginning of the universe. In that sense, none of us are responsible for any of it, any more than we are responsible for any of our behaviors (such as writing poems or murdering people, to refer back to Bertrand Russell).

Indeed, the latter statement is true under physicalism even if strict determinism is false. Whether the physical world functions in a fully predictable way entirely according to laws, or in a partly unpredictable way because of quantum effects, it is still the case that human behavior is entirely *natural* and is devoid of free will. In other words, even if we allow unpredictable quantum effects under the umbrella of physicalism, we still have to view the current state of things, and the results of all human activities, as unavoidable if not inevitable. It is all the result of purposeless decisionless movements of physical particles. Only random luck and not any sort of human choice could have made things different. The only thing responsible for the environmental destruction we are now experiencing—from lost ozone over the South Pole to the dramatic decline of polar bears due to lost ice at the North Pole—is the universe itself. We have no more choice about the polluting we have already done than water has a choice of whether or not to flow downhill, eroding soil and even rock as it goes. And the question of whether we keep destroying the earth or instead change our habits and try to stem or reverse the decline has also already been determined since the moment the universe came into existence. In fact, in this philosophy, the notion of destroying nature must be understood as a misnomer. Nature is whatever exists, in whatever state it is in.

Now, we need to be clear. Snyder was not trying to promote toxic wastes, atomic energy, or the growth of the next New York City. In fact, he would want to dissuade us from at least the first of those three activities, and probably the second and third as well. The world would do well to heed the warning issued by Snyder in his writings and to more closely follow some of his suggested lifestyles. Nor was he promoting a sort of fatalism—that whatever is going to happen will happen, because it was already determined. Snyder, like many other great nature writers of the past few decades, would have his ideas motivate a change in our actions so that we live in ways that are healthier for the world in which we and our fellow creatures live. Snyder was simply being honest about the philosophical implications of the worldview of naturalism.

Our first question, however, is whether this understanding of our human nature helps motivate what might otherwise be called "healthy environmental behavior." Certainly there are plenty of people who hold Snyder's philosophy who are also model citizens with respect to environmental practices. But the worldview itself doesn't seem to promote it. In particular, we cannot label any human behavior as "unnatural" if by definition everything is "natural." I can express a *personal* distaste for toxic waste, especially in my own backyard, as the saying goes. But I can't complain that it is somewhat *un*natural or *against* nature, because everything we humans do, according to Snyder and the philosophy of physicalism, is by definition natural.

The best I can do is argue that these sorts of behaviors (toxic dumping, etc.), however natural they might be, will result in lives that are less desirable for the majority of humans. And then I must hope that those who wield the power to influence the decisions agree with me, or at least that they agree that it will be less desirable for them also.

But at the same time, I also—if I hold to physicalism—need to understand that whatever is going to happen is already in the programming of the universe (which may or may not have a random number generator in the form of quanta, but is a computer program nonetheless, according to strict naturalism and causal closure). The future, including my own future behavior as well as the future of polar bears, is outside of the free will of any human. If I argue against toxic dumping, or for cleaner high-mileage cars, or for a reduction in coal-based electricity, or for cleaner but more costly coal-based energy, it is only because I am programmed to do so. If I prefer clean air and water, biodiversity, and a world in which polar bears still roam the arctic (even if I never get to see one), it is only because I am programmed to do so, and not because my preferences are somehow better or more natural. And, of course, the opposite is true; if I prefer a consumptive and exploitive lifestyle, and the luxury and material comfort that can often go along with that (at least for the minority who have money or power), it is also because I am programmed to have that preference and to behave in that way.

And then we ask the second question—the one that is behind chapters 2 through 4 of this book. We ask not whether this understanding of our human nature helps motivate healthy environmental behavior, but simply whether it feels or rings true to us. Does this make sense as the truth about the world in which we live? Can you really believe that polluted rivers and toxic waste dumps are *natural*? If you cannot, then you are denying physicalism from which this conclusion inevitably follows; you are affirming that we humans are more than physical beings in a causally closed universe.

The Absence of "Other"

The final set of implications of physicalism explored in this section are akin to those of the previous section. The argument is, once again, that the physicalist philosophy (if taken seriously and followed to its natural conclusions) not only has the strong potential to lead to unhealthy ecological practices—and is ultimately therefore unlivable in the long run for us as a race—but also that it contradicts what we intuitively understand to be true about ourselves and our relationships with those around us.

The central argument of this section is as follows. If physicalism were true, then there would be no meaningful concept of an individual autonomous self, only a single causally closed system composed of a huge number of material atomic particles each obeying laws of physics. If there is no individual *self*, then there is no individual *other*. If there is no *other*, then there is nothing and nobody *else* to care for, and also no real *ecology* to speak of—no interactions of distinct beings.[19] Furthermore, as we noted in the previous chapter's discussion on heroism, under physicalism there is no ultimate purpose, and there are no moral choices, because there are no real choices at all. And even if we had free will to make choices, without the *spiritual* man or a purposeful universe, there is no objective morality and no objective basis for evaluating these choices. Ultimately, then, under physicalism and determinism (strict or broad) there is no moral imperative to choose to care *for* or care *about* other creatures. That is so because:

1. There are *no morals*.
2. There are *no choices*.
3. There are *no others*.

The claim that under physicalism there are no real, existing individuals may be the most important and also the least obvious, and thus it requires the most explanation. To put it in full and as clearly as possible, the claim is this: according to strict naturalism, there is no meaningful distinction between selves; there is no real individual. We may all have a *sense* of self, and we may have a conscious awareness of what we *think* of as ourselves as individuals. In Kurzweil's terms, we have something we call *consciousness*. But this, we are told, is just an illusion and not a meaningful insight into any deeper reality. What we call consciousness is part of our programming, and computers can be programmed with the same experience as embodied humans. The idea of the individual is based on the old-fashioned notion of free will and autonomy, from which ardent naturalists like B. F. Skinner are trying to free us (as we saw in the previous chapter). We are taught to say goodbye to the autonomous or homunculus man. Indeed, much of Skinner's *Beyond Freedom and Dignity* is designed precisely to explain away the notion of individual persons. He complains that human behavior "is still attributed to human nature," and about an "extensive 'psychology of individual differences' in which people are compared and described in terms of traits of character, capacities, and abilities."[20] He argues that we should do away with these notions. And a few pages later, he again complains: "Unable to understand how or why the person we see behaves as he does, we attribute his behavior to a person we cannot see, whose behavior we cannot explain either but about whom we are not inclined to ask questions." In arguing for a shift in our thinking, he then states more clearly:

> Autonomous man serves to explain only the things we are not yet able to explain in other ways. His existence depends upon our ignorance, and he naturally loses status as we come to know more about behavior. The task of a scientific analysis is to explain how the behavior of a person as a physical system is related to the conditions under which the human species evolved and the conditions under which the individual lives.[21]

So Skinner acknowledges some concept of an individual—that is to say, he uses the word *individual*—but in the same breath he denies that this individual is really in any sense an actual individual, one who can behave as an autonomous self with any self-will. Rather, the so-called individual is no more than a "physical system." In particular, the behavior of a person *must*, Skinner argues, be understood entirely in terms of that system.

But now we take the next step. Under physicalism, not only are humans simply complex biochemical computers, or physical systems, but *the entire universe* is nothing more than one large, complex computer system. Consider what this means. A computer is composed of *hardware* and *software*. The software is divided into data (information) and instructions (the program). The hardware deterministically carries out its instructions based on its data. The hardware of the universal computer system is the physical universe itself—which, we are told, is all that exists. The universal computer system's *data* are the current state of all its physical particles. The program of this big computer system that is the universe is the laws of physics, which determine what each and every particle of the hardware will do next, based on its current state. The "each and every particle" part is the key notion, here. In this thinking, we, as humans, must be understood to be not only physical systems, but actually *part of* the big physical system.

B. F. Skinner argues for all of these details separately, though it is not clear that he consistently combines them to their conclusion. He writes,

> Behavior which operates upon the environment to produce consequences ("operant" behavior) can be studied by arranging environments in which specific consequences are contingent upon it. The contingencies under investigation have become steadily more complex, and one by one they are taking over the explanatory functions previously assigned to personalities, states of mind, feelings, traits of character, purposes, and intentions.[22]

Our behaviors are determined by our environment (or the system), Skinner argues repeatedly. All the things we might have thought of as who we are as *selves* or *autonomous individuals*—personalities, states of mind, feelings, traits, etc.—are slowly being replaced; they are no longer explanations of who we are. But Skinner also calls upon us to engage in behaviors to change the environment (or the system). That, indeed, is the primary point of his book. Thus, our behaviors collectively determine the environment, or program the system, while the environment determines or programs us. So, in fact, our behaviors *are* the environment. If Skinner is right, then we are inseparable from the system. Individuals are illusions. There is simply one, large, complex physical system, or environment, composed of many particles (some of which happened to be clumped together in bunches called humans).

Consider all of your activities in a given day, especially your interactions with other living creatures. You get up in the morning and feed a pet. You meet somebody coming into or going out of the bathroom. You make a pot of coffee and serve a cup to your partner, or perhaps he or she pours your cup, while you watch birds on your feeder. You get up to chase a squirrel off your feeder. You commute to work and interact with other commuters and then colleagues. You use electricity that was generated in some far-off place, and your transportation consumes gasoline drilled and refined in another far-off place, both with all sorts of (unknown to you) ramifications to other living creatures, and thus you interact indirectly but perhaps significantly. The coffee you drank earlier, as well as the second cup you buy at the gas station, was grown by people you will never meet but who are impacted by your purchase, on a piece of land with creatures impacted by the coffee plants. But what if we are simply components in one cohesive central system, all following one computer program that governs us all? Then these interactions are all simply the motions of molecules, or at a lower level of atoms, or at a lower level still of electrons and subatomic particles, all following physical laws with no purpose or intent. Everything you think of as your own purpose or intent—doing your job, finding a new job, getting a raise, getting a date, recycling, or consuming—is reducible to purposeless molecules following laws. If this is the true view of the universe, then the concept of individual is an illusion: I don't really interact in any meaningful way with my children, or my wife, or my colleagues, or the stranger at the local café where I stop for an espresso, *as real separate entities*. All of these interactions are simply controlled components of a single computer carrying out its program.

Here is perhaps a clearer way of thinking about it. Consider all the physical particles in some volume of atmosphere with roughly the same number of particles as my body. Like my body, these particles all follow the laws of physics. They may be proximate to each other for a few seconds, minutes, months, or perhaps even years—some small fraction of history. But in what sense does that collection of particles form a "self" or "individual"? Now ask, under physicalism in what way is a human "self" different? A bunch of particles have clustered together for some finite moment of history. But all of their behaviors are determined by the laws of physics, and by the system as a whole, and not by their decisions or will as human persons.

Of course if there is no individual *self*—if the idea of self, at least as an autonomous entity, is an illusion, as B. F. Skinner suggests and as I have argued is the case if physicalism is true—then it also immediately follows that there are no individual *others*. An other is simply a different autonomous self. And here is where the ecological implications begin to emerge. A strong argument can be made that healthy environmental practices, at their core, stem from caring *for* and caring *about* other creatures. I understand a polar bear to be something other than myself. It is not simply a part of the system, but it is a distinct individual. And so, while I have no ethical obligation to a purposeless system that doesn't even have any goals in mind, I may have an ethical obligation to an individual if any individuals actually exist. To view the bear as *other*, and as an individual, is a first step in my wanting to preserve its habitat so that it can, as an individual and as something other than me, survive and prosper. The very notion of bio*diversity* is based on the concepts of real individuals that differ from one another. As philosopher David O'Hara wrote in one of his sections of a book we coauthored, "We feel our difference from one another and from our world, and that feeling is instructive. We are different, and in that difference our ethical obligations to one another are exposed."[23]

To see this in another light, consider a computer system. It may be important for a computer system as a whole to have all its parts functioning. So somebody *outside* the system is motivated to replace or repair any malfunctioning components. If the graphics card goes bad, the user of the computer needs to get a new card—or a new computer. But it is only important for the user who exists *outside* the system that a computer system function properly. It is not important to a computer itself whether it functions in any way that is useful. Under the tenets of naturalism however, there is nothing outside the system. The system has no purpose and no real meaning or concept of *mal*functioning; however it functions is how it *must* function. Likewise, there is no concept of a broken component, because everything is functioning exactly as it *must* function.

Now, here the physicalist might chime in with a counterargument. It may be that the notion of an autonomous individual is an illusion—that all we have are particles following the laws of physics, which (because of those laws) clump themselves together in various ways—but even if all we have is one big universal system, we still should care about that system and want it to be healthy. In fact, we might want it to be healthy precisely because we are a part of it. And caring about that system may require us to care about components within that system that we call "individuals." Thus, biodiversity is still a useful system-level concept to describe the idea that the system as a whole is healthy if its particles choose very diverse ways to clump themselves together.

I grant this argument. And I sincerely hope people follow it. But we then need to ask, what is meant by healthy? The health of a system is judged in terms of some ideal: either how the system *ought* to function or what its goals and objectives are. But a computer system as a whole has no goal. Or, rather, its goal is determined by a user outside the system. A CPU simply carries out its instructions based on its state. It has no objective to accomplish. If there are real individuals—say, the polar bear—then we might act in a way that acknowledges their value. But if there is only a system, then the value of an individual is determined only by some systemwide goal. What is that? Or, to cut to the point for humans, how do we choose to act? Ultimately, we are left with trying to engineer the environment—or trying to define health—in a way most beneficial to us as a species.

Of course, this whole problem assumes that we are free to make choices and struggle to determine what the best choices are: do we act for some individuals or for the system? If there are no significant individuals, then we act for the system, which means for some arbitrary goals that *we* make *for* the system. And under physicalism, not only is there no ultimate purpose for the system, but we don't even make any choices. We do only what we are programmed to do. Thus, on several grounds, there is no moral imperative to choose to care for or about other creatures, because there are no morals, no choices, and no others.

Before closing this chapter, one important point must be made. I have explored what I argue are logical ecological conclusions of a certain worldview. I believe these ecological conclusions, if really followed, would be disastrous. In fact, it would seem that we are living in a world already experiencing many of the ecological consequences of a worldview that affirms only the material and denies human spirit or human free will. But I am not saying, in any way, that all of those who hold this worldview of physicalism are responsible for environmental degradation. In fact, many leading environmental activists do hold to this worldview and yet continue to write, speak, and act in ways that we agree promote ecological health, not only for "the universal system," but for individuals (of many species) within that system. For this, we can be glad, because my argument is that if naturalism really were followed consistently, it would be far more destructive.

C. S. Lewis, who studied and then taught philosophy at Oxford before he became a famous literary scholar and writer, and who himself held strongly to a worldview of naturalism until he was about thirty years old, makes a similar point about aspects of naturalism in his essay "On Living in an Atomic Age." Addressing the possibility—though he himself did not hold to the view—that the universe is both ultimately meaningless and also destined eventually to wind down, and that all life is to come to an end, he gives three possible responses. The first is despair, the second is decadent hedonism, and the third is to say, "Let [the universe] be merciless, I will have mercy. . . . I know the universe will win in the end, but what is that to me? I will go down fighting. Amid all this wastefulness I will persevere; amid all this competition, I will make sacrifices."[24] Thankfully, many who hold the assumption of naturalism have taken this third approach.

4

Reason, Science, and the Mind as a Physical Brain

This chapter starts with one simple but important question: Is human reason a trustworthy means of discovering truth—or any *more* trustworthy than any of numerous other ways that humans have come to belief (such as myth, religion, imagination, intuition, astrology, etc.)? In particular, to use a more technical term, *if* the assumption of physicalism is correct, ought we to trust human reasoning as *normative*?[1] A second, related question and subject of this chapter pertains to science: Should the assumptions of physicalism and causal closure lead to a higher or lower faith in the ability of science to accurately discover truth about our natural world?

Before seeking to answer this question, I should begin by defining *reason*, at least as I am using the term. Reason is an attempted means of dealing with the truth of *propositions*. A proposition, simply put, is a statement that is either true or false. Grammatically speaking, it is a *declarative*, as opposed to an *imperative* (command) or *interrogative* (question)—the other two types of complete sentences—or an *exclamatory* (a display of emotion).[2] The following are all examples of propositions.

All birds have wings.

All birds can fly.

A bird flew past my office window while I was typing this chapter.

Some cats chase birds.

If an animal has feathers and wings and lays eggs, it is a bird.

If all birds have wings, and a sparrow is a bird, then a sparrow has wings.

As the second example also illustrates, declaratives need not be true in order to be propositions; consider penguins, emus, and ostriches. Propositions may be true *or* false; they must be one or the other. Reason is a tool for determining the truth of propositions. We might even say that the *purpose* of reason is to determine whether certain propositions are true or false.[3]

The final two propositions above also illustrate the concept of *implication*. They are compound propositions involving more than one simple proposition. For example, we could consider four separate propositions about a particular animal referred to symbolically as X.

X has feathers.

X has wings.

X lays eggs.

X is a bird.[4]

These propositions can be considered separately with respect to some specific animal X, but the proposition "*If an animal has feathers and wings and lays eggs, it is a bird*" combines them to form a new proposition claiming that any and every animal X having feathers, wings, and laying eggs is a bird; the first three properties of having wings, having feathers, and laying eggs collectively *imply* the property of being a bird; *if* the first three are true, *then* the fourth is also true.

The two most common and broad forms of reasoning are known as *deductive* and *inductive*. Deductive reasoning is based on a collection of principles or laws, called *rules of inference*, which state when the truth of one proposition *must* follow from the truth of another proposition (or propositions). Or, to use the earlier terminology, it tells us when certain propositions *imply* other propositions. As an example, one of the most famous rules of inference is known as *modus ponens*, which states that if proposition *P* implies proposition *Q*, and furthermore proposition *P* is known to be true, then proposition *Q* must also be true. Computer scientists and some mathematicians write this as follows: $((P \rightarrow Q) \wedge P) \rightarrow Q$ where "$\wedge$" is a logical symbol for *and*, and "$\rightarrow$" is a logical symbol for *implies*. Philosophers often use a different notation:

$$\begin{array}{c} P \rightarrow Q \\ P \\ \hline \therefore Q \end{array}$$

where "$\therefore$" is a logical symbol for *therefore*, which is another word that gets at the idea of *implication*. Regardless of the notation, however, computer scientists, mathematicians, and most philosophers (namely those who accept reason) accept as "law" the modus ponens rule of inference.

An example of modus ponens using natural language can be found in the final example of a proposition above: "*If all birds have wings, and a sparrow is a bird, then a sparrow has wings.*" Here, the proposition *P* is that a sparrow is a bird, and the proposition *Q* is that a sparrow has wings. To say that *P* is true is to say that sparrows are birds. To say that *P*→*Q* is to say that *if* a sparrow is a bird, *then* it must have wings. And to say that *Q* is true is to say that sparrows have wings.

An argument is said to be *valid* if the conclusion is guaranteed by the premises (sometimes called assumptions or hypotheses). That is, an argument is *valid* if it follows accepted rules of inference. Both of the following arguments are valid.

> All birds have wings, and a sparrow is a bird, so a sparrow has wings.
>
> All birds have wings, and a cat is a bird, thus a cat has wings.

Both of these arguments follow the modus ponens rule of inference, and so in both cases if the premise were true, then the conclusion would also have to be accepted as true (assuming one accepts deductive reason itself, including the law of modus ponens). Note, however, that the premise "*a cat is a bird*" is false, and so is the conclusion that "*a cat has wings*." An argument can be valid and yet have a false conclusion if it begins with a false premise. An argument is said to be *sound* if it is both valid and has true premises. Only the first of the two arguments above is sound.

An argument can also be *invalid*, or even *unsound*, and yet still have a true conclusion. Neither of the following arguments is sound, and yet both of them have a true conclusion.

> All birds have wings, and a cat is a mammal, so a sparrow has wings.
>
> All animals have wings, and a sparrow is an animal, thus a sparrow has wings.

The first of these is not valid (and therefore is also not sound); the premises are true, but the conclusion does not follow a rule of inference. The second of these is valid but not sound; the first premise, that all animals have wings, is not true. In both cases, the fact that the conclusion is true is just a good guess, or luck, and has nothing to do with the attempted reasoning process by which we arrived at the conclusion.

One important aspect of deductive reasoning (as the modus ponens rule of inference may illustrate) is that it is *nonampliative*, meaning that the argument introduces no new knowledge. Everything in the conclusion of a valid deductive argument is completely present in the combination of the assumptions (or premises) and in the rules of inference. This is the very definition of a valid argument: the conclusion is guaranteed by the premises because it follows from rules of inference. Deductive reasoning begins with accepted generalities (abstract assumptions, definitions, and rules of inferences) and moves toward the truth of particulars.

Deductive reasoning is at the heart of mathematics, because mathematicians work by *defining* systems at a completely abstract level, without any necessary dependence on anything in the physical world. Integers, real numbers, and complex numbers are abstract concepts (though with unquestionably important applications to the real world). Integers follow mathematical rules governing integers, rather than physical "laws" governing particles. So deductive reasoning can fully prove the truth of various mathematical theorems. This is because there are certain assumptions we can know to be true *by definition*, rather than by just accepting them as true through observation or experimentation. However, deductive reasoning does not provide a tool for dealing with physical reality *until* or *unless* we agree upon assumptions about that world. Gravity, for example, must be discovered inductively; it cannot simply be defined. If we begin with assumptions, which themselves may be unprovable, then deductive reasoning may be able to tell us what conclusions are implied by those assumptions. It cannot tell us what assumptions to make.

Inductive reasoning, by contrast, is at the heart of science. Inductive reasoning begins with observations about the concrete particulars and then attempts to generalize conclusions from these particulars. Gravity on the earth is observed through countless daily particulars (such as dropping your toast or spilling your milk at breakfast). More generally, we daily observe—both on earth's surface and in the motions of planets and stars—the attraction of two objects with mass (such as the earth and the moon). From these observations, through much experimentation, inductive reasoning leads us to the general truth about the Universal Law of Gravitation:

$$F_g = G\frac{m_1 m_2}{r^2}$$

Note, however, that this law—though not doubted by anybody I know—cannot be *proven*, at least not in a deductive sense. What we learn from inductive reasoning may always later be shown to be false by some observed counterexample. (It might have seemed like excellent inductive reasoning for early Western Europeans who'd never seen an ostrich, an emu, or a penguin to conclude that all feathered winged creatures could fly.) Yet the conclusions of inductive reasoning are broader and more complete than the specific observations, and so inductive reason really does introduce *new* knowledge. Inductive reason is thus simultaneously more powerful than deductive reasoning (because it is *ampliative*) and less powerful (it cannot actually prove anything).

A third type of reason, known as *abductive*, is also worth mentioning. Abductive reasoning is often associated with intuition or insight. Abductive reasoning may be the step that leads the mathematician to *attempt* to prove something deductively, believing the conclusion to be true before formalizing a proof. It may be the step that leads a scientist to *attempt* some experiment that will later provide inductive evidence for some conclusion. Some philosophers would not use the term *reason* to describe abduction, either because abduction is *too informal*, or because it really does not provide any *convincing arguments*, or indeed it is not even an easily *identifiable process*. Others would argue that abduction is the most important type of reasoning, because it is what leads people to conclusions in the first place, and without some sort of abductive reasoning we might never be led to deductive or inductive reasoning.

There are two final but important points to be made about reason in general. Both should be kept in mind throughout this chapter. The first applies to both deductive and inductive reason (and thus also to mathematics and to science): *We cannot use reason to argue that reason is trustworthy*. Put more formally, an argument *from* reason cannot show that reason itself is *normative*. To attempt to do so would be circular: before I could reason with you that you ought to accept reason, you would already need to have accepted reason to accept the validity of the argument. In fact, there are philosophies widely held in various cultures that reject some of the fundamental rules of inference that are the backbone of reason. For example, postmodernism has brought into doubt the important *law of noncontradiction*: that a statement cannot be both true and false. There are many other rules of inference (for example, *double negation* and *reductio ad absurdum*) that are dependent on the law of noncontradiction, and so a denial of one leads to a denial of all three. In short, then, to accept the normativity or trustworthiness of human reason is a nontrivial assumption, and something *other* than reason needs to lead to that acceptance. What we are left with, then, is the question of *why* we ought to believe that reason is normative.

The second point is a related observation. As has often been pointed out, among the main hindrances to human knowledge of truth are what are often called *psychological effects*. That is, there are many things that humans believe *not* because they are true or reasonable, but because we have been psychologically conditioned to believe them. Assume for a moment that we have already accepted that reason is normative. Then, if we want to bring into doubt somebody's beliefs, we must show that those beliefs are not reasonable. We can succeed in this if we can show that the beliefs actually arise from psychological causes; when psychological causes are shown to be the sources for belief, we can discount the belief itself.

B. F. Skinner, Bertrand Russell, Richard Dawkins, and Daniel Dennett all do this on numerous occasions with respect to a belief in God, explaining away an acceptance of theism by arguing that it arises from psychological sources rather than from reason. For example, we earlier cited Dawkins explaining away faith in God as the psychological result of "childhood indoctrination." Dennett psychologically explains away opposition to naturalism in terms of wishful thinking: "Darwinians suspect their opponents of hankering after a . . . miraculous gift of genius."[5] Bertrand Russell writes, "I do not think that the real reason why people accept religion is anything to do with argumentation. They accept religion on emotional grounds."[6] The list of examples could go on and on. Interestingly enough, the Christian apologist C. S. Lewis also agrees with Dennett, Dawkins, and Russell on the basic premise that explaining a belief in terms of its psychological causes (such as wishful thinking) is a good way to discredit it. He writes,

> Wishful thinkings, prejudices, and the delusions of madness, are all caused, but they are ungrounded. Indeed to be caused is so different from being proved that we behave in disputation as if they were mutually exclusive. The mere existence of causes for a belief is popularly treated as raising a presumption that it is groundless, and the most popular way of discrediting a person's opinions is to explain them causally—"You say that *because* . . . you are a capitalist, or a hypochondriac, or a mere man, or only a woman."[7]

In short, when a belief is rooted in and explained by psychological causes, then we find it difficult to trust that belief. The belief may coincide with what is true, but that might be only by accident, as it were, and not because the process by which one arrived at belief was a trustworthy process.

So we can now turn to the implications of physicalism for reason and science. We ask, under the assumptions of physicalism, whether we can accept reason and science as normative. Ought we trust them as reliable guides to truth? In what follows, we will focus on inductive and deductive forms of reasoning. Though different, both inductive and deductive reasoning share one fundamentally important trait: they both begin with certain propositions (whether from observation and experimentation, from definition, or simply from assumption), and from these propositions they draw conclusions. Our argument about reason in the following section applies equally to both deductive and inductive reasoning, which are the two forms of reasoning that actually argue for the truth of propositions.

The Possibility of Reason

Now we can get to the central argument of this chapter. I claim that if the philosophy of physicalism were true, then reason itself could not be considered as normative: it should not be accepted as an objective standard for discovering what is true, and we should doubt the reliability or trustworthiness of its conclusions. If mind reduces to brain, and all the thoughts of the brain are determined (either predictably by laws of physics or unpredictably by random quantum effects), then what we call reason is at best *descriptive* of one possible human approach to knowledge (as religion is also *descriptive* of another possible approach to knowledge), but neither is *normative*; reason is not a way we ought to pursue knowledge if our goal is to know what is true. The conclusions to which we are led by reason may be true, like those of any faulty but lucky argument, but that is accidental, and any *truth* corresponding to our beliefs owes itself to something other than reason itself.

This applies to the belief in physicalism itself. It may be that physicalism is true and that humans are reducible to complex biochemical computers, but if this is true, then any reasoning process that leads us to this conclusion is only accidentally correct. We might roll dice and decide that if we roll an odd number, then some form of physicalism is true, and if we roll an even number, then some form of dualism is true. It is certainly possible that the dice will provide the correct answer. And similarly, it might be possible that we could use reason to come to the correct answer. But the reasoning process, if physicalism is correct, is no more valid than the rolling of the dice, and it should not be trusted.

This is not a new argument. One well-known presentation of it is that of C. S. Lewis in a critique of naturalism published in 1947 in his book *Miracles*. His argument appears in chapter 2, "The Cardinal Difficulty of Naturalism." In introducing his argument, he gives the following summary: "But Naturalism, even if it is not purely materialistic . . . discredits our processes of reasoning or at least reduces their credit to such a humble level that it can no longer support Naturalism itself."[8] Charles Taliaferro has done an excellent job summarizing Lewis's argument,[9] and in the appendix to their book *Naturalism*, Taliaferro and Stewart Goetz also provide a new and tighter version of this argument. Many other philosophers have also presented versions of the argument and affirmed its validity—though of course other philosophers don't accept the arguments of Lewis and of Taliaferro and Goetz, and still others accept the reasoned argument that reason is not normative but put faith in reason anyway.

We will not attempt to reproduce the argument here in its fullest philosophical form, in part because fine treatments already exist, and also because the versions of Lewis and of Taliaferro and Goetz are more complete than are needed here. They deal with broader forms of naturalism, whereas this book focuses on physicalism—that is, a strict naturalism applied to the human mind. What I will do is summarize the argument and then try to illustrate it directly from the writings of naturalists such as Richard Dawkins. I will show that if you accept what Dawkins argues for in *The God Delusion*, then you are left with the impossibility of any trustworthy or normative reason, and ultimately with a discredited scientific method.

To start our argument, remember that reason, in both its inductive and deductive forms, draws conclusions from various propositions. Reason deals with inference. In more formal language, we might say that reason is based on the *ground-consequent* relation, which states that we believe something *because* of some evidence. The evidence is *ground* for our drawing our conclusion; we infer our conclusions from the evidence.

Late in the evening before I wrote the first draft of this section, lying in my bed, I heard *plinks* and *plunks* on the metal roof of my house. I concluded it was raining outside. The plinks were not the *cause* of the rain, but they were the *cause* or *reason* for my conclusion that it was raining. Even though it was dark and I could not *see* any rain, and I was under a roof and could not *feel* any rain, I *reasoned* from the observation of metallic roof noises coming from above me to the conclusion that it was raining. This ground-consequent relation between my observations and my conclusion is at the heart of what we call reason.

By contrast, the cause of the rain itself has to do with atmospheric conditions such as moisture in the air—that is, with the physical conditions of the universe and the *laws* of physics such as the gravitational force that will pull the water droplets toward the earth. The atmospheric conditions and the laws of physics together form a *cause-effect* relationship producing the rain. The rain is the *effect*, and laws of nature and atmospheric conditions together form the *cause*.

Note the difference between the ground-consequent relationship and the cause-effect relationship. Reason, if it is a normative process for acquiring knowledge, must be based on the former; it must involve the ground-consequent relation. Correct reasoning means that we think something *because* the evidence has convinced us of its truth. But physicalism and causal closure tell us that everything—not just the falling of the rain, but all the thinking that goes on in our minds—is determined ultimately by cause-effect relationships. No person has any choice about what they will believe or disbelieve. Your thought process may involve some sort of pondering of evidence, and then concluding with some belief, but at the most basic level all that is really happening is that physical particles are following laws of physics as they rearrange themselves in that portion of physical reality that includes your brain. These rearrangements are causing your brain to be convinced of some truth. Considered at a higher level, we would say that under the assumption of physicalism *everything* that we ever think is the result of our environmental conditioning, of psychological *causes* rather than rational *grounds*, and therefore should be discredited as we noted at the start of this chapter. This is what the naturalists whose writings we have looked at in the first four chapters of this book repeatedly tell us.

To help see why this invalidates reason, consider what Dawkins tells us about computers.

> Computers do what they are told. They slavishly obey any instructions given in their own programming language. This is how they do

> useful things like word processing and spreadsheet calculations. But, as an inevitable by-product, they are equally robotic in obeying bad instructions. They have no way of telling whether an instruction will have a good effect or a bad. They simply obey, as soldiers are supposed to. It is their unquestioning obedience that makes computers useful, and exactly the same thing makes them inescapably vulnerable to infection by software viruses and worms. A maliciously designed program that says, "Copy me and send me to every address that you find on this hard disk" will simply be obeyed, and then obeyed again by the other computers down the line to which it is sent, in exponential expansion.[10]

Why this is important, of course, is that we're told that *we* (persons) are computers. If this is true, then what Dawkins tells us about computers is also true about humans. So let's visit what Dawkins says in this light, inserting "humans" for "computers" in this passage. "[*Humans*] slavishly obey any instructions given in their own programming language." Well, that's what the writings of Skinner, Dennett, and Dawkins have also explicitly told us—though, as noted, there is some disagreement on exactly what our "programming language" is, and to what extent it is genetic as opposed to environmental. But then comes the interesting part. "But, as an inevitable by-product, [*humans*] are equally robotic in obeying bad instructions. [We] have no way of telling whether an instruction will have a good effect or a bad. [We] simply obey." If we are programmed beings, then our reasoning itself is also programmed. We will follow our program no matter what, slavishly, like soldiers—or, rather, as computers. We have no means of determining whether reason is good or bad. We follow our brain program whether or not it leads to true knowledge. What we call the reasoning process is not trustworthy.

Now the physicalist convinced of the inherent trustworthiness of reason may respond at this point by appealing to our very strong intuition supporting reason. The rules of inference, for example, are *obviously* true. As the physicalist might point out, anybody with intelligence and education can look at these rules—modus ponens, for example—and see without question that they must be true. We can say the same thing more broadly about the standards of reason, including inductive reason: it is clearly and objectively a trustworthy means toward knowledge—an assumption that Dawkins himself repeatedly relies on. But then we must remember what the naturalist philosopher Daniel Dennett pointed out in arguing against the dualist explanation of human consciousness. "That belief, that very gripping, powerful intuition is, I think, in the end simply an illusion of common sense. It is as gripping as the common-sense illusion that the earth stands still and the sun goes around the earth."[11] Dennett argues that even our most gripping, powerful intuitions and most basic common sense—such as our gripping belief that the tools and rules of reason are objectively trustworthy and true—can be wrong and may need to be discarded.

To see that this is the case, we need only look at what Dawkins correctly points out about computers. They have no way of knowing whether their instructions are good or bad. We humans, also, if we are physical computational devices, will think *whatever we are programmed to think*, whether it is true or not. In fact, the theists whose beliefs Dawkins ridicules are just as convinced that their path to knowledge is true and trustworthy as are the Enlightenment rationalists who are committed to reason and science alone. If we are biochemical computational beings, entirely physical devices, then we must acknowledge the implications: if we think that reason is normative and trustworthy and accords with truth, it is only because we are programmed to think this. Likewise, according to this view, if we think reason is not normative, and there are no objective criteria for accepting it as a path to knowledge and truth, it is also only because we are programmed to think so.

Even this very argument—this reasoned discourse—if physicalism is true, is only accidentally correct and should not be trusted simply because it is reasonable. C. S. Lewis, in *Miracles*, argues this conclusion as follows:

> Now a train of reasoning has no value as a means of finding truth unless each step in it is connected with what went before in the Ground-Consequent relation. . . . On the other hand, every event in Nature must be connected with previous events in the Cause and Effect relation. But our acts of thinking are events. Therefore the true answer to "Why do you think this?" must begin with the Cause-Effect *because*.
>
> Unless our conclusion is the logical consequent from a ground it will be worthless and could be true only by a fluke.[12]

Once we have reduced thoughts to physical events, then they are completely governed by the laws governing physical events. Then everything any human has ever thought or will ever think is controlled by those physical events. Our thoughts, including what we call our *reasoned* thoughts, are determined events, in the broad sense of that word, and not rational connections. They are fully explainable by psychology.

In this light, reason is no different from any other belief system we might be programmed to accept, including religion. Dennett, Dawkins, and Russell are quick to dismiss religion as untruthful and harmful, and to explain it away by the means above: that we believe it only because of our postevolutionary programming. If they are correct in their assumption of physicalism, then we can concede that they are also correct in their assessment of religious belief: it has material causes that allow us to explain it away psychologically and in terms of evolution. As we noted at the start of this chapter, even C. S. Lewis would agree. But under physicalism, the same critique must be true also of reason itself. We believe it only because we are psychologically conditioned to believe it by our environment and evolutionary development. *But reason is true!* they might dogmatically repeat. To which I could repeat that theists say the same thing about their religion.

One possible objection to this argument is the claim that reason evolved as a trait that helped us survive and pass on our genes. In other words, we can trust reason because it has *proven* itself to be successful. How do we know it is successful? Success is defined, in Darwinian terms, by what survives and passes on genes. And humans have evolved to our present state of reason. What this really means is that we can trust that human reason, at times, will help us pass on our genes, or the genes prevalent in our culture. But this is a very different thing from saying it correlates with the truth, or that it is a normative means of determining whether one proposition follows from another through the ground-consequent relation. The very people who might argue that reason is valid and helps us discover truth, and thus has evolved, also discredit religion; they claim religion does not correlate with the truth, and explain it away as something that also evolved, either because it enabled genes to be passed on, or because it was an undesirable by-product of something else that enabled genes to be passed on. Perhaps this critique *is* true of religion. But under physicalism it must be equally true of reason. Again think back to what Dawkins wrote: "Of course, dyed-in-the-wool faith-heads are immune to argument, their resistance built up over years of childhood indoctrination using methods that took centuries to mature (whether by evolution or design)."[13] If what he writes is true of the "faith-heads," it must also be true of the adherents to reason; they are immune to argument against reason because their resistance has built up over years of evolution. It is true of *every* belief system.

We could repeat this argument, or variations of it, against the possibility of reason under physicalism, using the writing of others of the naturalists whom we have cited in this book. Consider what B. F. Skinner writes in his chapter "Freedom" in *Beyond Freedom and Dignity*:

> The content of the literature [of freedom] is the philosophy of freedom, but philosophies are among those inner causes which need to be scrutinized. We say that a person behaves in a given way because he possesses a philosophy, but we infer the philosophy from the behavior and therefore cannot use it in any satisfactory way as an explanation, at least until it is in turn explained. The literature of freedom . . . does not impart a philosophy of freedom; it induces people to act.[14]

Let's consider this closely. Skinner is writing about philosophies and what it means to hold a particular philosophy—in this case, the philosophy of freedom. But what is a philosophy? It is a system of thought or a set of principles relating to what we know and how we know it. For most philosophers, a philosophy is a carefully thought-out and reasoned belief system. What Skinner is telling us is that, rather than looking to philosophies as causes for how we act, we need to explain the causes of the philosophy itself. That is, our philosophies are caused *by* our environments. Since reason itself is a philosophical system, and an acceptance of the validity of reason is a philosophy, we must also then say that our reasoned thoughts and our reasoning processes are also simply causes that can be explained by something outside of our thoughts themselves. Thus, ultimately reason is not produced by thoughts, but by the mechanics of the universe.

This is the point of the final sentence in the passage cited above, in which Skinner blames the literature of freedom as an environmental factor for what he considers to be an untrue way of thinking. But since he has already denied any real value of thoughts as independent things, he jumps immediately to the actions caused by the literature of freedom. What we need to understand is that, if Skinner is right that we are not free, then the same argument holds for anything we might think or think that we think. It is no more likely to be true than the thought that we are free.

In fact, a few pages earlier in explaining his use of certain "casual expressions," Skinner explicitly refers to the "mind" as "an explanatory fiction" and an "idea" as "simply an imagined precursor of behavior."[15] This, it is clear from his writing, is how he believes we are all supposed to think about the mind and ideas, despite the fact that even he uses casual expressions suggesting something to the contrary. If *mind* and *ideas* are illusory, then certainly so is *reason*, which is based on our use of the mind to explore the validity of ideas.

Or we might return to the passage cited earlier from Bertrand Russell's essay "Has Religion Made Useful Contributions to Civilization?" Russell writes, "Materialists used the laws of physics to show, or attempt to show, that the movements of human bodies are mechanically determined, and that consequently everything we say and every change of position that we effect fall *outside* the sphere of any possible free will."[16] If Russell is correct here and elsewhere, then what he says applies equally to our thoughts and attempts to reason: "the [thoughts] of human [minds] are mechanically determined." But if our thoughts are mechanically determined, they could equally be mechanically determined in a way that does or does *not* correspond with truth, and the mind itself would have no way of knowing. It would believe whatever it was mechanically determined to believe, and it would furthermore believe that it was justified in that belief: that its conclusions were reasonable and therefore true.

In many ways, the possibility of reason being normative comes down to whether reason is a real mental event or a physical event. Only something involving a real mind and thoughts that are not just physical events might be normative. To quote again from Goetz and Taliaferro, strict naturalists "affirm a principle akin to but stronger than the causal closure principle." What this means is that "anything that is physical can be explained only in terms of something else that is physical or not mental. According to this stronger principle, anything, whether physical *or mental*, can be explained only in terms of something that is not mental in nature." The conclusion, then, is that what we call reason, as well as any other means to belief, and all of our "believings," "must always be explained causally by events that are not mental in nature."[17] C. S. Lewis phrases his own conclusion as follows:

> Any thing which professes to explain our reasoning fully without introducing an act of knowing thus solely determined by what is known, is really a theory that there is no reasoning.
>
> But this, as it seems to me, is what Naturalism is bound to do. It offers what professes to be a full account of our mental behaviour; but this account, on inspection, leaves no room for the acts of knowing or insight on which the whole value of our thinking, as a means to truth, depends.[18]

The Presuppositions of Science

The argument against the possibility of scientific knowledge under the assumption of physicalism is even stronger than the argument against reason. To see this, we need to review some of the presuppositions that make science possible. What do we need to accept a priori about the world and ourselves before we trust science? We will see that many of these a priori assumptions fail to hold under strict naturalism.

In the discussion that follows, by *science* we are speaking specifically of *natural science*. Given how often the term science is used, and how broadly it is accepted, it is more difficult than one might expect to find a commonly accepted definition or understanding of natural science that would be acceptable to the majority of scientists, while also understandable to educated people outside of the sciences. *The Oxford Dictionary of English* (2nd edition revised) defines *science* as "the intellectual and practical activity encompassing the systematic study of the structure and behaviour of the physical and natural world through observation and experiment."[19] The Encyclopedia Britannica defines *science* as "any system of knowledge that is concerned with the physical world and its phenomena and that entails unbiased observations and systematic experimentation."[20] *The New Zealand Oxford Dictionary* refers to science as "a branch of knowledge conducted on objective principles involving the systematised observation of and experiment with phenomena, esp. concerned with the material and functions of the physical universe (see also natural science)."[21] Finally, the *McGraw-Hill Encyclopedia of Science & Technology* opens its article describing science with "The study of nature and natural phenomena" and goes on to note, "There is also usually the implication that the subject matter of the individual science is something in the world of phenomena. Thus it is not usual to speak of the 'science' of mathematics or the 'science' of logic, even though both these disciplines are capable of the highest precision."[22] We will return later to the question of whether any science can be done in a completely unbiased way—that is, whether any human scientist can be totally free of bias—as is suggested in the Encyclopedia Brittanica definition. The main point that all of these definitions have in common is that science deals with the natural (that is, physical) world, and with natural (that is, physical) phenomena.

It is also instructive to review what is meant by the *scientific method*, which is what we are exploring as a possible means of knowledge. McGraw-Hill Encyclopedia of Science & Technology, in the article on *the scientific method*, begins by noting: "All the sciences referring to real or putatively real things are supposed to abide by the scientific method." It then goes on to summarize this method as a long sequence of steps. The eighth step is an "actual empirical test of the hypothesis, involving a search for both favorable and unfavorable evidence (examples and counterexamples)." And the ninth step is "critical examination and statistical processing of the data (for example, calculation of average error and elimination of outlying data)."[23] Thus something is scientific only if it involves empirical data collection from an observable experiment on real world phenomena.

So we can now turn to the assumptions (often hidden) that make science and the scientific method trustworthy sources of knowledge. In doing so, we must remember that these concerns are fundamentally philosophical in nature. We cannot scientifically defend the trustworthiness of science as a means to knowledge of the truth.

Before we can start depending on science to answer certain types of questions, we must have a nonscientific reason to accept the scientific approach in the first place, else we are once again stuck in circular reasoning. I note also that, in making explicit the assumptions of natural science, I am in no way trying to deny the validity of science (which I will defend in chap. 7). But it is important, if we are properly to trust science and understand *why* we trust science, to raise the question of what presuppositions we must place our faith in. The philosophical presuppositions behind science are often left unstated, and yet one's philosophical position on (for example) the question of physicalism impacts to what degree these presuppositions can and should be held.

I list several necessary or supporting presuppositions—each of which takes the form of a proposition—and briefly explain why it is a prerequisite to accepting science as a reliable means to truth.

Presupposition 1: *There exists a material universe outside your mind*. The truth of this presupposition may seem so obvious that it is not worth stating, but as noted in the introduction to this book, it is a philosophical position that is impossible to prove. It is also an important one. If it were false, then science would in some sense be meaningless, since science is the study of physical evidence, which presupposes a physical world. And there are competing philosophies that deny the existence of a material universe, or at least the possibility of any knowledge of that universe. This is true of various forms of idealism (more common in Eastern philosophies and religions like Buddhism or Hinduism). As Taliaferro has noted, "An eliminative idealist holds that there are no material objects whatever."[24] Taliaferro also points out that the great American philosopher Charles Peirce, while not denying the validity of scientific endeavor or being embarrassed about the success of science, "thought of the natural sciences as taking place within an altogether mental world."[25]

Presupposition 2: *The material universe has material causes*. Again, the importance of this presupposition is immediate from our working definition of what science is and does. It is worth noting, however, that we need not suppose that *all* causes are material in order for science to have value; we need only assume that *some* causes are material. However, in the presence of a nonmaterial cause, science (which assumes a material cause) will be inadequate to provide an explanation that is both true and complete *with respect to the particular events resulting from that cause*. A stronger presupposition, that the material universe operates *only* under material causes—the presupposition of *causal closure*—is a basic belief of strict naturalism. The causal closure presupposition is *not* necessary for one to accept science as valid and as providing knowledge. It is necessary only if one wants to see science as the *only* possible source of, and as an infallible source of, knowledge of *all* reality. It is also important to remember, as we noted in chapter 1, that this presupposition (as are all the others in this list) is philosophical and not scientific in nature. It is a statement *about* science, and not a statement *from* science. Science depends on this assumption but cannot prove it.

Presupposition 3: *The material universe is consistent and ordered*. These are really two assumptions, but they function collaboratively. Science is based on observations of the physical universe. It observes particulars and then reasons inductively to generalities. In order to *generalize*, we must assume that the universe is consistent and ordered *over both space and time*—that physical properties observed in one place at one time hold true in a different place and a different time. Alone of all the presuppositions listed here, this one might be supportable by mere observation without a priori assumptions. As I write this book, I am forty-six years old. I have caught trout in twenty-three US states, three Canadian provinces, and two European countries. During what to me is a broad temporal period (my entire life, to date), and a diverse spatial area (hundreds of different streams and rivers in multiple states, countries, watersheds, and mountain ranges), I have observed firsthand a consistency in the universe. In every trout stream in which I have fished, water has flowed downhill, and trout have breathed through gills and eaten insects. Though this is not enough to deductively prove consistency, it is certainly good evidence for me personally. But, of course, this is a minuscule fraction of the temporal history of the universe. It is also a very small fraction of the earth, and an infinitesimally small fraction of the universe. It isn't even a very large sample of the streams in my small home state of Vermont. There are several well-known Vermont trout streams I have yet to fish, including the Dog, Barton, Black, and Battenkill Rivers. It is a large leap to assume a consistent ordered *universe*—though it is a leap I have taken; if I do one day get to fish one or more of these rivers on my list, I will expect to find water flowing downhill, and the trout breathing through gills and eating insects.

Presupposition 4a: *Humans are capable of accurate observation.* Science is based, as the definitions above suggest, on observable evidence, or observable experiments, or on the collection of data through observation. This requires that humans be capable of making accurate, trustworthy observations. If we cannot do this, we cannot trust our scientific results or the truth of our theories. J. P. Moreland has noted, "Science assumes that our senses are reliable guides in knowing the external world. . . . Scientific theories . . . are the products of thinking and sensing selves, and their reliability depends, in part, on the reliability of the senses and the intellect."[26]

Presupposition 4b: *Accurate transmission of historical events is possible; humans can have knowledge based on recorded history.* This presupposition goes hand in hand with the previous one. We not only need to be able to make accurate observations, but we also need to record and disseminate those observations in documents. For one thing, the idea of a repeatable experiment requires that we be able to compare current observations with previously recorded observations, which means we need a reliable record of those past observations—observations that have entered into historical record. More significant is the simple idea that we don't continuously carry on every scientific experiment that justifies every scientific theory as though we were all forever high school students still learning the basics of the sciences. We trust theories in part because we trust the historical records of countless scientific experiments. In short, scientific knowledge requires historical knowledge—that we have an accurate record of what has already happened. (Indeed, as numerous examples illustrate, certain scientists have not always been truthful or reliable in their records.)

Now some might be tempted to argue that the very nature of science spares us from dependency on history, because all experiments are repeatable. But to show the naiveté of this, just note two things. First, in the very instant in which the experiment you are re-creating is completed, the results immediately enter into historical record just like the other experiments whose historical record you were hoping not to have to rely on. Second, nearly every experiment requires the comparison of data to other experiments, which are also historical records.

Moreover—and this could be listed as a separate presupposition, as is done by J. P. Moreland—the dependence on historical record requires a deeper dependence on the ability of language to objectively describe the world. Even apart from historical record, scientists need to be able to describe their ideas and results to other scientists using language. That this can be done is itself an assumption that has been brought into question by many philosophers of language. Moreland points out, "Scientific laws and theories are expressed in language. Science, therefore, is subject to philosophical disputes about the adequacy, use, and function of language. . . . Suffice it to say that science presupposes that language is an adequate medium for referring to stated truths about the world."[27]

Presupposition 5: *Humans are capable of reason.* This may be the most obvious of the presuppositions. But it may also be the least considered. Science is fundamentally rooted in inductive reason and also makes use of abductive and deductive reasoning, meaning that if science is to lead to knowledge, then the human mind must be capable of reliably moving from specific observations to general conclusions or beliefs. Taliaferro has noted, "It is very difficult even to imagine the sciences proceeding if there are no such things as beliefs. . . . Scientists have worked on gaining clearer and better-grounded beliefs about the natural world."[28]

This should not be underestimated, and the implications go far beyond science. C. S. Lewis is correct in his observation:

> All possible knowledge, then, depends on the validity of reasoning. If the feeling of certainty which we express by words like *must be* and *therefore* and *since* is a real perception of how things outside our own minds really "must" be, well and good. But if this certainty is merely a feeling in our own minds and not a genuine insight into realities beyond them—if it merely represents the way our minds happen to work—then we can have no knowledge. Unless human reasoning is valid no science can be true.[29]

In other words, if reason is merely *descriptive* of human minds rather than *normative*, then we lose not only the trustworthiness of the reasoning process, but the trustworthiness of science and of all knowledge. To cite Moreland again: "Scientists justify their scientific models . . . by appealing to reasons and observations as normative courts of appeal for their theories." And, in case one is tempted to *use* scientific results to justify the reliability of the senses and of the mind's reasoning, he adds, "It would be question begging to use a scientific theory about the senses to justify the senses themselves. That justification is a philosophical matter, and the reliability of the mind and senses is a philosophical presupposition of science."[30] (This is a comment that also lends support to our argument about reason in the first half of the chapter.)

Considering the Presuppositions

There are also other presuppositions necessary for scientific knowledge to be trustworthy.[31] However, those listed above are sufficient for our discussion. We now have to ask whether physicalism in general, and physicalist determinism in particular (broadly or strictly understood), give explicit reasons for accepting these presuppositions, or possibly for rejecting them. Let us consider them one at a time.

There exists a material universe outside your mind. This is one of those questions to which, even if we were to try to argue that the answer were "no," we would be functioning as though the answer were "yes," for we would be attempting to argue with *somebody*, and that would be acting as though somebody *else* exists (in addition to ourselves). If that somebody existed only in our minds, then we would be arguing only with ourselves. Like most worldviews (including dualism), physicalism accepts this presupposition as true, though it cannot be proven. Indeed, it assumes something even stronger: that we have a physical brain that functions under rules of physics. Physicalism cannot prove that this is true, but it certainly doesn't contradict the idea. Note that assuming the existence of a physical world or physical objects outside your mind does not imply that you can actually know anything about that world. Certain philosophical idealists may acknowledge the existence of some physical reality but still deny the meaningfulness of a *discussion* of physical objects apart from reference to our own minds. But what we are concerned with here is just the existence of a material reality.

The material universe has material causes. A philosophy of physicalism certainly affirms this also, and thus can affirm the validity of science at least with respect to this presupposition. In fact, naturalism (independent of the question of determinism) affirms the stronger presupposition that there are *only* material causes. The strong faith in science held by most naturalists comes primarily from considering *only* this presupposition and typically none of the others (as we will soon argue). It often comes from an implicit holding of this presupposition by faith, without an acknowledgment that it is even an assumption that must be held.

The material universe is consistent and ordered. Here, again independent of the question of determinism or the unpredictability of quanta, the naturalist might argue (as we noted above) that we have a history of observing a consistent ordered universe. And so, rather than holding this presupposition by faith, as it were, those accepting strict naturalism who wish also to hold a high view of science may claim to accept this *by observation* and through inductive reason, moving from the particulars of our daily experience of consistency and order to the generality of a consistent universe. Indeed, they may claim that this is not a presupposition at all, but a conclusion of science. Here, of course, the reasoning is circular, for we cannot accept the validity of science and of inductive reason, and in particular of this specific supposed conclusion of science, without holding this presupposition to start with. So it must be understood as a presupposition and not a conclusion. Nonetheless, naturalism certainly does not explicitly contradict this.

On the other hand, naturalism still does not answer the question of *why* the universe is consistent and ordered—why it *should* be or *ought* to be. The strict naturalist understands the universe to exist without any inherent purpose or meaning. It may be said to be *random*. For example, the complexity of life is explained via random mutations and the evolutionary process. It may be that it isn't really random and that all of history, including evolutionary history, is determined. Whether it is truly random or not depends on quantum physics. The important thing meant by *random*, to which naturalists hold whether quantum theories prove true or not, is simply that the universe is "without any controlling force." Some have used the word *accidental*, which may be a better word than *random*. In any case, we are back to the universe or cosmos as being without purpose, meaning that there is no *inherent* or *inherited* or *intended* order or structure in the universe. If this is the case, it is certainly reasonable to ask *why* and *how* something purposeless and random could bring about something consistent and ordered.

The most common response to this, from the naturalists, is simply to point to reality and argue that it *is* ordered, and it is pointless to ask why. It is what it is. Of course, this order and consistency must still be accepted as a presupposition that validates science and induction. The naturalist must either circularly accept the presupposition of order and consistency as being validated *by* induction and science, or must accept it a priori even though the underlying philosophy gives no reason for it. C. S. Lewis has noted, "If we have no notion why a thing happens, then of course we know no reason why it should not be otherwise, and therefore have no certainty that it might not some day be otherwise."[32]

Nonetheless, Lewis's warning aside, we have seen nothing in physicalism that would *explicitly* deny any of the previous group of assumptions, even if these philosophies also give no reason for accepting some of them. But now we begin to run into trouble. Consider the next assumption.

Humans are capable of accurate observation and accurate transmission of history. Dawkins makes a very interesting observation about the human brain.

> The human brain runs first-class simulation software. Our eyes don't present to our brains a faithful photograph of what is out there, or an accurate movie of what is going on through time. Our brains construct a continuously updated model: updated by coded pulses chattering along the optic nerve, but constructed nevertheless. . . . The brain, having no basis for choosing between them, alternates, and we experience a series of flips from one internal model to the other. The picture we are looking at appears, almost literally, to flip over and become something else.[33]

The point of Dawkins's comment was to discredit certain types of alleged religious experiences. A large number of persons throughout history have claimed to have seen visions (or seen angels, or witnessed miracles) and appeared to have been genuinely convinced that those visions were real. Dawkins explains away these visions by appealing to how easily we may be fooled, by optical illusions in particular, and by our senses in general. He argues that the large number of claims doesn't mean that there is validity to any of them. He goes on to make that point explicit.

> I say all this just to demonstrate the formidable power of the brain's simulation software. It is well capable of constructing "visions" and "visitations" of the utmost veridical power. To simulate a ghost or an angel or a Virgin Mary would be child's play to software of this sophistication. And the same thing works for hearing. When we hear a sound, it is not faithfully transported up the auditory nerve and relayed to the brain as if by a high-fidelity Bang and Olufsen. As with vision, the brain constructs a sound model, based upon continuously updated auditory nerve data.[34]

Let's suppose that Dawkins is right. His argument brings into doubt not only the claims he wishes to discredit, from persons alleging to have had sensory input from supernatural sources, but it also brings into doubt the trustworthiness of *all* sensory perception. If, as he claims, "our eyes don't present to our brains a faithful photograph of what is out there, or an accurate movie of what is going on through time," then how can we trust any science, which is based on human sensory input, to take observations and collect data? The answer is, we should not. And the problem is not solved by allowing a computer to take data for us, or to process it for us, since we still need our senses to read the output of the computer. Ironically, if Dawkins is right in this particular observation about the unreliability of our senses—a conclusion he claims to have drawn *from* science—then we should begin to distrust science itself, because we should not trust the human capacity to make or record accurate observations based on our senses.

We should add, at this point, what may be an obvious comment. Some are fond of making claims such as, "The only type of truth is scientific truth," or "I will accept as true only what science proves to be true." It should be clear that before one can accept scientific truth, one must accept several *philosophical truths*. And, to get to the point of this assumption, before we can have any faith in scientific truth, we must also be able to have faith in *historical truth*. If one will accept only what science proves to be true, then that person must begin by rejecting science itself, since it cannot be scientifically proven to be true.

Humans are capable of reason. Here we get to perhaps the central issue. Science is based on reason, but according to the tenets of physicalism reason is merely a description of what humans do. It is not a normative process that can be understood as a trustworthy means to knowledge of truth. Reason may lead us to a true belief just as rolling a die or flipping a coin might lead us to a true belief. But the correlation between the truth and the process by which we arrived at belief (whether reason or luck) is accidental. And when reason falls, so does science. To do science, we must believe that reason is normative and trustworthy. Ultimately, we may choose to act in a way based on reason and science because we have been programmed to do so by an evolutionary process at work during an era in which those who act scientifically have passed their genes on. But our actions, like our beliefs, are programmed. It is self-refuting to try to argue that they are true.

In conclusion, then, if the argument of this chapter is reasonable, it seems that there are three possible things we can do. One possibility is that we deny reason and science from the start, but we may still accept by faith the precepts of physicalism. That is, we deny that reason has any normative value; we put no trust in reason or science as means to truth, but perhaps we continue to practice them (with complete intellectual skepticism) only because they will help (at least for a time) to propagate our species. This allows us even to reject the reasoned arguments of this chapter, since reason has no real normative value. Of course if we begin by denying reason, then we don't need this chapter in the first place, because we already agree with the conclusions (just not by way of reason).

A second approach is that we could start by trusting reason, and affirming physicalism. But if we do this, then reason—as shown in this chapter—ought to refute itself, and we are left where we were with the first possibility above, without any trust in reason or science.

The third possibility is that we put a high faith in reason and science; we trust our intuition and common sense that both of them are trustworthy and, indeed, normative—that they are more than *descriptive* of how humans seek truth, but are *prescriptive* of how we *ought* to seek truth if we want reliable knowledge. Charles Taliaferro has noted the following:

> In ordinary life we certainly seem to act as though our beliefs and desires make a difference in what happens. In the course of reasoning with others, whether it be shop talk or legal debate, we presuppose that reasons and beliefs make a difference in each other's lives. If beliefs, intentions, and other psychological items are causally irrelevant, then our entire framework for thinking of each other as *bona fide* responsible agents is threatened.[35]

In other words, we normally act as though reason and belief were not merely an untrustworthy phenomenon of physicalism; we act as though our beliefs were not only effects caused by the physical realm, but could also be causes of effects in the physical realm. In which case we must affirm the existence of something more than physical nature; we must deny physicalism and causal closure and open our eyes to the possibility that humans may be spiritual as well as physical beings, and that from this dual nature comes a real possibility for both reason and science. This leads us to the second part of this book, where we explore the implications of an understanding of humanness that does not preclude a spiritual reality.

PART 2

THE SPIRITUAL HUMAN

In the previous four chapters, we sought to explore the implications of accepting a worldview of physicalism—a philosophy of strict naturalism and causal closure with respect to the universe in general and, in particular, to what it means to be human. We argued that such a view denies the possibility of individual human creativity and heroism. So it is likely (if followed consistently) to devalue the physical or natural world itself and the motivation for healthy ecological practices among humans. It also denies the validity of reason and science as normative means toward true knowledge.

In the next three chapters, we will explore the same set of topics, but from a different worldview: one that affirms both a physical and a spiritual reality, understanding the human as a bodily as well as a spiritual being. We will use, as our vehicle for exploring the possibility of this *dualistic* reality, a theistic worldview common to both Judaism and Christianity. It is a form of dualism (as I will argue again in our final chapter) that does not reduce to Cartesian dualism, or a ghost-in-the-machine worldview, or to a Platonic view of the soul.[1] We will also explore some implications of an incarnate creator that are particular to Christianity.

As in the first part of this book, I will draw from the writings of well-known thinkers who espouse the views I am critiquing. In this case, we will explore, among others, two of the twentieth century's most well-known Christian writers and thinkers: C. S. Lewis and J. R. R. Tolkien. Their writings present not only aspects of a Christian form of dualism, but also the implications of these ideas. Of course, in a critique of a Christian or Judeo-Christian worldview, we will also look directly at the Bible as well as at the writings of theologians and philosophers who seek to explain or defend the ideas of Christianity.

In the concluding chapter, I will return to some bigger questions, including the claim raised in the first chapter that a ghost-in-the-machine reductionism is not the only form of dualism or the only alternative to naturalism and determinism. In doing so, I will try to answer a few final closely related objections to this Christian and dualist worldview, including the concern for how a "ghost" could actually move the physical parts of a "machine" without itself being a physical entity inside of a causally closed system.

5

Affirming the Creative and the Heroic

In the second chapter, we pointed out that the assumption of physicalism, in denying personal freedom and any possibility of autonomy, also eliminates the possibility of real creativity and any real heroism. Yet our human self-awareness seems universally rooted in some awareness of our own creativity, while also being drawn to the possibility of true heroism. Is this a pointer to reality or just an illusion?

For most members of our race, the importance of creativity is difficult to shake. Thus, even determinists like Kurzweil laud examples of what we call "creativity." But while he and others might provide tools or exercises for enhancing creativity, they must ultimately view these tools as means of programming humans or as extending the programmed human into a programmed computer. The physicalist may teach her child to play violin and to compose music, but if she is honest and consistent with her worldview, she would have to admit that teaching music to a child is no different from writing a computer program so that a computer can play chess or compose music in imitation of Puccini.

Is there a worldview that takes creativity seriously—one that explains it, rather than explaining it *away*? Is there a worldview that looks not only at the *source* of creativity, but also at its *purpose*?

At least one worldview that takes creativity very seriously is Judeo-Christian theism, which sees humans as both physical and spiritual creatures who are the handiwork of a divine creator rather than the product of blind, purposeless chance. This worldview not only affirms that creativity is real but explains where creativity comes from, and takes seriously why it is important.

One of the clearest—and, indeed, one of the most creative—exemplars and proponents of these ideas is J. R. R. Tolkien. The twentieth-century Oxford professor, philologist, scholar of Old English and Old Norse language and literature, and mythopoet is most famous for his body of Middle-earth mythology, poetry, and heroic fantasy, including *The Hobbit* and *The Lord of the Rings*. Rooted in a Christian (and dualistic in the broader sense) understanding of what it means to be human, his writings provide one understanding of the source and the purpose of human creativity. It is an understanding contrasting sharply with that of Kurzweil and Skinner. Indeed, the importance of creativity, and especially of creative art, is so central to the ideas of J. R. R. Tolkien that it surfaces in nearly everything he writes. However, his ideas on creativity may be clearest in his autobiographical[1] short fairy tale "Leaf by Niggle" and in his essay "On Fairy-Stories."

In this chapter, as a contrast to the physicalist understanding of creativity and heroism presented in chapter 2, we explore these two works of J. R. R. Tolkien, plus two of his posthumously published works, titled "The Debate of Finrod and Andreth" and "Of Aulë and Yavanna." Both of these latter stories are mythical dialogues, or collections of dialogues, expressing important philosophical and theological ideas, much as do the dialogues of Plato.

Mythical Dialogues: The *Hröa* and *Fëa* of J. R. R. Tolkien

In our current age, strongly influenced by Enlightenment rationalism and twentieth-century scientism, it is tempting to dismiss or even to deny the value of myth, story, and imagination. Certainly it can be easy to miss the philosophical significance of Tolkien's ideas, since they most often come to us in mythical form (and involve mythical creatures such as Elves, Dwarves, and Ents). But if we dismiss

Tolkien's discourses for that reason, we would also have to dismiss the importance of the philosophical ideas of Plato, one of the most famous and important philosophers in history.[2] Many of Plato's important ideas are also communicated in the form of myth and dialogue. Plato apparently believed that this was the best form to communicate these ideas, which have been taken seriously and discussed for more than two millennia since his time. As we saw, even a naturalist and nondualist such as Kurzweil takes seriously Plato's ideas, including his ideas about human nature, and sees that the ideas and their form have substance that can be explored and understood, and with which one might agree or (as in Kurzweil's case) disagree.

So before turning to Tolkien's explicit explorations of creativity in his essay "On Fairy-Stories" and his short story "Leaf by Niggle," it is valuable to look first at an exploration of his ideas about body and soul in the form of mythical dialogue. The first dialogue we explore takes place in the First Age of Middle-earth, centuries before the events of *The Lord of the Rings*. It is between a wise and learned human woman named Andreth and an Elven king named Finrod. Finrod was considered among the wisest and most trustworthy of the highest race of Elves living still in Middle-earth at the time. Though the story, titled in Elvish *Athrabeth Finrod ah Andreth* (in English, "The Debate of Finrod and Andreth"), was not published until 1993, twenty years after the author's death, the author's son Christopher Tolkien describes it as "a major and finished work" of his father, and notes that "it is referred to elsewhere [in J. R. R. Tolkien's notes] as if it had for my father some 'authority.'"[3] The author intended the story to have been included in a published version of *The Silmarillion*, and he argued (unsuccessfully) in a letter of some twenty-six thousand words that *The Silmarillion* ought to be published in conjunction with *The Lord of the Rings* as an indispensable part of understanding that latter work.

One interesting aspect of "The Debate of Finrod and Andreth," as a fictional dialogue, is that Tolkien wrote his own commentary on it, intending that the commentary would also be published as the "last item in an appendix" in the same volume as the dialogue itself.[4] In fact, he wrote not only commentary on the dialogue, but also extensive notes on the commentary, which are longer than the commentary itself. So we have a very clear idea what Tolkien was trying to communicate through that dialogue. In the commentary, he explains several tenets that King Finrod would have held as his starting point in the debate. In particular, he explains what Finrod understood and assumed about the nature of Elves *and Men* (humans). "With regard to King Finrod," the commentary states, "it must be understood that he starts with certain basic beliefs, which he would have said were derived from one or more of these sources: his created nature; angelic instruction; thought; and experience." The commentary then sets out seven of these basic beliefs, all of which relate directly to the subject of this book. The first provides a foundation for all the rest, while the second and third are particularly interesting regarding the spiritual nature of humans.

1. There exists Eru (The One); that is, One God Creator, who made (or more strictly designed) the World, but is not Himself the World. This world, or Universe, he calls *Eä*, an Elvish word that means "It is," or "Let It Be."
2. There are on Earth "incarnate" creatures, Elves and Men: these are made of a union of *hröa* and *fëa* (roughly but not exactly equivalent to "body" and "soul"). This, [Finrod] would say, was a *known fact* concerning Elvish nature, and could therefore be deduced for human nature from the close kinship of Elves and Men.
3. *Hröa* and *fëa* [Finrod] would say are wholly distinct in kind, and not on the "same plane of derivation from Eru," but were designed each for the other, to abide in perpetual harmony. The *fëa* is indestructible, a unique identity which cannot be disintegrated or absorbed into any other identity. The *hröa*, however, can be destroyed and dissolved: that is a fact of experience. (In such a case he would describe the *fëa* as "exiled" or "houseless.")[5]

In the second of these tenets, Tolkien introduces his concept of *hröa* and *fëa*, describing them as similar to, but not *exactly* the same as, *body* and *soul*. Tolkien is not only using the Platonic approach of mythopoesis[6] and fictional dialogue to communicate philosophical ideas, but his reference to "body" and "soul" brings to mind Plato's concept put forward in mythical dialogues two and a half millennia earlier. "And this composition of soul and body," Plato writes in the *Phaedrus*, "is called a living and mortal creature."[7] Tolkien must have felt that Plato was on the right track, understanding that men, while bodily beings, are not *merely* bodily; we also have some identity that is eternal and will continue in existence even if the body is destroyed. It is an identity, Tolkien notes, that "cannot be disintegrated or absorbed into any other identity." Presumably, in this view, there could *not* be multiple copies of that identity; we could not download our consciousness to be *absorbed* into a computer, and we especially could not have it simultaneously exist in several different computer programs.

Indeed, just as writers like Bertrand Russell consider the complete materialism of humans to be indisputable, Finrod accepts as a "known fact"—clear from both divine revelation and observation—that human (and elvish) nature is at once *both* biological and spiritual. Yet this concept is also different from the Platonic idea, if only subtly so. Tolkien's commentary on "The Debate" describes body and soul as "designed each for the other, to abide in perpetual harmony." They are intimately related, even if fundamentally different in nature. They are more like story and plot, or wave and particle, than like a ghost in a machine. Whereas for Plato—at least in many interpretations—the goal of the mind or soul is to *escape* the body, to move from the imperfect physical to the perfect ideal, for Tolkien by contrast the body and the soul, or *hröa* and *fëa*, are *made for each other*. "The separation of *hröa* and *fëa* is 'unnatural,' and proceeds not from the original design."[8] Indeed, great evil befalls in Middle-earth in the one instance in which an Elf (Miriel, the mother of Fëanor) intentionally abandons her *hröa* so that she may forget her existence and continue only as an incomplete, bodiless *fëa*.[9]

In the dialogue itself, the Elven king Finrod explains to Andreth what he believes to be the nature of the race of Men. After speaking of Men as *Children* of the creator Eru, Finrod goes on to say:

> When we speak so, we speak out of knowledge, not out of mere Elvish lore; and we proclaim that ye are our kin, in a kinship far closer . . . than that which binds together all other creatures of Arda [the Earth], and ourselves to them.
>
> Other creatures also in Middle-earth we love in their measure and kind: the beasts and birds who are our friends, the trees, and even

> the fair flowers that pass more swiftly than Men. Their passing we regret; but believe it to be a part of their nature, as much as are their shapes or their hues.
>
> But for you, who are our nearer kin, our regret is far greater.[10]

In other words, while Finrod's fellow creatures—trees and animals and flowers—have worth and value, and though he may mourn the passing of a beloved animal, or an ancient tree, or even a passing bird needlessly killed, these other creatures do not have an eternal nature akin to his. Humans have a nature at once both bodily and spiritual, and when the body of a human friend dies, Finrod loses a spiritual as well as a physical relationship.

Let us begin to consider, then, what are the implications of this dualist view of humans to our understanding of creativity.

The Source of Human Creativity

As we have noted several times, humans seem to be creative. We act as though we are creative. We *feel* our creativity. Even the most ardent physicalists, though they may explain creativity away in one of several ways, seem unable to escape from living *as though* they were creative and exercised free will. So it makes sense to ask the question, why are we creative?

This question can be interpreted in two ways, both of which are important. The question can refer to the efficient cause: *Where does creativity come from?* Put another way, the efficient-cause question asks: *How did humans end up being (or at least appearing to be) creative?* The question can also refer to the final cause, or *telos* of creativity: *For what purpose, or to what end, are we creative?*

One approach to the question, why? is to deny creativity altogether. This relieves us of the problem of answering either meaning of the question (and the denial is necessary if we have a worldview such as physicalism that cannot give an answer). You don't need to find the source of something that doesn't exist. A river has a source. A mirage does not. We look for the source of a river by following it upstream to smaller and smaller tributaries. We explain a mirage not by telling where the water comes from (since the water is not real), but by explaining why we *seem* to see, or are tricked into believing that we see, water.

If creativity is real, then it is like a river and not a mirage, and we are led to ask where it comes from. In answer to that question, one of the most important ideas in Tolkien's mythic exploration of human nature is captured by the word *creature*. The very word crea*ture* implies something that has been creat*ed*. A creature is not merely an animal or a plant or a human being whose existence is attributed to purposeless chance; it is a *created being*. There are at least three important implications of creaturehood. One is that a creature is distinct from its creator; a creature owes its existence to the creator, but not the other way around. The second is that a creature is the result of a purposeful act: a creative act. Men, Finrod's second tenet tells us, are "made" beings, and made beings are not accidents or mere random happenings. The third implication is that a creature owes not only its existence, but also its very nature, to the creator. As I noted earlier in the book, my children have been responsible for countless Lego constructions over the past decade and a half. Each construction—house, space station, castle, city, land or air or space vehicle—has been given its form and purpose, its very nature, by its creators: from the imagination and hands of my children, as well as from the Danish designers who created the Lego bricks to start with.

And the third implication of creaturehood may go even deeper—as in the case of Tolkien's understanding of human creaturehood. If I see on the floor of our playroom a Lego space vehicle for some hostile alien being, I don't assume that my child who built it is himself a hostile alien being. If creativity is real at all, and not merely illusory, it would appear that we are capable of creating things that are different from us and that have a different purpose, though the purpose came from us. But to some degree, everything we create bears *something* of our imprint. For a time, I could look at Lego creations in our playroom and determine (from their symmetry or lack thereof, the use of doors and hinges, the color choices, etc.) which of my three children had made them from the nature of the objects (no matter how foreign they looked).

Some of our creations are even more like self-portraits or like the bearing of children than they are like my children's creations of alien Lego space vehicles. In these cases, the nature of the creature is very much like that of the creator. Finrod's third tenet states that our nature is "derived" from Eru, the creator, whose name means

"The One," and who is also called Ilúvatar, which means "Father of All." And this is the central idea of this chapter. If our source is a creative being (God, the divine creative being), and we derive our nature from that source, then our own nature must also be creative; or to phrase this in terms of our question: Why are we creative? The answer is straightforward but profound: we are creative because we were created by, and in the likeness of, a creator. To bear a creator's nature is to be creative—to be a creator. In this context, our creativity makes perfect sense. We have an explanation for it and don't have to view it as illusory.

This is such an important idea in Tolkien's worldview that it surfaces in many places in his writing. We see it, for example, in yet another of his Middle-earth myths: the story of the creation of the race of Dwarves by the angelic being Aulë, told in the chapter of *The Silmarillion* titled "Of Aulë and Yavanna." This chapter presents three mythic dialogues: one between Aulë and the divine creator Eru, one between Aulë and his spouse, Yavanna, and one between Yavanna and Manwë, the regent of Eru.[11] The tale tells how Aulë, impatient for the promised coming of Elves and Men into the world, creates Dwarves from his memory of what Elves and Men will look like. However, he has no power to gives Dwarves their own free will, so they are only his puppets. Furthermore, he has no authority from the creator Eru even to do this. When Eru confronts Aulë, chastising him for his act of impatience and for exceeding his authority, Aulë repents but also gives this defense: "Yet the making of things is in my heart from my own making by thee; and the child of little understanding that makes a play of the deeds of his father may do so without thought of mockery, but because he is the son of his father."[12]

This is a profound answer to the question of where our creativity comes from. It could well be Tolkien's own defense for his whole lifetime of created works, as well as his defense of all creativity. *The making of things is in our hearts*. We are creative by nature. Why? Because we are children of a creator. We are made by a maker. Our image is derived from our creator's just as a child derives her image from her parents. And while Eru does not condone Aulë's action, neither does he deny the basic truth of Aulë's reasoning. Eru, we are told, has "compassion upon Aulë and his desire," and he gives the gift of free will to the Dwarves.[13]

The importance of our freedom and creativity as gifts of our creator also comes out in another way in this story. Aulë himself cannot give free will to the Dwarves. He cannot make them creative beings. They are only his puppets. As Eru tells him, "The creatures of thy hand and mind can live only by that being, moving when thou thinkest to move them, and if thy thought be elsewhere, standing idle."[14] Eru might well have pointed out to a computer programmer that his computer programs can do only what they are programmed to do; they cannot choose to disobey their programmer. Tolkien seems to be suggesting here that one created being inside of creation cannot give the capacity for free will to another object inside of creation. Creativity must come from something outside of creation. Philosophically speaking, causal closure cannot account for creativity. But Tolkien did not believe in a causally closed universe. Eru is able to make the Dwarves free, and as a gift of mercy to Aulë he does that: he gives them "life of their own."[15] The Dwarves, like Men and Elves, become Eru's children—though they are called children "by adoption" rather than by birth. And though Dwarves are capable of doing evil (as are Men and Elves) they are also capable of creativity, and they create some of the most splendid works of art and craft and beauty in the history of Middle-earth.

For those still wary of seeking important philosophical ideas in myths—whether in Plato's myths or in the more recent myths of J. R. R.Tolkien—Tolkien also makes the same point in one of his best-known essays, a nonfiction work titled, "On Fairy-Stories." In explaining why humans create stories, he writes, "We make in our measure and in our derivative mode, because we are made: and not only made, but made in the image and likeness of a Maker."[16] Here, Tolkien puts in his own words, speaking about himself and his fellow human writers of creative fantasy in our own world, the same argument put forth by Aulë in a mythic context. We are *making* beings because we are *made* beings; not only that, but we are beings made in the image of a Maker.

Here, also, Tolkien's language is closer to the biblical language from which he draws his ideas. The first chapter of the Bible gives the following account of the divine and creative source of humankind. "Then God said, 'Let us make man in our image, in our likeness. . . .' So God created man in his own image, in the image of God he created him; male and female he created them" (Gen. 1:26–27). And if we turn a few verses earlier, to the very first verse of the Bible, we see something very important about the God who created male and female. "In the beginning, God created the heavens and the earth" (Gen. 1:1). The first verb associated with God in the entire Bible is the verb *create*. Thus, the first thing we learn about God, other than that he already existed in the beginning, is that he has a creative nature. It is this creative nature that humans have inherited—or, rather, the creative nature with which we have been created.

If you ask how this is possible, it is because this worldview affirms that we are spiritual as well as bodily beings, we have a *fëa* as well as a *hröa*. Thus, our actions are not *entirely* caused by physical laws that govern material bodies. Our spiritual nature is also derived from our creator, who breathed spirit into the dust to create us. We share our creator's creativity, in part because we share our creator's spiritual nature. The answer may not be pleasing to those who deny the existence of a creator, but it does provide an explanation of where human creativity could come from in a way that materialist presuppositions cannot. It is an answer that takes our creativity seriously.

Tolkien's Threefold Telos of Creativity

The source of creativity is not, however, the only aspect of creativity we may wish to explore. If we take creativity seriously, we ask not only from whence it comes, but also to where it leads. That is, what is the *telos* or purpose of creativity? Though the question is not strictly necessary to this chapter, an exploration of the answer provided in the works of J. R. R. Tolkien illustrates how seriously creativity is considered in the Christian dualism he represents, and thus gives further insight into the contrast between physicalism and integrative dualism and the implications of each.

Indeed, the very question, "What is the purpose of creativity?" doesn't make sense from a standpoint of physicalism. Remember Kurzweil's definition cited earlier: "Free will is purposeful behavior and decision making."[17] A computer does not have the freedom to have a purpose or to make decisions. If it had a purpose and could make decisions based on that purpose, a computer would have free will. It does not. It follows its program. In that sense, returning to our earlier example, from the perspective of the computer a program to automatically raise and lower a garage door at different times and in different circumstances is no different from a program to compose music. I may prefer the sound of music to the sound of a garage door going up and down, and so I (the user or programmer of the computer) may have a different purpose for the two programs, but the programs themselves and the computer running them do not act based on any purpose of their own. Likewise, if we, as humans, are complex computer programs, then we have no purpose for our creativity. That is, if we cannot carry out purposeful decision making, then we cannot *choose* to be creative as a result of some purpose any more than we can choose anything else. The *telos* of creativity, and in particular of creative art, is irrelevant from the point of view of the computer program that is designed to "create the art."

By contrast, the Christian worldview as seen in Tolkien's writing takes seriously what ought to be our *telos* for creativity, just as it takes seriously the source of that creativity. A threefold purpose for creative art that is fully consistent with, and is rooted in, J. R. R. Tolkien's Christian faith can be seen in his short autobiographical allegory "Leaf by Niggle," and in his essay "On Fairy-Stories."

The first of the three ends of creativity relates directly to what we have already pointed out in this chapter. According to Tolkien, we were created with the very purpose of being creative: *to put our creativity to use is to glorify our creator simply by being what we were intended to be*. Creative art, in particular, and expressions of creativity in general, do not need any further justification. Though the simplest and most obvious purpose of creativity, it also may be the end or goal most easily overlooked even by those who share Tolkien's view that humans are beings of both body and spirit, and moreover are created in the image of a creative God.

"Leaf by Niggle" is about a painter named Niggle who must go on a journey. Because the journey is expected to be unpleasant, he puts it off. (As we later discover, he also puts off or ignores many, though not all, of his obligations to his neighbors in favor of spending his time working on a painting.) The first paragraph of the story introduces Niggle's journey. The second introduces Niggle himself. It does so with a simple sentence: "Niggle was a painter."[18] The narrator does not say that Niggle painted, nor that Niggle liked to paint, nor that painting was something Niggle did. It says, rather, that a painter is who Niggle *was*: his very nature was to create, and specifically to create with paints on canvas. Tolkien might have pointed out in his essay that Niggle was a painter because he was made in the image and likeness of a painter.

The journey Niggle must take is best understood as the journey of death and, more specifically, a journey toward heaven. This is suggested strongly by several aspects of the imagery: the journey comes after an illness, and it starts with a trip down a dark tunnel; Niggle is taken on the journey by a man dressed all in black and is not allowed to bring anything with him; the journey involves forgetfulness; and Niggle seems to pass out of time itself. At some point on this journey, Niggle ends up in a purgatorial workhouse under the care and authority of a doctor and two voices, called simply the First Voice and the Second Voice. Together this trinity forms a "medical board," or perhaps a "court of inquiry," or both at once. It is from this court of inquiry that Niggle also passes through a sort of judgment, as does his former neighbor Parish. In the context of judgment several important points are made with respect to the value of creativity and of creative art. The first is an explicit affirmation of what we surmised from the introduction to the story: Niggle "was a painter by nature," the Second Voice tells the First Voice. We also learn that Niggle took care to paint *well*, to do good creative work simply for the sake of doing good creative work. "He took a great deal of pains with leaves, just for their own sake," the Second Voice says in Niggle's defense, noting also that, "a Leaf by Niggle has a charm of its own."[19] This simultaneously gives value to the art itself, and to the importance of being committed to the careful practice of creative art. The First Voice agrees, and this fact of Niggle's care to do good artistic work is one of the important points in his defense.

On the other hand, the neighbor Parish is judged for *not* having appreciated the worth of Niggle's painting. The narrator explains, with a tone of criticism:

> When Parish looked at Niggle's garden (which was often) he saw mostly weeds; and when he looked at Niggle's pictures (which was seldom) he saw only green and grey patches and black lines, which

> seemed to him nonsensical. He did not mind mentioning the weeds (a neighbourly duty), but he refrained from giving any opinion of the pictures. He thought this was very kind, and he did not realize that, even if it was kind, it was not kind enough. Help with the weeds (and perhaps praise for the pictures) would have been better.[20]

Toward the end of the tale, Niggle and Parish meet the shepherd, who will eventually guide them into the Mountains. The shepherd—a figure drawn from biblical imagery and associated with God (Pss. 23; 80; Isa. 40; Mic. 5; John 10:11–18; etc.)—also points out Parish's shortsightedness in not seeing the value of art, and even for wanting to use Niggle's canvases and paints to mend his leaky roof. Parish believed that only practical things like vegetable gardens and house roofs were important. He did not glimpse the worth of art, and he is chastised for acting on that belief. "You might have caught the glimpse [of the beauty of Niggle's work]," the shepherd tells him, "if you had ever thought it worth while to try."[21]

So J. R. R. Tolkien, beginning with the view that human creativity has its source in a creator, and that we were created to be creative, takes the consistent next step of seeing the practice of creativity and the making of creative art to be a worthwhile endeavor. To be creative is to be who we, as humans, were made to be; it is a following of the creator's plan. In particular, this suggests that the expression of creativity does not need some other *practical* or *useful* end to justify its existence. This gives a very high view of creativity and creative art in Tolkien's Christian worldview, and we will return to this later in this chapter. But first, we see two other ends toward which human creativity ought to strive that may give it value.

Creativity, Beauty, and the Enrichment of Creation

A second purpose, or *telos*, of creativity is the enrichment of the world: the bringing into being—through creative art and more generally through the practice and use of our creativity—new beauty. We were made to be creative beings *in order that* we might add to the beauty of the world through our practice of creativity. Whether our creativity is expressed in cooking or carpentry, architecture or visual arts, sports or scientific endeavor, philosophy or farming, parenting or pottery, or poetry or computer programming, in teaching, quilting, homemaking, or any other of myriad ways in which creativity is put to use, we can enrich the world through our bringing into being new and beautiful creations of our own thoughts and hands and voices.

At the very end of his essay "On Fairy-Stories," Tolkien reflects on the importance of the Christian story of the incarnation and God's redemption of humankind. In doing so, he explores the implications of the Christian belief that the creator of the universe entered into and redeemed his creation. This idea of incarnation is pivotal for our discussion, because it is an explicit example of dualism: a spiritual being (God, the creator) taking on physical form (as a human person in a human body). Jesus, according to Christian teaching, was both fully human and fully divine—both flesh and spirit. He performed miracles, including turning water into wine and walking on water. He also ate fish, slept, walked from town to town, and got dirt on his feet when he walked. Tolkien explores implications of this by looking at the creative labors of humankind in light of it.

> The Christian has still to work, with mind as well as body, to suffer, hope, and die; but he may now perceive that all his bents and faculties have a purpose, which can be redeemed. So great is the bounty with which he has been treated that he may now, perhaps, fairly dare to guess that in Fantasy he may actually assist in the effoliation and multiple enrichment of creation. All tales may come true; and yet, at the last, redeemed, they may be as like and as unlike the forms that we give them as Man, finally redeemed, will be like and unlike the fallen that we know.[22]

There is a great deal to unravel in this passage, which addresses both what a Christian *ought* to do and what he or she can *hope* for. Though the specific topic of Tolkien's essay is the creative literary endeavor of fantasy and myth, the context of his comments pertains more broadly to the human use of imagination—the image-making and imagery-making facility, which is an essential part of creativity. In all creative endeavors we may "assist in the . . . multiple enrichment of creation." The created physical world is good and valuable, as is attested by God coming and dwelling in it in bodily form. God, the creator, has given humans the gift of adding to his creation in countless ways through the practice of our own creativity. This, of course, assumes that we really are capable of creativity and originality. If this is true, then in creativity humans can become God's partners, as we were made to be. This is a "purpose" toward which we direct our "bents and faculties," our thoughts and our labors, especially our creativity. What a great gift, a "bounty," this is, in Tolkien's view.

Now, Tolkien also acknowledges that we are a "fallen" (or sinful) race. That is, we have turned away from God and his original purpose for us. And so our creative endeavors are corrupted, to one degree or another, by our fallen nature. At best, our creative endeavors are marred and fall short of perfection, even those of the most well-intentioned artists. At worst, we intentionally put our creativity to work only for selfish gain at the expense of others, or to manipulate or hurt others. History has no shortage of evil creative geniuses. This is an important point, and it separates humans from computers. According to Tolkien, the creator of humankind had a *telos* for making us as creative beings; this *telos* was that we use our creativity to partner in the continued act of creation, of bringing into being new forms and new beauty. The difference between human persons and computer programs is that humans are free whether or not we strive toward that *telos*. We have our own *telos* that may or may not be in accord with our creator's. Indeed, in a fallen world, the *telos* of human creativity will never be fully in keeping with that of our creator. Tolkien presents what he believed to be the ideal *telos* of creativity but makes it clear that as free-will beings we are not constrained to use our creativity toward that end.

Consider, for example, what Tolkien writes about goblins in his most famous story, *The Hobbit*.

> Now goblins are cruel, wicked, and bad-hearted. They make no beautiful things, but they make many clever ones. . . . Hammers, axes, swords, daggers, pickaxes, tongs, and also instruments of torture, they make very well, or get other people to make to their design. . . . It is not unlikely that they invented some of the machines that have since troubled the world, especially the ingenious devices for killing large numbers of people at once.[23]

Goblins do not lack creativity. The narrator explains that they are clever, ingenious, and capable of invention. The fact that they design things that others build shows that they are not merely skilled with their hands, but actually *originate* ideas. But their creativity is put to evil use: enslaving and destroying. Hopefully, few of us *intend* to put our creativity to evil purpose. (Even the goblins would not describe *themselves* as evil.[24]) Yet even when we (humans) desire to use creativity for good or for beauty, either our motives are mixed or we fail to be able to fully realize our vision. What Tolkien points out, however, is that our flawed creative efforts can be redeemed because of God's work through the incarnate Messiah who took bodily form in the person of a first-century Jew named *Yeshua* (or *Jesus* in an Anglicized name form) and experienced the fullness of humanity and what it means to be a being of both *hröa* and *fëa*, body and spirit.

The creator's redeeming work, on the one hand, doesn't free humans from the obligation of practicing creativity. Nor does it mean that human creative efforts become perfect. We still need to work with body and mind and to practice creativity, and our efforts will (for a time) still be flawed. Suffering has not been removed from the world. But when we strive to use our creativity toward God's intended *telos*, we can imagine a day when our flawed creative efforts will be made perfect, and the beauty we envisioned complete. The narrator of "Leaf by Niggle" makes the reader aware of numerous flaws in Niggle's character, and Niggle himself is aware of the flaws in his painting stemming from his imperfect skill. Yet at the end of "Leaf by Niggle," through an act of grace the flawed painter's flawed painting is brought to its perfect completeness.

Indeed, throughout the story we see the worth of beauty affirmed; the use of human creativity to bring beauty into the world is shown to be a valuable *telos* of that creativity. The First and Second Voices of the story affirm the efforts of Niggle simply to create a beautiful leaf. Perhaps the clearest expression of the value of beauty as an end toward which creativity may work comes in a dialogue near the conclusion of the story. Here, Tolkien presents an opposing view through the highly unsympathetic character of Councilor Tompkins. Some time after Niggle has died (or "gone on his journey"), Councilor Tompkins has a conversation with a schoolmaster named Atkins. Atkins raises the possibility of preserving a surviving fragment of one of the paintings of the late Niggle—which, indeed, he later does, "one beautiful leaf" that he frames and puts into the town museum. Atkins believes there is value in the paintings and worth in preserving them. He is surprised that Tompkins does not. "Then you don't think painting is worth anything, not worth preserving, or improving, or even making use of?" Atkins asks. Tompkins's reply is telling.

> "Of course, painting has uses," said Tompkins. "But you couldn't make use of his painting. There is plenty of scope for bold young men not afraid of new ideas and new methods. None for this old-fashioned stuff. Private day-dreaming. He could not have designed a telling poster to save his life. Always fiddling with leaves and flowers. I asked him why, once. He said he thought they were pretty! Can you believe it? He said *pretty*! 'What, digestive and genital organs of plants?' I said to him; and he had nothing to answer. Silly footler."[25]

Our first clue about what Tolkien thinks of Tompkins's view may be suggested by the name. Tompkins is a diminutive of Tom or Thomas. Thomas is the Bible's most famous doubter, whom posterity dubs with the moniker "Doubting Thomas." Hence, the name Tompkins could be translated as "the Little Doubter" or "the Little Unbeliever." That would be a good description of his character; Councilor Tompkins does not believe in any spiritual reality, nor even in the concept of the journey.

In short, Tompkins is a physicalist. What little we see of him in the story is enough to make it clear that he holds essentially the same view of human nature that can be seen in the writings of B. F. Skinner, Richard Dawkins, and other real physicalists whose ideas had become widespread during Tolkien's life. (Consider also Richard Dawkins's condemnation, cited earlier in this book, of medieval cathedrals as having no use and therefore being wasteful of resources.) By denying any spiritual reality, Tompkins views humans as automata. This is evident in an earlier comment when he notes that Niggle "could have been made into a serviceable cog," if the "schoolmasters knew [their] business."[26] The term "cog" itself implies a machine, or automata. Even more telling is the notion that Niggle "could have been made into" one, meaning that humans are simply raw material to be worked with and conditioned through their education and the shaping of their environment. Tompkins goes on to deny any meaning or ultimate purpose of creativity. The only value he sees in art is economic or political: designing posters to sell products or ideas, to make money, or to help condition other people. He explicitly ridicules the notion of beauty, reducing the beauty of a flower (or a painting of a flower) to mere reproductive biology—viewing flowers as nothing more than "digestive and genital organs of plants."

The portrayal of this character provides Tolkien an opportunity to contrast a physicalist view of creative art with his own theistic view, expressed elsewhere in the story, and to suggest that Tompkins's physicalist view, which devalues art, is both shallow and untrue. Readers should realize immediately that Tolkien believed Tompkins's view to be untrue. The story is about the very journey that Tompkins denies; it makes it clear that the journey is real, while Tompkins claims it is a fiction. Furthermore, the value of Niggle's painting is strongly affirmed at the end of the tale, and *not* for any economic reason. His great painting *is* finally preserved for eternity (though not, as Atkins planned, in a museum). In short, Tolkien was entirely critical of Tompkins's view of—which is to say, his devaluation of—creative art. The story critiques that view and presents an alternative.

Niggle, by contrast—though his view is ridiculed by Tompkins—expresses a belief that a painting may be valuable simply because it is "beautiful" (as he says early in the story), or at least "pretty" (a word he uses later). This is also the view of the narrator, the First Voice, the Second Voice, the shepherd, and even presumably of Atkins. And, the readers may clearly surmise, it is the view of the author Tolkien himself. Niggle is not interested in posters. He is interested in painting flowers, because by doing so he can create his version of their beauty. So Tolkien's theistic worldview, in contrast to the physicalist view of his character Tompkins, affirms the value of creativity, and also the value of created art for the sake of beauty.

Art and Truth

The final *telos* of creativity seen in Tolkien's story, and which flows from his theistic worldview, is both the simplest and most complex to explain—and the easiest to misunderstand or trivialize. Creativity, imagination, and art are means by which we both understand the universe in which we live and by which we communicate that understanding to others. Through our creativity we come to know what is true, and we help others to know what is true. This simple idea is especially important as a *telos* of artistic endeavor: poetry, painting, sculpture, story, the composition of music, etc.

What Tolkien does *not* mean by this is that art should be—or even *can* be—reducible to a message or moral or any form of abstract propositional reason or truth. This is why this third purpose of creativity and of art, though simple, is the easiest to misunderstand. Creative imagination and reason go hand in hand as means to make sense of the world, but they are not the same thing. Indeed, this third point may be misapplied in two different directions. On the one hand, we may mistakenly try to reduce a work of art to some simplistic message or moral it is supposed to convey, and thus miss the art *as art*. That is, we may view a work of creative art only for the sake of its message and thus devalue its beauty and its creative significance, reducing the work of art to mere propaganda. This might be akin to, or no better than, Tompkins's attitude of valuing the creativity only for its poster potential.

On the other hand, we may be so opposed to such a reduction of beauty and art to a mere propositional truth that we miss the idea that art can be true. With respect to his own creative art, the writing of mythic and fantastic literature, Tolkien argued in various places that it *must* contain truth, even religious truth. He argued also that it must be applicable. He also simultaneously claimed that he disliked explicit allegory, a form of story that often assigns such an inflexible and narrow message or interpretation to a story that it devalues the artistic aspects. (Although, in fact, he did write a small number of allegories or stories with allegorical significance, including "Leaf by Niggle.") So Tolkien rejected both extremes. This was the central subject of a previous book, *From Homer to Harry Potter*, that I coauthored with David O'Hara. I will not repeat all of our previous arguments from that book here but will explore just a few ways Tolkien explored truth as a *telos* of creative art both in his famous essay "On Fairy-Stories" and in his story "Leaf by Niggle."

Toward the end of "Leaf by Niggle," Niggle's painting is given the gift of primary reality; it becomes no longer a *painting* of a tree, but the *tree itself* as Niggle always imagined it. Niggle and his former neighbor Parish then live for a time in a cabin near the tree, taking care of it and completing it, while they continue their own journeys of both personal growth and reconciliation. (Their prior relationship had been less than perfect.) One day they take a walk, and they meet the shepherd coming out of the high and distant Mountains that appear in the background of the painting. The shepherd takes Niggle back to these Mountains with him, and the reader is left with the impression that these Mountains are the promised paradise. The tale then ends with the First Voice and Second Voice discussing Niggle's painting. "It is proving very useful indeed," the Second Voice comments. "As a holiday, and a refreshment. It is splendid for convalescence; and not only for that, for many it is the best introduction to the Mountains. I am sending more and more there."[27] It is very interesting to note here that Niggle's creative art eventually does prove "useful"—far more useful than Tompkins could have imagined. Its most important use, however, contrary to the view of Tompkins, is certainly *not* economic or political; the painting cannot be reduced to a mere poster or to some message or moral in propositional form. Indeed, the ultimate "use" of the creative work is one that even Niggle never imagined. Instead, it is a use bestowed by divine grace. Moreover, the creative work was shown to have value well before it was proven to be useful. The value of the work did not stem from its usefulness, and it is not economic. Nevertheless, it does become useful. Tolkien might well be suggesting that the usefulness of art comes from its worth and beauty, rather than vice versa.

Tolkien also seems to be suggesting that the painting is useful in more ways than one. First, Niggle's creative work proves to be restful and emotionally healing for both himself (the creator) and for his neighbor Parish (who had a lame leg, and for whom it is also physically healing); it is both a "holiday" and a place of "convalescence." And not only for them, but for many who come there after them. Art can heal both the artist who creates it and the viewer who participates in the art. In fact, in the case of Niggle and Parish, it is healing for the two of them *together*, and for their relationship. The art brings them together, in part by helping them to understand (through living with the art) the truth about each other and about their world.

As for the second use, the Second Voice tells us that the painting also ends up providing, for some growing number of people, an "introduction to the Mountains." From near the start of the tale readers learn that Niggle's painting, while by conscious intention of its creator was just a painting of a tree—or, more specifically, a collection of leaves—provided a glimpse through the branches and leaves of the Mountains behind. The Mountains, we learn, are true and real and eternal. The painting, which gains those properties only in relation to the Mountains, thus becomes a pointer to something that is true and real and eternal. It provides a glimpse of, or insight into, some underlying truth. And this is a vitally important *telos* of creativity and imagination in general, and of creative art in particular. Through creative art, flawed though it is, we gain a glimpse of transcendent truth. Art, like metaphor, can point to something beyond itself.

Thus, of his own favorite creative endeavor, the making of myth, fantasy, and fairy story, Tolkien writes in "On Fairy-Stories," "The peculiar quality of the 'joy' in successful Fantasy can thus be explained as a sudden glimpse of the underlying reality or truth."[28] Again, if we try to turn story into sermon, a painting into poster, or art into an agenda, our creativity will almost certainly fail *as art*, because we have reduced creative imagination to propositional reasoning or, worse still, propaganda. To speak of art as a vehicle of truth—or, more specifically, to reduce the *telos* of art to "getting across some message"—is dangerous, but it is equally dangerous to deny altogether the *telos* that through our creativity we come better to understand the world in which we live and to communicate that understanding. Tolkien grappled with these ideas precisely because he understood just how important our creativity is, how easily it can be corrupted, and thus how important it is to understand. In short, his view of human nature caused him to take human creativity seriously. That he spent so much time exploring the importance of creativity, and of art, and of story, suggests how important it is in his Christian worldview that sees humans as more than machines.

Taking Heroism Seriously

We end this chapter by turning to the subject of heroism, again contrasting the view of Tolkien with that of the physicalists we explored in the earlier chapters. We need say much less about heroism, not because it is less important than creativity, but because Tolkien's view, and the contrast with that of physicalism, ought to be much clearer even to the casual observer. Tolkien's main body of work is heroic literature. It could even be defined as the English language's quintessential work of heroism of the past century. While B. F. Skinner and Bertrand Russell explicitly deny the possibility of heroism, and criticize those who promote it, Tolkien presents it, models it, and defines it.

At the heart of Tolkien's model of what it means to be a hero is free will, which is the opposition of automation. Certainly, as we saw in an earlier chapter, the models of heroes in Tolkien's tales—Frodo, Sam, Merry, Pippin, Aragorn, Faramir, Beren, Éomer, Elrond, Galadriel, Legolas—are those who make difficult choices, often at great risk or personal sacrifice. Their heroic choice is usually a decision to do what is right rather than what is easy. These examples are difficult to explore in a short amount of space, and would involve a considerable amount of plot summary. Yet we can see in just a few brief dialogues that Tolkien not only affirms the reality of heroism, but also that his understanding of heroism comes down to the choices made by the heroes.

These choices and the free will of the characters are emphasized repeatedly through the tale. There are, for example, the words of Elrond to Frodo when Frodo chooses to take the ring to Mordor, cited in the first chapter of this book. There are the words of Legolas to the Dwarf Gimli, when Gimli chooses to remain on the quest after the visit to Lothlórien. "For such is the way of it: to find and lose, as it seems to those whose boat is on the running stream. But I count you blessed, Gimli son of Glóin: for your loss you suffer of *your own free will*, and you *might have chosen otherwise*."[29] There are the words of Aragorn. When Éomer first meets him on the Plains of Rohan and asks, "What doom do you bring out of the North?" Aragorn replies, "The doom of choice."[30] We could consider as well Galadriel's choice to refuse the One Ring and to help Frodo with his quest even though the success or failure of that quest will bring about the doom of her beloved Lothlórien. As she tells Frodo, she and her people have made the heroic choice to "cast all away rather than submit to Sauron" even though it will mean that they will be "diminished, and Lothlórien will fade, and the tides of Time will sweep it away."[31] There is even a chapter titled "The Choices of Master Samwise."[32]

We need not belabor this point. Most physicalists would not deny that Tolkien takes heroism seriously in large part because he also takes seriously our moral nature as free-will beings. The question is not what he portrayed, but whether he was correct. The question is whether all the potent aspects that have made his storytelling so real and his heroes so attractive are mere illusions. Can we explain it all away as a mere evolutionary device to pass on our genes? Or is it possible that a writer of fantasy literature has presented a *more* true view of human nature than that of the seemingly reasonable physicalists who view human persons as computational devices?

6

Body, Spirit, and the Value of Creation

This chapter, in many ways, is the most difficult chapter of this book to write. In chapter 3, we claimed that a worldview of strict naturalism, and in particular a view of humans as mere computational beings, has many facets which, if followed seriously and consistently, will lead to human behavior with devastating environmental consequences. This is especially true of the ideas of Raymond Kurzweil put forth in books such as *The Age of Spiritual Machines*. In this chapter, we argue that a philosophy that affirms and takes seriously both body and spirit as important parts of human nature *ought* to lead to the healthiest sort of environmentally responsible behavior.

What makes the chapter difficult is that, on the one hand, it appears impossible or nearly impossible for physicalists actually to live their lives day to day *as though* their philosophy were true. In particular—despite the warnings issued in chapter 3 about the increasing escapes from the real world into virtual worlds so common in our culture today—there are, thankfully, still many people who, while holding to the same underlying philosophy as Kurzweil, have not (yet) abandoned the physical world of nature or sought to replace it with a virtual reality. Similarly, there are many who deny any objective moral basis for healthy ecology or for any *telos* for the cosmos, and yet who (again, thankfully) have practices widely viewed as ecologically healthy, such as eating locally and organically, reducing waste and energy consumption and fossil fuel dependence, and more broadly eschewing lifestyles of unsustainable consumption.

What of those who affirm a human being who is both bodily and spiritual? Certainly many of the leading environmental thinkers and activists in the past few decades, as well as important nature writers and philosophers of the past several centuries, who have paved the way for healthier ecological practices, have been strongly motivated by explicitly theistic thinking, or at least by a belief that human persons are both physical and spiritual. (This fact is sometimes not acknowledged in contemporary environmental discourse.)

On the other hand, however, there are also some religious theists who seem to be at least antienvironmental*ist*, if not antienvironmental in their words and actions. Thus, Wendell Berry notes in his essay "Christianity and the Survival of Creation" (an essay to which we will return later in this chapter): "The indictment of Christianity by the anti-Christian conservationists is, in many respects, just. . . . The certified Christian seems just as likely as anyone else to join the military-industrial conspiracy to murder Creation." What Berry goes on to point out, however, is that these ecologically unhealthy behaviors, often practiced by Christians, not only do *not* stem from a Christian worldview but are explicitly contrary to it. "The conservationist indictment of Christianity is a problem," he notes in the next paragraph, "because, however just it may be, it does not come from an adequate understanding of the Bible and the cultural traditions that descend from the Bible." He then tells his readers what is needed: "very precise distinctions between biblical instruction and the behavior of those peoples supposed to have been biblically instructed."[1]

The goal of this chapter, then, is to look at the theological ideas in the Bible itself, and at their philosophical implications, as well as at the writings of some of the most careful and thoughtful Christian thinkers (such as Wendell Berry), in order to see what is said about nature and about our relationship with nature. (For further exploration, see the recommended reading list on "Christianity and Ecology" at the end of this book.) We will argue that, just as these ideas lead to a high view of art and creativity (as explored in the previous chapter), so they also lead to a high view of nature and to an important moral imperative to care for the earth and its creatures. In particular, we hope to show how the potential environmental problems that arise out of naturalistic thinking are answered by a worldview affirming a spiritual as well as a physical reality.

Purposeful Creation and Ecological Practice

A starting point of this discussion is to look at the starting point of the universe. The Judeo-Christian account of the origins of the physical universe begins with a creator bringing a cosmos into existence. This cosmos includes the earth as well as the stars and the other planets—the entire physical universe. The creation account proceeds with the creator causing that earth to teem with life. So we begin with a universe and with life, which are neither random nor accidental, but rather are purposeful and meaningful. To use a word from the previous chapter, the universe itself has a *telos*. Philosophically speaking, accepting this *telos* comes from accepting that the universe has its origin or cause in something—or, rather, some*one*—who is personal and who simultaneously dwells within the cosmos and yet is not a part of it. (This, of course, means denying causal closure.) As the result of a purposeful act by a personal being, the cosmos therefore has a transcendent purpose.

To see the ecological importance of a cosmic purpose, a pair of examples might be helpful. Consider walking into a scrapyard or dump, and seeing a pile of lumber, old doors, hinges, and used hardware strewn about. Contrast that with walking into a carefully arranged and organized workshop where you might find the same sorts of supplies (though presumably in newer condition), perhaps alongside some project in progress. In the first case, you would feel justified in assuming that there was no particular purpose for the materials lying about. That is, you might understand that door hinges *in general* have an intended purpose, but the *particular* old hinge lying on the ground in front of you was only accidentally or coincidentally in that particular place. Nobody had any reason that it should be there or remain there, and it wasn't intended for any particular use. You would thus also likely feel justified in making whatever use you wanted of this material for your own project;

it would be merely a resource to be consumed as you wish. On the other hand, seeing the same materials in a well-organized workshop, before you simply grabbed something and started using it for your own project, you would (I hope) want to know why it was there and what was its purpose. You would have some obligation to the person who organized that workshop—either not to use those supplies at all or to use them only in a manner or for a purpose for which they were intended.

Or consider walking into a kitchen and finding freshly baked cookies on the counter. After a moment of surprise and delight at the pleasant aroma, but before you actually pick up a few of the cookies and eat them, your thoughts ought to turn next to the question of *why* those cookies are sitting out. Since cookies don't just appear on their own, you should appropriately surmise that they are there for a purpose. Again, before choosing to take one, you ought to try to determine what that purpose is, and whether your consumption of one (or two) meets that intended purpose. If you are fortunate—perhaps it is your own kitchen or you are an expected guest in somebody else's—the cookies were made by somebody *for you*; the *telos* is your own delight. Either way, however, understanding those cookies as having a purpose should impact how you view them and how you use them.

Note that we are asking a philosophical question. Is there a *telos* for the building supplies or for the cookies? The answer to that question has important implications. The same applies to the physical world around us. If the cosmos, and more specifically our home planet earth, has no intended purpose, then we can't possibly be guilty of using it in a way *contrary* to its purpose. A purposeless cosmos might well be seen, therefore, as reducing to so many *natural resources*—which may be why, in the world today, we so often refer to everything from water, to soil, to coal beneath the mountaintops of West Virginia and eastern Kentucky as "natural resources." It is why we refer to a stand of trees as *lumber* or *timber resource* rather than as *trees*. Even the terms *environment* and *nature*, as opposed to *creation*, suggests something less meaningful, less purposeful, less under the care of a divine creator. The term *environment* suggests something that is around us and exists only in reference to us. Of course, this still does not mean we should just waste it or destroy it, because doing so might have negative consequences for ourselves, but in seeing it as lumber or a timber resource, we still view it from only a pragmatic and utilitarian view, free of the implications of *telos*.

If, on the other hand, we understand the cosmos as being made with a purpose, then we should also understand that there are restrictions on how we ought to make use of it, or whether we are even free to make use of it *at all*. This latter view is precisely what the Judeo-Christian creation account tells us, and the ecological implications are profound. The Bible begins in Genesis 1:1–2 by telling that the cosmos was created, and that it was created by a God who cares about it and is involved in its continued being. God does not simply look down upon it from afar, but his spirit hovers over the waters (Gen. 1:2). The New Testament echoes this. Colossians 1:15–17 tells us not only that God created all things through Jesus, "things in heaven" and "invisible" (the spiritual reality) as well as things "on earth" and "visible" (the physical reality), but also that "in him all things hold together"; he continues to uphold and sustain that which he created.

Wendell Berry comments on several implications (or discoveries) stemming from a biblical account of Creation: an understanding that God created the universe, that he proclaimed it good, and that he sustains it and dwells in it.

> We will discover that we humans do not own the world or any part of it. . . .
>
> We will discover that God made not only the parts of Creation that we humans understand and approve but all of it. . . .
>
> We will discover that God found the world, as He made it, to be good, that He made it for His pleasure, and that He continues to love it and to find it worthy, despite its reduction and corruption by us. . . .
>
> We will discover that the Creation is not in any sense independent of the Creator, the result of a primal creative act long over and done with, but is the continuous, constant participation of all creatures in the being of God.[2]

And the final discovery that flows from this understanding gets at the practical applications and philosophical implications of the previous ones: "We will discover that for these reasons our destruction of nature is not just bad stewardship, or stupid economics, or a betrayal of family responsibility; it is the most horrid blasphemy. It is flinging God's gifts into His face, as if they were of no worth beyond that assigned to them by our destruction of them." Berry then goes on to point out the following. "The Bible leaves no doubt at all about the sanctity of the act of world-making, or of the world that was made, or of creaturely or bodily life in this world. We are holy creatures living among other holy creatures in a world that is holy."[3] Every important word here—*sanctity*, *holy*, *creaturely*, *creature*, *making*, and *made*—while affirming a "bodily life," also flows from a belief that there is a spiritual reality and that the cosmos was created with purpose. And each word also ought to lead to a profound and healthy environmental ethic: a respectful and nonexploitive way of living on this holy created earth. The environmental implications of viewing the physical universe as a purposed creation of a transcendent being—as part of, and flowing from, a broader reality that is not merely physical—are profound.

Just the idea of purpose is so important that it is worth exploring further. One purpose for the earth, according to the biblical creation account, is to be a habitation for creatures who dwell on it, and one purpose for those creatures is that they be fruitful and multiply, and thus fill the earth with the goodness and adornment that comes from their presence: flowers and trees and shrubs as well as birds who sing and are adorned in bright feathers, and creatures who dwell in the depths of the sea or the remotest jungle and may never be seen by human eyes. Much has been made of Genesis 1:28, which tells of God's blessings on the newly created humans, male and female. "God blessed them and said to them, 'Be fruitful and increase in number; fill the earth and subdue it. Rule over the fish of the sea and the birds of the air and over every living creature that moves on the ground.'" Some have argued that this is religious justification for exploitation and human overpopulation. Regarding the idea of being fruitful and filling the earth, however, we must see the whole picture of the first chapter of Genesis. Prior to this, Genesis 1:11–12 gives a description of the purpose of the land with respect to plant life.

> Then God said, "Let the land produce vegetation: seed-bearing plants and trees on the land that bear fruit with seed in it, according to their

> various kinds." And it was so. The land produced vegetation: plants bearing seed according to their kinds and trees bearing fruit with seed in it according to their kinds. And God saw that it was good.

And a little later, Genesis 2:20–22 and 2:24–25 gives the purpose of the earth—the land and the water—with respect to living animals.

> And God said, "Let the water teem with living creatures, and let birds fly above the earth across the expanse of the sky." So God created the great creatures of the sea and every living and moving thing with which the water teems, according to their kinds, and every winged bird according to its kind. And God saw that it was good. God blessed them and said, "Be fruitful and increase in number and fill the water in the seas, and let the birds increase on the earth." . . . And God said, "Let the land produce living creatures according to their kinds: livestock, creatures that move along the ground, and wild animals, each according to its kind." And it was so. God made the wild animals according to their kinds, the livestock according to their kinds, and all the creatures that move along the ground according to their kinds. And God saw that it was good.

Thus, not only humans, but *all* living things—vegetation, sea creatures, birds, and later all sorts of land creatures—are intended to reproduce and be fruitful, and indeed are blessed by God with fruitfulness. Or, to put this in terms of the earth, the water is intended or purposed to *teem* with life, and the land to *produce* vegetation and animals. We also must add, as Wendell Berry eloquently noted, that the creation itself is *good*, that it was pronounced good *prior to* human arrival on the scene, and that its goodness is independent of any usefulness as a *resource* to humans. So, according to this theistic, nonphysicalist philosophy, any human understanding of our human purpose, and the purpose of the cosmos, must keep its fruitfulness and created goodness in mind.

This, alone, could be considered a prime ecological directive that comes from a Judeo-Christian worldview affirming the earth as a created and purposeful place. Understanding this, we should not feel free to approach the cosmos as mere consumers, taking from it what we want for our own pleasure. What Cal DeWitt says of this passage is a good summary:

> The fish of the sea and the birds of the air, as well as people, are given God's blessing of fruitfulness. . . . God's Creation reflects God's fruitful work of giving to land and life what satisfies. . . . As God's work brings fruit to Creation, so too should ours. As God provides for the creatures, so should we who were created to reflect the God whose image we bear. Imaging God, we should provide for the creatures.[4]

The Cosmos and Human Moral Responsibility

And this leads us to a second philosophical aspect of a Judeo-Christian theistic worldview as it applies to ecology. As spiritual beings, we are both free-will beings and moral beings, meaning that we are morally responsible to the creator for how we care for creation. In fact, all of creation has a purpose, including the cosmos that is our habitation as well as human persons as moral inhabitants of the cosmos. Part of our purpose, according to the Bible, is to care for creation, to enrich its fruitfulness and to bless it. This is explicitly stated in the creation story in Genesis 1–2. Genesis 2:15–17 presents both a purpose for humankind and a command to be followed in keeping with that purpose. "The Lord God took the man and put him in the Garden of Eden to work it and take care of it. And the Lord God commanded the man, 'You are free to eat from any tree in the garden; but you must not eat from the tree of the knowledge of good and evil, for when you eat of it you will surely die.'" The first part of this gives a purpose for humanity, to *work and take care of* God's creation. The second part gives a particular imperative specifying what Adam was and was *not* allowed to do. Having long ago left the garden of Eden, the narrower conditions of that particular imperative (not to eat of one particular tree) no longer apply to us, and so I won't comment on it except to note that from the beginning, according to the biblical account, humans were *never* given permission to do or to consume whatever we wanted. Both the earth and its human inhabitants have a purpose, and those purposes and relationships imply certain restrictions.

Regarding the purpose of taking care of creation, it has been pointed out that the Hebrew word *shamar*, used here, and translated as "take care of" (or in some English translations as "keep"), is the same word used in the Aaronic blessing that prescribes how priests are to bless the people of Israel (Num. 6:22–27). The direct implication is that we (humans) ought to care for God's creation with the same sort of blessing, keeping, and care-taking that we desire from God for ourselves. This is another profound basis for a healthy environmental ethic. With this in mind, W. Dayton Roberts makes the following comment on the Genesis passages:

> The verbs used in Genesis to describe Adam's responsibilities—*serving*, *watchful care*, *ordering* and *controlling*—make us think of a benevolent overseer, one who reflects the Creator's own concern for the well-being of creature and Creation. In the words of theologian William Dyrness, Adam's ministry is "a reflection of the loving, ordered relationships of God himself."[5]

Cal DeWitt also comments on the importance of this passage in his principles defining environmental stewardship that should follow from a theistic account of creation:

> Genesis 2:15 expects human people and their descendants to *serve* and *keep* the garden. The word "keep" is the Hebrew word *shamar*, which means a loving, caring, sustaining kind of keeping. This word is used in the Aaronic blessing, "The Lord bless you and *keep* you" (Num. 6:24). When we invoke God to keep *us*, it is not that God would keep us in a kind of preserved, inactive state. Instead it is that God would keep us in all of our vitality, energy and beauty. . . . It is the kind of rich and full keeping that we should bring to God's garden, his creatures and to all of Creation. As God keeps his people, so should people keep Creation.[6]

The context of all of this is to remember that we are not merely biological beings, but spiritual beings as well, made in God's image. As spiritual beings, we have not only moral freedom, but a certain moral authority. If this is a correct view, then unlike animals, we *can* act in ways that are not natural. Which is to say, we can acknowledge that certain human activities go *against* nature—a possibility that strict naturalism denies. Despite what Gary Snyder says, this allows us to point at toxic wastes, dead zones in the ocean, and depleted ozone—caused by human activity—and to say it is *not* natural. It is *un*natural or even *anti*natural. The human activities that cause these things may also be—and in some if not all cases certainly are—immoral.

Put another way, as spiritual beings who have freedom to act outside of nature, we have power and responsibility; we can change nature. We thus have not only the freedom and ability to "rule over the fish of the sea and the birds of the air and over every living creature that moves on the ground," but as moral beings made in God's image we have the responsibility to do so wisely and in keeping with God's character and plan. Christian theologian Stephen Bouma-Prediger summarizes this well.

> The [human] earth-creature is called to subdue and have dominion over other creatures. We are called to dominion. What does this mean? Does dominion, as is often assumed, necessarily mean domination? A larger canonical perspective sheds light on this important question. For example, Psalm 72 speaks most clearly of the ideal king—of one who rules and exercises dominion properly. The psalm unequivocally states that such a ruler executes justice for the oppressed, delivers the needy, helps the poor, and embodies righteousness in all he does. In short, the proper exercise of dominion yields shalom—the flourishing of all creation. This is a far cry from dominion as domination. And Jesus, in the Gospel accounts, defines dominion in terms clearly contrary to the way it is usually understood. For Jesus, to rule is to serve. To exercise dominion is to suffer, if necessary, for the good of the other. There is no question of domination, exploitation, misuse. Humans, therefore, are called to rule, but only if ruling is understood rightly.[7]

This worldview also tells us both that humans, as moral agents, have a purpose, and also that we are responsible for our actions. We are not mere machines. If this theistic dualism is correct, and physicalism is not, then we cannot simply say, "Whatever happens was unavoidably destined to happen." We cannot be let off the hook so easily. Rather, we must acknowledge that whatever happens, we (as a race and as individuals) have some responsibility for it.

In short, while the particular moral imperative of Scripture might be said to be more theological than philosophical (and would take more than a few pages to explore), the idea that there even *can* be moral imperatives with respect to our care for creation, and that we have freedom to obey them, is a fundamental philosophical fact that follows from a worldview that accepts a universe that can be touched by something outside of it, and a view of humans as spiritual as well as physical beings. The dualist worldview provides a philosophical basis from which we can begin to explore some objective moral foundations for ecological activities that transcend our personal preference for what we would like the world to be. We also need not buy into the fatalistic view that comes from physicalism (whether of a strictly determinist vein or not) that whatever destructive thing happens to nature—including the destructive things we ourselves do—is simply destined to happen.

To connect this with the previous chapter, if the dualist philosophy suggested by a Judeo-Christian worldview is true, then we can portray healthy and self-sacrificial care for our earth as *heroic*, and (contrary to B. F. Skinner) we can write and read literatures of freedom that are both true and good, and that motivate people to behave freely in ways that are good for the earth. This, in fact, is precisely what Tolkien did in *The Lord of the Rings*. His philosophy leads not only to a high view of creativity and heroism, but also to a high view of the value of the created earth. As noted earlier, Frodo is presented as heroic for his difficult choices and selfless courageous actions. And these choices and actions are in turn motivated to a large degree by his desire to save his land, the Shire. The Shire is a healthy agrarian community with wild forests, clean rivers, good soils, and indefinitely sustainable small family farms. Frodo understands that Middle-earth in general, and the Shire in particular, is good and to be valued and protected. Thus, at the start of the story, when first confronted with his enormous task, he says, "I should like to save the Shire, if I could—though there have been times when I thought the inhabitants too stupid and dull for words. . . . I feel that as long as the Shire lies behind, safe and comfortable, I shall find wandering more bearable: I shall know that somewhere there is a firm foothold, even if my feet cannot stand there again."[8] Note first that his desire is to save the Shire *in its wholeness*—its forests, fields, rivers, animals, and soils, as well as its houses, farms, cornfields, and perhaps especially its inns that serve fine ale—and not merely to save his fellow Hobbits (though they are certainly included). This is clear in that he distinguishes the inhabitants of the Shire from the Shire itself.

Note also that his desire to save the Shire is not merely so that he can enjoy it for himself. He is doing it for others, and for the Shire itself, even knowing that he himself is not likely to find a firm foothold there again. Again at the end of the story, he says, truly, "I tried to save the Shire, and it has been saved, but not for me. It must often be so, Sam, when things are in danger: some one has to give them up, lose them, so that others may keep them."[9] Tolkien's underlying philosophy makes possible this sort of environmental ethic and this self-sacrificial heroism. If we had more people following that model today, giving up their own selfish and consumptive desires for the good of the land about us, and its inhabitants, we would go a long way toward taking care of the environmental woes currently plaguing this earth.[10]

Ecology and the Bodily Resurrection

There is one more important topic to explore—one that is both theological and philosophical in nature, relates directly to a particular type of dualism affirmed by both traditional Judaism and Christianity, and is manifest especially in the Christian understanding of a bodily resurrection.

Judeo-Christian theism affirms both body and spirit and, moreover, affirms both as *important*. What is often popularly emphasized is the Christian teaching that humans have on the one hand an immortal spirit, but on the other a body destined to die a natural death. This idea must be explored, especially as the Judeo-Christian idea of *spirit* is often confused with the Platonic idea of *soul*. Whereas Plato saw the soul as desiring to be free of the body,[11] Christianity proclaims instead *a bodily resurrection*. On several occasions during his life, Jesus spoke about resurrection and either hinted at or prophesied his own bodily death and resurrection (e.g., Matt. 16:31; 17:23; 20:19; Mark 9:9; Luke 9:22; 18:33; 20:37; 24:7; etc.). The apostle Paul proclaims that this bodily resurrection is of first importance to Christianity and to Christians (1 Cor. 15:1–34).

C. S. Lewis, in his book *Miracles*, makes an accurate (though for some people somewhat startling and surprising) observation. "The earliest Christian documents give a casual and unemphatic assent to the belief that the supernatural part of a man survives the death of the natural organism. But they are very little interested in the matter." At first glance, it may seem odd to suggest that Christians—especially the early Christians—are "very little interested" in immortality, but the lack of interest is in regard to Platonic ideas about immortality of the *soul*. Lewis goes on to explain. "What they [the earliest Christians] are intensely interested in is the restoration or 'resurrection' of the whole composite creature by a miraculous divine act."[12] In other words, the biblical Christian account of eternal life does not correspond to the popular image of disembodied spirits hovering on clouds. Rather, the Christian idea of eternal life is once again that of embodiment: a life of both body and spirit. The body is important.

Put another way, Christian teaching about the death of the mortal body does not promise that the *soul* will go to *heaven*. Rather, the Christian hope given in the Bible is that *heaven will come to earth*, and the individual will be given a *new body*—or, perhaps, will be resurrected in a new body. That is, both the created earth and our bodies will be renewed or restored. Paul writes in Romans 8:18–25 that the entire creation, and not just the human race, awaits that restoration. According to the Bible, heaven is a kingdom defined by the presence of God; it is not a place to which we escape from earth. To dwell in heaven will be to dwell on this earth, though it will be a restored earth. Thus, heaven, which is also earth, in the Bible is most often pictured in physical terms: a city with walls and gates made of the material stuff of this world: jasper, gold, sapphire, chalcedony, emerald, and so on (Rev. 21). It is described as being filled with trees and having a great river running through the center (Ezek. 47; Rev. 22). This may be why the book of Revelation also uses strong language of judgment with respect to those who destroy God's creation: "The time has come for judging the dead . . . and for destroying those who destroy the earth" (Rev. 11:18). Again, this is theological in nature, but relates philosophically to the particular view of dualism. It is an affirmation not only of the eternal nature of humans as spiritual persons, but also of the importance of the body and the physical earth. What a sharp contrast this is to the body–soul dualism of Plato or the disembodied brain of Kurzweil.

Such an affirmation of the importance of the physical body and cosmos is yet another way that human care for the creation is validated. If this type of theistic dualism is correct, the best training to be a good citizen of heaven must involve being a good caretaker of this world and its current inhabitants. Jesus says as much in many of his sermons and parables, most notably in his parable of the good Samaritan (Luke 10:25–37), his parable of the sheep and the goats (Matt. 25:31–46), and in the Sermon on the Mount (Matt. 5–6).

And this all relates to what we saw in the first section of this chapter. The creator did not merely create a cosmos and then sit back, detached, to let the cosmos run (or run down) on its own. We do not have causal closure—a purely naturalistic cosmos devoid of spiritual presence. Judaism and Christianity both tell us that the creator continues to care for his creation, to be present within it, and to uphold it. The Bible is full of references to the creator feeding his creatures and causing rain to fall to quench the thirsts of beasts and to water his plants that they may grow. It tells us that God cares about the birds of the air and the flowers of the field, the wild goats and coneys atop the mountains, and the sea creatures of the deep. (Read Psalm 104!)

The Christian doctrine of incarnation, proclaiming a creator who came and lived on earth in bodily form, especially affirms this philosophical idea. Jesus's first recorded miracle was changing water into wine—and not cheap wine either, but the very best of wines, so that physical taste buds and noses (which he created) could delight in the taste and scent. He performed this miracle at a wedding, to help celebrate a marriage, which itself involves the bodily union of a man and a woman, and the highest form of bodily delight. Norman Wirzba was correct to ask the question quoted in chapter 3: "Can we *properly* engage the world if we despise the bodies in terms of which such engagement occurs, or despise the natural bodies upon which our own lives so clearly depend?"[13] What Christian theism and dualism offer is a philosophy that affirms the possibility of heroism, affirms moral imperatives to care for creation, affirms the free will that comes with a spiritual human, and also affirms (rather than despises) the bodies through which we may achieve all of the above.

7

A Biblical Defense of Reason and Science

We turn now to our final pair of related subjects: reason and science. The goal of this chapter is to argue for the value of reason itself, starting from a philosophical system rooted in a theistic dualism that affirms a spiritual and physical nature of humans and the universe. In chapter 4 I claimed that if physicalism were true, then reason could not be considered normative and would be no more objectively trustworthy as a reliable source of knowledge than is the most *un*reasonable superstition. Here I argue briefly that a person who believes in a creative and good God, and in human beings created in the image of that God, has philosophical grounds to trust reason. I show also that the teachings of Christianity explicitly affirm the importance of reason, even as a basis for faith. I conclude the chapter by arguing that a Judeo-Christian worldview provides a strong basis for the trustworthiness of science as a means toward knowledge, but that it also makes it clear that science and reason are not the *only* means to knowledge.

Can Reason and Spirituality Sleep in the Same Bed?

In some sense, this section does not need to be written. Chapter 4 argued that in a strictly naturalistic world—a causally closed universe—reason is not, and cannot be, normative. In less philosophical terms, but terms that perhaps speak even more clearly and strongly, a computer cannot reliably trust itself (or its programming) to produce correct results. However, if our presuppositions do not exclude the possibility of something beyond nature, then there is no reason we are required to deny that reason could be normative. If we accept that humans may be spiritual as well as material beings, then we may accept also that we are fully capable of some sort of reasoning process that transcends mere computation and that reliably leads to knowledge.

Of course, even if we are spiritual as well as physical beings, we may still fail to reason properly and thus end up with false beliefs not corresponding to the truth, but this is a failure in ourselves, not a failure of the notion of human reason itself. Until somebody comes along and provides an argument (comparable to chap. 4) that reason is impossible under dualism, dualists are not explicitly forced to argue for reason but may simply accept it because it *seems* to be consistent and trustworthy. (Physicalists cannot do this, as there is an explicit argument against reason from physicalism.)

Nonetheless, it is worth a few comments suggesting that Judeo-Christian theism provides an actual *positive* philosophical basis for reason (and for reasoning). If reason *as a normative process* cannot be explained naturalistically, then it must have a *super*natural source. Judeo-Christianity posits a source for that supernatural reason: a divine Reasoner, God. It tells us not only that we are spiritually capable of thought that is not merely mechanistic—that our minds do not reduce to our brains—but also that God upholds our thoughts with his divine thought. Reason comes from God and is, to humans, a gift, an act of divine grace.

C. S. Lewis claims, "The human mind in the act of knowing is illuminated by the Divine reason."[1] Drawing on the title of Lewis's book, reason is in one way or another, *miraculous*. The capacity to reason is a created capacity that is part of who we are as spiritual as well as physical persons. There are two ways we might view this, both of which may be true and either of which alone is sufficient to justify Lewis's claim. The first is to understand reason as something done by the entire human person, who makes use of a biochemical brain *designed* to reason, but who is not merely *reducible* to a brain. That is, there is a spiritual as well as a physical aspect to human reason. Thus, reason is not wholly explainable by physical laws. A second, complementary way to view this is just to note that under the assumption of theism even the physical brain itself—all its collections of neurons—is the result of something nonphysical: the purposeful work of a creator. The brain was designed. In either case, when we reason, we are exercising supernatural ability.

Using different terms a few pages later in his book, Lewis posits the existence of "an eternal self-existent Reason, which neither slumbers nor sleeps." He goes on to describe how our human reason can be based on that eternal Reason, and in doing so argues that if we accept reason as normative—or "valid," in his terminology—then we *must* believe in some higher source of reason than the merely physical:

> Yet if any thought is valid, such [an eternal self-existent] Reason must exist and must be the source of my own imperfect and intermittent rationality. Human minds, then, are not the only supernatural entities that exist. They do not come from nowhere. Each has come into Nature from Supernature: each has its tap-root in an external, self-existent, rational Being, whom we call God. Each is an offshoot, or spearhead, or incursion of that Supernatural reality into Nature.[2]

In short, then, just as we explained the source of human creativity by answering that we are spiritual as well as physical beings—creatures created in the image of a creator, and bearing something of his creative personality—so we also answer that we are reasoning beings because we are spiritual (not merely natural) beings, created in the image of a Reasoning Being. (That reason is part of the nature of our creator can be seen, among other ways, in the orderliness and structure of creation, which we return to in the final section of this chapter.) We are capable of reasoning because God, the divine Reason, makes us capable.

Charles Taliaferro, in his book *Consciousness and the Mind of God*, states this in a sort of double negative.

> It would be puzzling to suppose that an all-good God constructs creatures with cognitive faculties designed only to mislead and generate systematically mistaken views. It would be less odd, I think, for us to be in such a sorry state of cognitive failure if the world were

> the outcome of mere chance or the outcome of natural laws which do not themselves reflect the intelligence of a good agent or, to wax fantastic, the outcome of a malign agent.[3]

In other words, if one believes that humans were brought into existence by a good God, then it does *not* make sense to *not* trust reason.

Now, there are two possible objections to this answer that should be addressed. The first is an old philosophical objection that arises in many forms, one of which we will address in the final chapter of this book. How does our answer explain where reason comes from? Naturalism, if it tries to defend the possibility of reason, must tell us that reason is somehow inherent in nature itself. Our theistic answer tells us that reason is inherent in God. Both answers point to, as the source of reason, something that is outside the human person and preexisting all human persons. Isn't it the case, then, that either both are meaningful answers or neither is? Put another way, the objector to this argument could ask, "Whence does God get *his* reasoning ability? How did God become the divine Reason? If humans need a source for reason, then doesn't God?"

This line of questioning misses the point. The argument here is not that there is no ultimate source for reason. Reason, and in particular *human* reason, if it is normative, *must* have some ultimate source. The argument is only that such an ultimate source cannot be natural; it cannot be purely physical or computational. Put another way, there are two possibilities for such an ultimate source (of anything): the source is either entirely *in* nature (that is, the source is nature itself) or it is not, meaning the source (or some aspect of the source) is *outside* of nature. But we have already ruled out, in chapter 4 of this book, the first of these: the possibility that reason could be both normative and purely physical. To point to a computational human as the source of reason is one and the same as pointing to a computational (and causally closed) universe itself. Both of these attempts see reason as entirely natural, and as computational. The argument of chapter 4 simply points out that normative reason cannot be computational and purely physical; hence, it cannot come from *within* nature—either from humans or from the universe itself. The argument does not say that there cannot be a single ultimate source of reason *outside* of nature.

This leaves only two choices: either reason is not normative, or it is not natural. In other words, if we want to accept reason as normative, we must view its source as outside of nature—as somehow *super*natural. One who a priori rejects such a possibility (of the spiritual or supernatural) is left rejecting reason itself. But why reject such a possibility of the spiritual or superatural? We are free to accept reason and to point to a divine Reasoner as the source. If we accept some form of dualism, then we may also accept reason itself, and human reason in particular, as normative and trustworthy.

The second objection is more complex. If human reason has its source in divine Reason—if human reason is miraculous, a gift of grace—then why does human reason *ever* fail? Why do different people reason to different conclusions? Or, to pose the question in religious terms, if God grants reason, and is the source of reason, then how could anybody ever reason to the conclusion that there was no God? This is an objection that Jesus himself seems to have foreseen, and the answer gets back to the very nature of reason, that it must (if it is valid) involve free choice to choose among competing options. It also gets to our own nature as human beings. Though this book focuses on the first of Dick Keyes's philosophical questions raised in the introduction—"What exists?"—the answer to this objection gets to the second of his questions: "What is wrong?" Let us look at Jesus's answer.

Jesus tells a parable, or story, of a rich man and Lazarus. His story is recorded in the Gospel of Luke, as he told it to some of the wealthy religious leaders of his day (who were sneering at his teaching about the dangers of pursuing riches). Here is Luke's version of Jesus's words as he tells this story:

> There was a rich man who was dressed in purple and fine linen and lived in luxury every day. At his gate was laid a beggar named Lazarus, covered with sores and longing to eat what fell from the rich man's table. Even the dogs came and licked his sores.
>
> The time came when the beggar died and the angels carried him to Abraham's side. The rich man also died and was buried. In hell, where he was in torment, he looked up and saw Abraham far away, with Lazarus by his side. So he called to him, "Father Abraham, have pity on me and send Lazarus to dip the tip of his finger in water and cool my tongue, because I am in agony in this fire."

> But Abraham replied, "Son, remember that in your lifetime you received your good things, while Lazarus received bad things, but now he is comforted here and you are in agony. And besides all this, between us and you a great chasm has been fixed, so that those who want to go from here to you cannot, nor can anyone cross over from there to us."
>
> He answered, "Then I beg you, father, send Lazarus to my father's house, for I have five brothers. Let him warn them, so that they will not also come to this place of torment."
>
> Abraham replied, "They have Moses and the Prophets; let them listen to them."
>
> "No, father Abraham," he said, "but if someone from the dead goes to them, they will repent."
>
> He said to him, "If they do not listen to Moses and the Prophets, they will not be convinced even if someone rises from the dead."
>
> Luke 16:19–31

Much could be said about this passage with respect to how we treat other humans during our lives, especially how we treat the poor like Lazarus. We might, without stretching the story, generalize Jesus's lesson to the subjects of oppression, exploitation, and the accumulation of wealth at the expense of the welfare of those around us. These comments would be valuable in the context of the previous chapter on ecology, and the importance of how we live our lives as embodied beings on this earth. More important for this chapter, however, is the concluding interaction between the rich man and Abraham. If we focus on this part of the story, we might title it "The Rich Man and Abraham" rather than "The Rich Man and Lazarus."

The rich man requests that he be allowed to go warn his five brothers about judgment so that they will stop pursuing wealth while mistreating the poor. "If someone from the dead goes to them," the rich man argues, "they will repent." The thinking of the rich man seems clear at this point: if he were to rise from the dead and appear to his brothers and warn them, his appearance alone ought to provide sufficient evidence to convince them of the reality of judgment. That is, his brothers would *reason*, based on the evidence of his return from the dead, to the correct conclusion, which is some sort of knowledge about the consequences of their behavior with respect to judgment and an afterlife. Abraham's response gets right to the point: "If they do not listen to Moses and the Prophets, they will not be convinced even if someone rises from the dead." Abraham does not deny the importance of evidence and reason. What he points out is that, as free-will beings with our personal motives—in this case the desire for wealth or pleasure, or perhaps just stubborn pride—we can freely ignore evidence, and we can reason poorly. We can reason not from sound principles toward true conclusions, but from our selfish motives toward false conclusions, all the while convinced that we are correct. The apostle Paul makes a similar observation in his letter to the Romans, in Romans 1:18–23.

In fact, this objection applies equally to any explanation of human reason. If human reason is valid—whether it comes from God or any source—then we can ask, appropriately, why do any two people ever reason to different conclusions? That different reasonable humans come to different conclusions about all sorts of important questions seems like a simple, unquestionable fact, and any account of reason needs to give an answer for this. The Bible has an answer. It tells us that something is wrong with the universe: our relationship with God is broken, and that break—that brokenness—damages our ability to reason from the divine Reason, just as it negatively impacts our relationships with other creatures (our ecology). Our reason is flawed not because divine Reason is flawed, but because every human effort to reason (even for the most well-intentioned of us) bears the mark of our broken relation with God. Even if God, the divine Reason, is the source of our reason, our reason will still not be perfect, because the channel along which reason comes to us no longer functions as it should. It needs to be mended.

The Importance of Evidence to the Prophets and Apostles

We now turn from the underlying theistic philosophy that supports reason, and that ought to lead to a high view of the possibility of reason, to the actual biblical model of how reason should be practiced. Because so many people today tend to view faith as somehow blind and religion as being a subjective experience with no interest in objective truth, it is important to see the working out of a philosophy of reason—to dispel the idea of blind faith, at least as it pertains to the Christian faith.

The point of this section is simple. From the ancient Hebrew prophets, to the writers of the four Christian Gospels, to the teachings of the apostles, to the words of Jesus, time and time again the biblical call to faith includes or is centered on a call to reason. Contrary to inviting adherents to throw away their minds and their reason, and to believe blindly, the teachings of Jesus and the Bible repeatedly invite people to examine the evidence, metaphorically to weigh it on a scale, and then to believe because it is true and reasonable.

We do not have the space for a systematic exploration of all of Scripture on this topic. That would be the work of many books. Rather, we will look at just a few examples from each category of biblical literature, beginning with the ancient Hebrew prophets. One compelling example is the story of the famous prophet Elijah, who lived in Israel during the reign of the notoriously wicked king Ahab and his even more notorious wife, the treacherous Jezebel. King Ahab had turned away from the Lord, the God of Abraham, and turned to the gods (or idols) of Baal and Asherah. He had gone so far as to order the few remaining prophets of the Lord put to death. The prophet Elijah was thus living in hiding—but only after accurately prophesying a long and severe drought. Three years into this drought, with the nation of Israel suffering, King Ahab was still trying to find and kill Elijah. The prophet Elijah came out of hiding and sent word to the king that he would meet him on Mount Carmel. He had King Ahab bring along the four hundred fifty prophets of Baal and the four hundred prophets of Asherah, and summon the people of Israel. We can read the account of this in 1 Kings 18.

This is what Elijah says to the people. "How long will you waver between two opinions? If the LORD is God, follow him; but if Baal is God, follow him" (1 Kings 18:21). There are two important observations here. The first is Elijah's use of the phrase, "waver between two opinions." This is at the heart of what reason is about: choosing from among various competing ideas or opinions about what is true. Of course, there are ways other than reason to make decisions, so this alone does not constitute a call to reason. But it does set up the conditions and also draws implicitly from the logical rule of inference often called the Law of Noncontradiction, which states that two conflicting ideas cannot both be true: if *P* is a proposition, then *P* and *not P* cannot both be true; symbolically, $P \wedge \neg P = \text{False}$. Or, equivalently, *P* implies *not not P*; the truth of a proposition implies the falsity of its negation; symbolically, $P \rightarrow \neg(\neg P)$. Elijah claims that the God of Abraham is the only God. If this claim is true, then Baal and Asherah cannot be real gods. If Baal and Asherah *are* real gods, then Elijah's claim is false. Elijah points this out, which is itself an act of reason. He then calls the people of Israel to decide which they will believe. They must choose between competing truth claims.

The second observation is that Elijah does *not* tell the people to follow the Lord simply out of tradition, or because it is convenient, or because it is a nice idea. He does not ask them to blindly trust his word, or just to take his authority. He tells them to follow the Lord (the God of Abraham) *only* if he *really is* God. That is, Elijah calls them to believe what is true. If the Lord is truly God, then the people should believe because it is true; and if not, then they should disbelieve monotheism, because it is false.

What happens next is even more important. Elijah sets up a test or trial so that the people can look at the evidence and reason to the correct conclusion. After pointing out that he is alone among God's prophets, but that there are four hundred fifty prophets of Baal present, he gives the following command.

> Get two bulls for us. Let [Baal's prophets] choose one for themselves, and let them cut it into pieces and put it on the wood but not set fire to it. I will prepare the other bull and put it on the wood but not set fire to it. Then you call on the name of your god, and I will call on the name of the LORD. The god who answers by fire—he is God.
>
> 1 Kings 18:22–24

This is a simple test, with straightforward reasoning: a real God (and not just an idol made of wood or gold) should have the power to cause fire (out of nothing). The Israelites are invited to make their decision based on that reasoning and that evidence—though it should be noted that Elijah takes an extra step of allowing his enemies to dump water all over his altar just to make the evidence that much more compelling if and when fire really does come down.

Elijah is one of the most famous prophets of God in the Bible. His approach in calling the people of faith should be considered seriously. And he is not alone. Another of the famous prophets, Isaiah, has similar words for the people of Israel, recorded in the book of prophecy that bears his name. On different occasions, most notably in Isaiah 44:7–20, he invites people to reason about their practice of making and worshiping idols, suggesting first that it makes no sense to worship a piece of wood that just as easily could be thrown into the fire, and second that they should consider the evidence as to whether these idols can really hear and answer their prayers and come to their aid. Speaking of idols carved of wood, he writes:

> No one stops to think,
> no one has the knowledge or understanding to say,
> "Half of it I used for fuel;
> I even baked bread over its coals,
> I roasted meat and I ate.
> Shall I make a detestable thing from what is left?
> Shall I bow down to a block of wood?"
> He feeds on ashes, a deluded heart misleads him;
> he cannot save himself, or say,
> "Is not this thing in my right hand a lie?"
>
> Isaiah 44:19–20

The final three lines here contrast the sort of bad thinking that comes from a *deluded heart* with the *knowledge* and *understanding* and good reasoning of the *mind* mentioned earlier.

When we move to the New Testament, the calls to reason and to examine evidence become even clearer and often use a legal metaphor of a trial in which the judge or jury are invited to weigh evidence and reason to determine the truth. The New Testament Gospels of Matthew, Mark, Luke, and John are accounts of Jesus's life. Consider the explicit reasons given in two of the Gospels for why they were written. In reference to his account of the death of Jesus and the evidence that Jesus really was dead, the apostle John writes in his Gospel, "The man who saw it has given testimony, and his testimony is true. He knows that he tells the truth, and he testifies so that you also may believe" (John 19:35). John's stated concern here is for the truth of the events. The evidence of his eyewitness testimony is intended to point to that truth, and the central idea is that the belief of his audience is to be based on that evidence.

This approach is even clearer a chapter later. After he describes Jesus's resurrection from the dead, John writes, "Jesus did many other miraculous signs in the presence of his disciples, which are not recorded in this book. But these are written that you may believe that Jesus is the Christ, the Son of God, and that by believing you may have life in his name" (John 20:30–31). The word translated here as "miraculous signs" is the Greek word *sémeion*. It is used frequently in the New Testament, and the significance of it with respect to deductive reason is worth exploring. *Sémeion* (from which we get the modern English word *semiotics*) refers to a sign or token of the trustworthiness of a person and the truth of that person's claims. In a strict sense, the word refers to "miracles and wonders by which God authenticates the men sent by him, or by which men prove that the cause they are pleading is God's."[4] The idea of *authentication* and *proof* in this definition is important. Jews, and later Christians, were not supposed to blindly believe any person claiming to bring a message from God or to proclaim the truth; they were expected to test a person's authority. A *sémeion* provides evidence for, or reasons to believe in, a person's truth claims. If a person performs miraculous signs, then there is sufficient reason to believe that person has come from God and speaks the truth.

We could write this symbolically. Let P be the proposition that a person (in this case Jesus) performs a miraculous sign (*sémeion*). Let Q be the proposition that the person has authority from God and can be trusted to speak the truth. The deductive reasoning, symbolically written, is that $P \rightarrow Q$: performing a miraculous sign implies that one is speaking the truth and can be trusted—that this person really has come from God. This was widely accepted by John's Jewish audience. It was the reasoning of Elijah also (see, for example, John 3:1–2).

It is important to note here that the possibility of miracles in general, and this concept of *miraculous signs* in particular and the idea that $P \rightarrow Q$, does not in any way deny laws of nature. Quite the opposite, in fact; for a miraculous sign to have any evidential significance, people had to have a very good understanding of the laws of nature and the way that things naturally (or normally) worked when there was no supernatural intervention. If we are not able to recognize the *normal* (or natural) patterns of nature, then we cannot recognize that an event that does not follow the pattern is a miraculous sign. Causing an apple to fall when separated from its branch on an apple tree would not have been recognized as a miraculous sign.

Indeed, behind the concept of miraculous signs is not only a proper understanding of the normal functioning of nature (what we might today call a *scientific* understanding of the world), but also an example of valid deductive reasoning using the modus ponens rule. Modus ponens and the implication of miraculous signs is used explicitly numerous times in the Bible to reason, especially in the writings of John. As noted, it was accepted that $P \rightarrow Q$. This makes sense; a supernatural event is evidence of the supernatural. Even strict naturalists today accept this implication, which is why they deny that supernatural events could occur. The question is whether supernatural events do occur and, more particularly, in the examples in the Gospel of John, whether Jesus performed any legitimate miraculous sign. If he did perform miraculous signs, then P is true of Jesus, and thus with respect to Jesus we have $((P \rightarrow Q) \wedge P) \rightarrow Q$: *A person who performs miraculous signs is from God, Jesus performed miraculous signs, and therefore Jesus is from God.*

This deductive argument appears in several logical forms, most notably in John 9:1–34. John records how Jesus, on the Sabbath day when Jews were not supposed to work, heals a man who had been born blind. John then reports the responses of various persons or groups of persons to this healing. Also in consideration is the fact that the miraculous healing occurred on the Sabbath day and that healing would have been considered "work" by the religious leaders. In John 9:31–34, the blind man argues first that his healing constitutes a miraculous sign: "Nobody has ever heard of opening the eyes of a man born blind." Thus, since Jesus healed him, the proposition P is true of Jesus. The blind man then argues, "If this man were not from God, he could do nothing." Symbolically, he is claiming that $\neg Q \rightarrow \neg P$. But the proposition $\neg Q \rightarrow \neg P$, which is called the *contrapositive* of $P \rightarrow Q$, is logically equivalent to $P \rightarrow Q$. If $P \rightarrow Q$, then $\neg Q \rightarrow \neg P$, and vice versa. Thus, the blind mind first claims P and then reaffirms $P \rightarrow Q$. He is arguing from modus ponens in the form $((\neg Q \rightarrow \neg P) \wedge P) \rightarrow Q$. (He leaves the conclusion Q unstated because he assumes his audience will reason correctly.)

Interestingly enough, the Pharisees, who in this case were opposing Jesus, apply the same reasoning about miracles, that $P \rightarrow Q$.

However, they compound this reasoning with another example of modus ponens. John 9:16 states, "Some of the Pharisees said, 'This man is not from God, for he does not keep the Sabbath.'" Their first modus ponens argument is that a person who comes from God would keep the Sabbath, and Jesus did not keep the Sabbath (at least not in the way they thought it should be kept), and therefore Jesus was not from God. They then make use of the same modus ponens discussed above, that *if* Jesus had healed the blind man, *then* he must be from God. The Pharisees therefore conclude that Jesus could not have healed the blind man. That is, they reason that $((P \to Q) \land \neg Q) \to \neg P$, which is also logically equivalent to $((P \to Q) \land P) \to Q$: *if Jesus healed, then he would be God, and he isn't God (because he doesn't follow the Sabbath), and so he didn't heal.*

We now return to John 20:30–31, in which John gives his reason for recording his Gospel account of Jesus's life, based on the evidence of miraculous signs. The *formula*, if we may call it one, given here by John, is simple: evidence leads (by reason) to belief (or faith), and belief leads to (eternal) life. John's invitation is to reason about the evidence (as we would in a court of law) and then to believe what is true because of that evidence. More broadly, the biblical message is that God gives eternal life by grace (it cannot be earned, either by hard work or by good reasoning), but that grace works through faith. And the invitation to faith given here by John is an invitation to reason and examine evidence.

The Gospel of Luke suggests something similar, except it comes near the start of the Gospel rather than at the end. Luke's Gospel begins:

> Many have undertaken to draw up an account of the things that have been fulfilled among us, just as they were handed down to us by those who from the first were eyewitnesses and servants of the word. Therefore, since I myself have carefully investigated everything from the beginning, it seemed good also to me to write an orderly account for you, most excellent Theophilus, so that you may know the certainty of the things you have been taught.
>
> Luke 1:1–4

Note Luke's careful wording. He is interested in eyewitness account. He claims to have done a careful investigation. His goal is an orderly account. And, most importantly, his goal is to enable his readers to know "the certainty of the things" they have been taught. As with the Gospel of John, this does not mean that Luke's account is true, or even that Luke *thinks* it is true. It may be that he is trying to deceive people. (Though numerous well-reasoned arguments have been presented suggesting that the earlier followers of Jesus really were persuaded that the resurrection was true.[5]) What these accounts show is that Luke and John believed at least in the validity of reason as a means toward knowledge, and that their call to faith was a call to examine evidence. They were not calling their audience to believe their message blindly, or because it was a nice idea, but because it was *true*.

As with John and Luke, the example and teachings of the apostles Paul and Peter, Jesus's most famous followers in the early church, show that they had the same philosophical principles at work—that they too had a very high view of reason as a means toward knowledge. Paul's example can be seen in Acts 17–18, where he goes from city to city (Thessalonica, Berea, Athens, Corinth) proclaiming that Jesus rose from the dead and that he really is God—that some form of dualism is true, and spirit has come and been incarnate in flesh. Several different words are used to describe Paul's approach of reasoning about the truth of his message. For example, in Acts 17:2, 17 and 18:4, 19 the writer uses the Greek verb *dialegomai*, which is generally translated to English as "reason" or "argue";[6] so we are explicitly told on several occasions that Paul *reasons* with his various audiences about the truth of the Christian claims. Other verbs used to describe Paul's approach include "explaining and proving" (Acts 17:3),[7] with the result being that his audience is "persuaded" (Acts 17:4).[8] When Paul goes to Athens, he engages in philosophical "dispute" (Acts 17:18) with Athenian "philosophers" who "spent their time doing nothing but talking about and listening to the latest ideas" (Acts 17:21).

Again, this is not the approach of a religion that calls its adherents to blind faith, but of one that holds a very high view of reason. In fact, the author of Acts writes in Acts 17:11, "Now the Bereans were of more noble character than the Thessalonians, for they received the message with great eagerness and examined the Scriptures every day to see if what Paul said was true." What did the Bereans do? They tried to determine what was true by reason and careful examination. The Christian author of Acts speaks of this reasoned approach to knowledge as the "more noble" one.

The first of Paul's two preserved letters to the Corinthians adds to this picture. At the start of 1 Corinthians 15, he points out clearly that of first importance is the historical truth of the Christian claims. He then implicitly invites his readers to examine the evidence themselves, by pointing out that there are many eyewitnesses to Jesus's resurrection who are still alive, and he goes on to spend much of the chapter arguing that *if* the gospel story were just a nice idea, or a metaphor, and not the actual truth, then Christianity would be a waste of time. Likewise, the apostle Peter, in the first of his general letters to the first-century church, explicitly commands Christians to be ready to give a reasoned defense of their Christian hope (1 Pet. 3:15). He uses the Greek verb *apologia*, which refers to a verbal defense or a reasoned argument, and is the word from which we get the modern English word *apologetics*.

Jesus and Reason

We now turn directly to the claims of Jesus, and specifically to the reasons he gives for accepting those claims—that is, to aspects of Jesus's philosophical basis for approaching the question of where to place our faith. His words in the fifth chapter of the Gospel of John are especially relevant:

> If I testify about myself, my testimony is not valid. There is another who testifies in my favor, and I know that his testimony about me is valid.
>
> You have sent to John and he has testified to the truth. Not that I accept human testimony; but I mention it that you may be saved. John was a lamp that burned and gave light, and you chose for a time to enjoy his light.
>
> I have testimony weightier than that of John. For the very work that the Father has given me to finish, and which I am doing, testifies that the Father has sent me. And the Father who sent me has himself testified concerning me. You have never heard his voice nor seen his form, nor does his word dwell in you, for you do not believe the one

> he sent. You diligently study the Scriptures because you think that by them you possess eternal life. These are the Scriptures that testify about me, yet you refuse to come to me to have life.
>
> John 5:31–40

In referring to his own "testimony" about himself as "not valid," Jesus is not trying to cast doubt on his trustworthiness, but rather is making reference to a court of law. (In fact, he later argues that his testimony is trustworthy, even if made on his own behalf.) In a legal dispute, Jewish law required the testimony of multiple witnesses to decide important cases, and in particular did not allow one person to win a case against another by bringing testimony on their own behalf (see, for example, Num. 35:30; Deut. 17:6; 19:15; Matt. 18:16; John 8:13). Simply by appealing to the validity of certain types of testimony, Jesus is suggesting, as the appropriate approach to faith, the metaphor or model of a court of law—the idea of examining and weighing evidence and listening to testimony. He goes on to point to several other testimonies that ought to be taken as valid, including the evidence of his works. He invites his audience to look at this evidence. Once again, he does not ask his audience to believe blindly, to just take his word without evidence simply because it is comforting or appealing or sounds nice. He says they ought to believe because it is "true and reasonable," which is the claim Paul himself makes a few decades later at his trial before the Roman governor Porcius Festus (Acts 26:25).

There are many other passages where we could see the same sorts of ideas, such as John 10:37–38, where Jesus says, "Do not believe me *unless* I do what my Father does. But *if* I do it, even though you do not believe me, *believe the miracles*, that you may *know and understand* that the Father is in me, and I in the Father" (emphasis added). The weight of Scripture—from the Old Testament prophets to the apostles, understood by the Gospel writers, and taught by Jesus—suggests that *faith* should be rooted in *truth*, making use of *reason* and seeking out *evidence*. The biblical call to faith is, time and time again, a call to reason, to examine evidence, and to believe what is true.

And this leads us finally to one oft-cited dialogue involving Jesus and his disciple Thomas, who (as noted in a previous chapter) is often known by the moniker "Doubting Thomas." The dialogue takes place after Jesus's resurrection from the dead and is recorded by John in John 20:24–29. At first glance, this interaction between Jesus and Thomas appears to be a counterexample to the call for reasoned faith and might be raised as an objection to the conclusion of the previous paragraph. When Jesus had earlier appeared to his disciples, before the scene recorded here, Thomas had not been present. When told about Jesus's resurrection and postresurrection appearance, Thomas had expressed an unwillingness to accept the testimony of his fellows. So when Jesus later appears to a group that includes Thomas, and Thomas then acknowledges Jesus's divinity, Jesus tells him, "Because you have seen me, you have believed; blessed are those who have not seen and yet have believed" (John 20:29). Some see in this passage that Jesus, by blessing those who "have not seen and yet have believed," is promoting an *unseeing belief*—in modern parlance, a *blind faith*. But these words must be understood in both their immediate context and also in light of the rest of Jesus's teaching.

Consider first how John, who recorded this dialogue, understood it. His very next words are the statement we discussed earlier in this section: "Jesus did many other miraculous signs in the presence of his disciples, which are not recorded in this book. But these are written that you may believe that Jesus is the Christ, the Son of God, and that by believing you may have life in his name." So John, who knew Jesus as well as or better than any human alive, after writing Jesus's words to Thomas, immediately gives us his own model, which presents faith (or belief) as being motivated and upheld by evidence (miraculous signs). This strongly suggests that Jesus's words to Thomas were *not* intended to promote blind faith. So let us consider the events that led up to these words and make a few observations.

> Now Thomas (called Didymus), one of the Twelve, was not with the disciples when Jesus came. So the other disciples told him, "We have seen the Lord!"
>
> But he said to them, "Unless I see the nail marks in his hands and put my finger where the nails were, and put my hand into his side, I will not believe it."
>
> A week later his disciples were in the house again, and Thomas was with them. Though the doors were locked, Jesus came and stood

among them and said, "Peace be with you!" Then he said to Thomas, "Put your finger here; see my hands. Reach out your hand and put it into my side. Stop doubting and believe."

Thomas said to him, "My Lord and my God!"

Then Jesus told him, "Because you have seen me, you have believed; blessed are those who have not seen and yet have believed."

John 20:24–29

What do we observe about this interaction between Jesus and Thomas, as John records it for us? First and foremost, we see that Jesus provides for Thomas exactly the reasons for faith that Thomas requested, namely concrete evidence: without Thomas saying another word, Jesus first offers peace and then invites Thomas to put his finger where the nails were. Jesus does *not* require Thomas to believe without seeing. In fact, Jesus provides even more implicit evidence of his divinity than was requested by Thomas: he demonstrates that he knows exactly what Thomas had said. The story also shows Thomas professing faith in Jesus *after* being given some evidence.

So why, then, does Jesus make his proclamation about believing *without* seeing? What is perhaps less clear but seems like a valid understanding in light of Jesus's parable about the rich man and Lazarus, is that Thomas was being stubborn. In particular, Thomas has already been shown considerable evidence pointing toward Jesus's divinity. According to John's Gospel, which also records this interaction, Thomas had witnessed three years' worth of Jesus's *miraculous signs*: healing the sick, casting out demons, walking on water, feeding large crowds with only a small amount of food, and more. Regarding the resurrection, he had also heard reliable testimony from trustworthy sources. So—like the rich man's brothers, who Jesus pointed out should already have had enough evidence to change their lifestyles even without a resurrection appearance—Thomas had very good reason to believe even without seeing a resurrected Jesus with his own eyes. Yet Thomas is stubbornly refusing to believe. His words suggest an act of the will, an obstinacy about what he will choose to believe, as much as, or more than, a state of his intellect.

In the end, however, Jesus's words may be intended far more as a promise to other believers who have less evidence than as any sort of chastisement of Thomas for his desire for evidence. (Contrary to some impressions, Jesus does not chastise or condemn Thomas, or in any way criticize his desire for evidence.) The vast majority of Christian believers throughout history have had to believe, not *without* evidence, but certainly with *less* evidence than Thomas had in actually seeing and touching the resurrected body. So Jesus's words here are a blessing for the rest of Christian believers who would come after Thomas in history. Christians in the twenty-first century need not believe blindly, or in opposition to reason, but their belief, no matter how reasoned or reasoning, will have to come without that direct physical and visual contact that Thomas had.

Judeo-Christian Theism and the Validity of Science

We now turn from reason to science, and this section can be much briefer. The theistic, or *super*naturalist worldview of Judaism and Christianity allows for the possibility of reason as a trustworthy, reliable, valid, or normative means to knowledge. Indeed, it is even stronger than that, in that it provides *positive* reasons to think that spiritual and physical human persons, created by an orderly God who continues to interact with his creation, are capable of knowing by reason. Since reason is also a fundamental prerequisite for science, it follows that under a theism that affirms both a natural and a supernatural reality—even though it denies causal closure—science can also be held in high regard as a means to knowledge. Let us briefly consider the other presuppositions of science and how an assumption of theism akin to a Judeo-Christian concept of creation may or may not support them.

There exists a material universe outside your mind. The first few verses of the Bible tell us that God exists, so if we begin with that assumption, then we also accept that there is something outside our own minds. Indeed, God's existence precedes and is the necessary condition for the existence of our minds. Moreover and more specifically, those same verses also speak of God having brought into existence an actual cosmos: a physical universe. The physical universe is real, created by God, and exists independently and prior to the existence of any human. Since God made us of the stuff of this physical universe ("from the dust of the ground," as Gen. 2:7

proclaims), we are dependent on the cosmos for our existence even as we are dependent on God. The very name *Adam* comes from the word for "earth," *adamah*. Judeo-Christian theism, in affirming the spirit and the spiritual, does not deny the body and the material.

The material universe has material causes. It is also interesting and vitally important to note that Judeo-Christian theism, while denying causal closure and affirming the possibility of God's continued work as a supernatural agent within nature, in no way denies the reality of material causes. What it denies is that there are *only* material causes. In fact, the wording of the Bible repeatedly implies the reality of material as well as supernatural causes in God's created cosmos. This can be seen as early as the first chapter of Genesis, which, to describe God's creative activity in bringing about and ordering the cosmos, uses two different Hebrew words: *bara* and *asah*. The word *bara*, used in Genesis 1:1, 21, and 27, and often translated as "create," is the rarer word. It is used only thirty-three times in the entire Old Testament and always implies "some degree of supernatural activity on the part of God." Though it does occasionally allow for a "combination of miracle and process," it generally implies a "radical newness, something distinctively different."[9] The word *asah*, by contrast, is used much more frequently: 624 times in the Old Testament. It is often translated as "make," and appears in Genesis 1:7, 16, 25, 26, and 31. The word *asah* often refers to the "normal activity of people making or forming something." When the verb is used of God, it is occasionally used to describe a miraculous event—and can thus be used as a substitute for *bara* (as in Gen. 1:26)—but it often implies God's "providential care for His creatures in a customary way" (as in Zech. 10:1). That is, *asah* can refer to God's work through ongoing process—what we might refer to as "natural process", if we understood nature as being created and sustained by God.[10]

Certainly, one suggestion of the use of two different words in the creation account is that God, in bringing about and ordering life and the cosmos, did some singular acts that could *not* be described via natural process, but that he also frequently worked through the natural processes of a cosmos he created, understands, and governs. This idea of natural process is also strongly suggested by the wording of Genesis 1:24, which speaks of "*the land* produc[ing] living creatures" (emphasis added), rather than God creating all living creatures and then putting them onto the land. Walter Bradley and Roger Olsen, though they are both theists who affirm God's supernatural hand in the universe, in their article "The Trustworthiness of Scripture in Areas Relating to Natural Science," still conclude, "Arguments for a mechanism of creation that utilizes *only* fiat miracle cannot be based on the common usage of 'bara and asah.' . . . The 'bara' and 'asah' of Genesis 1 seem to suggest God working through a combination of fiat miracle and process."[11] In other words, the biblical use of these two Hebrew verbs imply that God operates through material or natural processes (of the kind open to study with the tools and methods of natural science).

There are numerous other examples. Various proverbs suggest the natural consequences of human activities. The Bible also has many agrarian references to the natural life cycles of plants and even of human life. Indeed, what we might call the *miraculous* activities of the supernatural within nature, which do not proceed from naturalistic processes, are (by definition, we might even say) the exception rather than the rule. As noted earlier, the very concept of a *sémeion*, or miraculous sign, requires a recognition of *natural* processes and of the fact that these natural processes are the norm. Miraculous causes must be relatively rare for them to be recognizable as miraculous signs. As C. S. Lewis notes in his book *Miracles*, "How could [miracles] be surprising unless they were seen to be exceptions to the rules? And how can anything be seen to be an exception till the rules are known. . . . Belief in miracles, far from depending on an ignorance of the laws of nature, is only possible in so far as those laws are known."[12] In short, then, a theistic belief in the possibility of miracles and the importance of miraculous signs would strengthen rather than diminish the significance of science and of understanding that nature runs according to certain laws or material causes.

Having acknowledged the reality of material causes, however, it is important to note that most biblical theists would argue that God's hand is also at work (supernaturally) even in upholding what we call naturalistic processes (as the apostle Paul points out with respect to Jesus in Col. 1:17).

In short, while the Judeo-Christian worldview affirms the possibility of supernatural intervention in nature, and indeed the reality of past, present, and future examples of this activity, adherents of this worldview look to *natural* processes as the normal means of continued life on earth and thus affirm the validity of the scientific method to study those processes. Indeed, they affirm the supernatural presence even in natural processes, and this gives more rather than less credence to the reliability of the study of those processes.

The material universe is consistent and ordered. Genesis 1 paints a picture of God giving order and structure to a cosmos whose initial condition is one of chaos. God separates light from darkness (1:4), earth from heavens (1:7), water from dry land (1:9). Creatures reproduce, not randomly, but *after their own kind* (1:11, 12, 21). The repeated picture is of an orderly creator giving order and structure to a created universe. The creator even ordains patterns of seasons, days, and years to give order and structure to life (Gen. 1:14–19; 2:1–3). If we have already affirmed the reliability of human reason, we could affirm order in the universe because we have observed it; and as reasoning beings we can inductively reason from the pattern and order of our observed particulars (over a very narrow window of space and time) to the pattern of order of the entire cosmos (across both space and time). But the Judeo-Christian belief in a creator gives an even stronger reason: the universe is consistent and ordered because it was created by a consistent and ordered God, and it takes its nature and purpose from him.

Nature is thus seen as something that reveals truth and is worthy of study and observation. This is even explicitly stated in various places in the Bible, such as Psalm 19, which reminds us in its first four verses:

> The heavens declare the glory of God;
> the skies proclaim the work of his hands.
> Day after day they pour forth speech;
> night after night they display knowledge.
> There is no speech or language
> where their voice is not heard.
> Their voice goes out into all the earth,
> their words to the ends of the world.

Indeed, while the second half of the psalm speaks of the truth that is revealed in the Bible, the first half (cited above) speaks of the truth revealed *in nature*. In the final chapters of the book of Job, God also calls Job to reflect on nature. We see this as well in numerous other psalms and in Romans 1:19–20.

Taliaferro draws a similar conclusion:

> Simply conceive outright of the physical workings of the cosmos as the outcome of the reasoned, purposive agency of a single intelligence, God. We can expect (and at times require) that physics and the other sciences proceed with descriptions of natural phenomena without referring to personal agency, but this by no means saddles us with leaving nonagentive explanations as somehow themselves unexplained. The underlying, cosmic agent should be thought of as powerful enough to account for the complex, uniform character of the world.[13]

Belief in a reasoned God as the source of the complex, uniform cosmos can and should lead not only to some trust in the ability of science, but even to a practice of science that does not continually refer to personal agency. In other words, there are *natural* phenomena, and these should be studied using *natural* science, which sees these phenomena as operating under physical laws with uniform character. Science ought to be exploring these physical laws. But this does not mean that the scientist needs to deny the reality of that personal agency behind the consistency in the world—or, I would add, the possibility that there are singular events whose explanation does not follow directly from merely physical agency.

To put this in terms of science, Judeo-Christian theists can trust the scientific process to discover and shed light on normal workings of the cosmos, because their worldview points to the universe as being created and upheld in an orderly and consistent way. Indeed, many of the most important early figures of modern science—the forerunners and founders of the scientific method—give as a reason behind their scientific work a belief in a supremely ordered creator and hence an ordered universe. Nicholas Copernicus in the early sixteenth century noted, "The universe has been wrought for us by a supremely good and orderly creator." This idea was powerful enough to motivate him in his scientific endeavors to look for order in the motion of stars and planets. As author Charles Hummel has noted, "Copernicus faithfully served his church with extraordinary commitment and courage. At the same time he studied the world 'which has been built for us by the Best and Most Orderly Workman of all.' Copernicus pursued his science with a sense of 'loving duty to seek the truth in all things, in so far as God has granted that to human reason.'"[14]

Likewise, Sir Isaac Newton, a century and a half later, would express similar ideas at the end of his *Principles* "The most beautiful system of the sun, planets, and comets, could only proceed from the counsel and dominion of an intelligent and powerful being. . . . The Being governs all things, not as the soul of the world, but as Lord over all."[15]

Humans are capable of accurate observation and accurate transmission of history. With respect to this final presupposition, we note first that large portions of the Bible, including at least the first seventeen books of the Old Testament, the first five books of the New Testament, and large portions of other books, are historical narratives presented as reliable sources. As we argued earlier with respect to the apostle Paul's treatment of reason and evidence, Christianity rests on being able to know something about history—at the very minimum, to be able to know the truth of the resurrection. Furthermore, most of this narrative comes to us through human *observers* of the events, and all of it comes through human *recorders* of the events even in cases (such as Gen. 1–2) where there must have been divine revelation about events that no human could have witnessed firsthand.

A significant part of the reason for accepting the validity of recorded documents is accepting the ability of language to accurately convey knowledge. The theist can accept this assumption because she or he starts with a belief that God is a God of language and communication. This aspect of God's nature is evident from Genesis 1–2, in which not only is language presented as the metaphorical vehicle for God's creative work (God speaks and it happens), but also God speaks to *himself*, declaring his plans and judgments of what he has made ("it is good"), and later God speaks to Adam and Eve in the garden of Eden. The Bible is then full of examples of God speaking to humans, at times telling those humans what to say to others, and moreover expecting the meaning of those words to be understood. If God is a God of language, and humans are made in God's image, then we expect ourselves to be creatures of language. This presents a worldview in which words have meaning, and language can correlate with reality and communicate real ideas. Indeed, when God himself is incarnate as a human in the person of Jesus, he is called by John "The Word[16] made flesh."

Limitations of Reason and Science

So a Judeo-Christian worldview affirming a spiritual reality including a spiritual and physical human nature provides a metaphysical basis on which to place some trust in both reason and science. It does not, however, suggest that we can trust *human* reason or *human* science either as *infallible* means toward knowledge or as the *only* means toward knowledge.

Regarding the trustworthiness of reason and science, there are a few important caveats to be made, some of which we have already touched upon. The first is that, while reason as a process can be considered normative, human reasoning always has the possibility of error. First of all, no human has possession of all knowledge. There is therefore a possibility of reasoning that is *valid* but not *sound*; even if the reasoning process is trustworthy, an argument beginning with false assumptions or assertions (that is, with imperfect knowledge) may end with false conclusions.

Second, the very idea of reason implies choosing between *possible* alternatives. (If there are not competing possible alternatives, then at some level reasoning is not even necessary.) This is true in particular about inductive reasoning, which (unlike deductive reasoning) is *ampliative*. Inductive reasoning requires steps (one might even say *leaps*) that do not simply follow from rules of inference. History is full of examples of intelligent, reasonable, and reasoning persons differing on their conclusions, as it is also full of examples of accepted scientific conclusions later being shown to be false.

Third, reason and science both are based on the ability of language to convey ideas. We argued that a Judeo-Christian view of human nature suggests that we have inherited from a creator the ability to use language. We can trust that language conveys meaning. But moving from a general philosophy of human nature to the theology of *fallen* human nature, the Bible claims that humans, having disobeyed God (Gen. 3; Rom. 3:23), are now limited and corrupted by that disobedience (called "sin") and by its consequences. Language, like all aspects of human nature, is fallen. It conveys meaning, but not *perfect* meaning. Indeed, apart from any theological explanation, the imperfections of human language use may be accepted simply from observation. To anybody who has ever had a misunderstanding with a spouse or close friend, this requires no explanation. On the one hand, this theistic view would tell us that, while human language use is never perfect, we are wrong to throw out language altogether (and thus also wrong to throw out reason and science simply because they are based on language). At the same time, we would be foolish not to acknowledge that language also presents difficulties.

To use an example, we might envision a truck driver en route from Florida to Maine, stopping for a cup of coffee. If he mistakenly pulls into a bakery-café, orders a coffee, and gets a four-dollar espresso drink or some flavored coffee instead of a black cup of joe, he might be disappointed (at the drink as well as the cost). His use of the word *coffee* would have failed to communicate exactly what he intended or desired—as perhaps would the use of the word *coffee* by a Parisian artist or an Italian cappuccino-lover who wanted an espresso drink, went to a truck stop, and got the cup of joe instead. The word *coffee* still communicated *something*; the word had meaning; what that person received, in each case, was indeed coffee. On the other hand, if the truck driver ordered coffee and got a plate of spinach, he would have reason to complain (and woe to the barista who served it); we all understand and accept that *coffee* has some meaning, and that a plate of spinach does not fall within that meaning.[17] Language and its human usage is not perfect, but it does communicate meaning, and when we take care with the precision of language, it is a vehicle that enables both science and reason.

Nonetheless, our fallen use of language is related to a fourth and final caveat, which is that our use of reason is susceptible not only to a lack of knowledge (incorrect assumptions), to faulty induction, and to shortcomings of language, but also to a deeper failure: we all have human motives that—though often unacknowledged and at times even unrecognized—can be stronger than our desire for the truth. Motives may have to do with pride or selfish desires, with a political or social agenda, or even with the desire to do something "good" for somebody else. All of these can lead to a willingness to ignore reason, or perhaps to reason poorly—even while we may be convinced that we are actually reasoning well.

Even for those who deny notions such as *sin*, or who find it hard to believe that a scientist or intelligent philosopher could ever reason poorly, it is not difficult to see that this sort of thing happens. The clearest examples may come from the area of romance. How many times has some otherwise reasonable person failed to heed or even to see obvious problems with a romantic interest? Yet the person acting unreasonably, even blindly, may be completely convinced that he or she is being completely reasonable in the handling of this romantic involvement. Michael McDonald's famous Doobie Brothers hit "What a Fool Believes" was insightful in its observation: the wisest person cannot reason away false beliefs that are captive to romantic inclination. Except that all of us can be fools in this regard.

With respect to our reasoning about religious truth, the Bible also makes this idea clear in several places: the parable of the rich man and Lazarus, the example of "Doubting Thomas," the teachings of Paul in Romans 1. Reasonable humans will often reason poorly or fail to reason in areas relating to God because we begin with a broken relationship with God, and we bring a certain stubbornness and selfishness to the table. Reason itself is normative and trustworthy. However, humans who attempt to practice reason are not; our reason falls short of the divine Reason.

Science has its own limitations also in addition to those of reason. These limitations should make it clear that neither scientists nor science itself are infallible in their approach to knowledge. For one, scientists have the same shortcomings as anyone: they do not have complete knowledge and may make false assumptions, or faulty inductive conclusions, or be hindered by the shortcomings of language. (This should be obvious, since science is dependent on reason.) Scientists also bring to their work all sorts of personal motivations and aspects of fallen human nature that may interfere with the search for truth. Examples include desires for funding, desires for fame or success, political agendas, or simply a commitment to metaphysical presuppositions that are not in themselves scientific and yet can cause a scientist to interpret observations in a certain way. History is full not only of knowingly fudged experiments and intentionally phony "scientific" data, but also of scientists who were not intentionally trying to falsify experiments or to deceive and yet drew incorrect conclusions because of preconceived expectations or beliefs.

And even if science were done by humans who never approached their disciplines with a shred of self-interest or any motivation other than pure scientific discovery—a difficult proposition to accept—there would still remain one limitation: if causal closure is a false assumption, then there are singular events in history that cannot be explained by natural causes, nor could they be repeated in controlled experiments. Thus, while science can tell us the patterns of how things generally work, under what we have observed as the consistent "laws of nature," and can thus *suggest* how certain historical events were *likely* to have happened *if* they worked under causal closure, it must admit uncertainty about causes of uncontrolled and unrepeated past experiences. If, for example, the assumption of strict naturalism is false, then we would have to admit not only to the possibility of miracles, but also to the inability of science to explain those miraculous events. This is a problem with trying to understand historical events in the past purely scientifically, if those events had some nonnatural causes. It could also be a problem with trying to fully understand human *mind*, if mind is more than brain.

Again, this in no way invalidates the ability of science to give us so-called laws. Those laws are patterns, and they explain how the cosmos works under natural conditions. This is invaluable in nearly every area of life, from treating disease to building bridges to testing soil for the planting of crops. Science helps us understand the patterns of a consistent and ordered cosmos. What we must acknowledge is that what we call "laws" are merely regular patterns that we should *expect* to be the norm, but which do not constitute a closed and unalterable system.

A final point is in order in this chapter, though it follows a different track from the previous few paragraphs. As noted, a philosophy stemming from Judeo-Christian theism supports the validity of both reason and science and, indeed, suggests that these pursuits ought to be held in high regard. However, while reason and science may lead us to knowledge, they are not the *only* paths to truth. The Bible suggests that humans also come to knowledge through our imagination, which is at work in literature and the arts. Contrary to the views of the strict rationalism of the Enlightenment, a painting or poem, symphony or sculpture, film or work of fiction has the capacity not only to entertain us, but to *inform* us as well. And that informing happens not only at the intellectual level *after* we have viewed or read or listened to the work of art, and then reasoned about it; it happens first and foremost *while we are engaged* in the work—that is, while our imaginations are engaged. Thomas Howard has said this eloquently in his book *An Antique Drum*: "Imagination is, in a word, the faculty by which we organize the content of our experience into some form, and thus apprehend it as significant. Put another way, it is what makes us refuse to accept experience as mere random clutter, and makes us try without ceasing to shape that experience so that we can manage it."[18] This point is central to J. R. R. Tolkien's essay "On Fairy-Stories" discussed earlier, as well as to his famous scholarly essay on the poem *Beowulf*, titled "The Monsters and the Critics." It is a point that could be—and has been—the subject of many books. In our learning we are dependent on imagination as well as on intellect—on reason and science.

And, finally, when it comes to knowing God, we are also dependent on revelation. Descartes tried to reason from his own existence to the existence of God. But if there really is a creator behind the universe, and all of the physical cosmos is the created work of that creator who himself is distinct from creation—though he may inhabit his creation and work within it—then it stands to reason that we can know very little about that creator *unless* he makes himself known within his creation. We may use reason, science, and imagination to study and make sense of that revelation *if* and *when* it comes to us, but if God keeps silent and does not speak within his creation, then we cannot know that God through reason and science alone (though we might know something about the physical creation).

8

The Integrated Person

In the second half of this book we have explored implications of a particular understanding of what it means to be a human. The worldview we explored affirms both a material body and an immaterial spirit. It understands the body and spirit to be metaphysically distinct from each other, and yet intimately related. Charles Taliaferro refers to this general philosophy as *integrative dualism*.

On one side, integrative dualism contrasts sharply with physicalism and strict naturalism, which deny the immaterial spirit. On the opposite side from physicalism, however, are worldviews that in one way or another deny or diminish the material world and affirm instead *only* some sort of immaterial reality (such as spirit, or soul, or mind, or even abstractions or ideas). These other worldviews, in affirming an immaterial reality, are often considered under a broad umbrella known as *dualism*. And here it must be noted that the sort of *integrative* dualism that flows out of a Judeo-Christian theology also contrasts sharply with these other forms of dualism. In particular, just as integrative dualism affirms the real existence of immaterial spirit (and thus contrasts with physicalism), it also affirms the importance and goodness of the body and of physical reality (and thus differs substantively from other forms of dualism).

Since these basic questions—questions about what it means to be human and about the existence of material and spiritual reality—are among the most important philosophical questions one could ask, it is not surprising that integrative dualism has some markedly different philosophical and practical implications from either physicalism or other forms of dualism. This book has emphasized the differences between physicalism and integrative dualism, especially with respect to their differing implications for creativity, heroism, ecology, reason, and science. However, the integrative dualist and the physicalist ought to agree on at least one thing: the danger of various worldviews that deny the importance of the bodily aspect of the human person or of the material world altogether. Indeed, many physicalists who reject dualism altogether often seem to be doing so more out of a reaction against these other body-denying forms of dualism than out of any real understanding of integrative dualism. As I conclude this book, therefore, it is important to reaffirm just what integrative dualism really is and how it is different from a Cartesian dualism, a ghost-in-the-machine dualism, or gnosticism. In doing so, I also try to answer a few remaining arguments against integrative dualism that come from the physicalists' side.

Ghosts and Buttons

As noted at the start of the book, one common attack on all dualist understandings of human nature is to reduce them all equally to the idea of a ghost in a machine. The gist of the reduction is as follows. The ghost is supposed to be our spirit (or soul), and the machine is our body. Of course, a machine is very real and physical, as we all know, while a ghost is ephemeral and ethereal, like a puff of smoke, which cannot be touched or held and lasts only a few seconds before it fades or is blown off by the wind. A ghost is somehow much less real than a machine. That is what our popular imaginations have been trained to tell us in modern times. So when we try to imagine this ethereal ghost somehow pushing buttons that make the machine work, we can't quite do it. If there were a spiritual reality, we think, it would have to be *less* substantive than the physical. (After all, it has no material substance, so how could it be substant*ive*?) Perhaps, in our imaginations, we can conjure up the concept of a ghost. We might think of Sam Wheat, the character played by Patrick Swayze (opposite Demi Moore) in the 1990 film *Ghost*, or the various ghosts at Hogwarts in the Harry Potter books. These imaginary ghosts hover around watching the physical life of the world (and maybe making occasional eerie noises or satirical comments), but they can't touch or interact with the physical world in any meaningful way. Lacking physical bodies, they are impotent.

And that is the argument against dualism (often expressed with the help of a comic drawing). How could a spiritual entity have any impact on the physical world, including the physical actions of humans: speaking, talking, or walking, writing this book, or reading this book? Or, to put a slightly different spin on the argument, *if* the spiritual entity can have physical impact on the world, then the entity isn't spiritual at all, but physical. Raymond Kurzweil expresses this precise opinion: "If God and spirit operate outside the material world and have no effect on it, then perhaps we can safely ignore them altogether. On the other hand, if they do affect and interact with the material world, then why not consider them part of it? Otherwise, our metaphysics becomes hopelessly elaborate."[1]

The first sentence above is one that I, and most dualists I know, would agree with. I am happy ignoring any nonmaterial entity that can have *no* impact whatsoever on the material world. (Note, however, that even the act of communicating with a material being would have to be accepted as having an impact on that material world, in that it impacts the behavior of a material being who receives that communication. Thus any nonmaterial entity that in any way makes itself known to a human person has an impact. So all Kurzweil is really saying is that any spiritual entity about which we can know absolutely nothing can be ignored, which isn't really saying very much.) His next leap makes less sense to me, however. That he would refer to integrative dualism—or any philosophy stating that something nonmaterial could impact the material world—as "hopelessly elaborate" (and presumably therefore untrue or unworthy of consideration) seems a bit odd. I can think of many things that are at least as elaborate as integrative dualism and yet have been considered and understood by humans, and are widely believed to be true and real: the nature of light, the force of rotational inertia, the organization of electrons in atoms, and quantum physics, to name four. Even if a metaphysics were highly elaborate—I must ignore the word "hopelessly" here, as it doesn't actually make sense as an adverb modifying "elaborate" in this context—does that make it untrue? Is the dual view of the nature of light in some way less true because it is more elaborate than a single-nature view of light?

In light of this, Kurzweil's comment seems more of a rhetorical device, like a comic strip depicting a ghost pushing buttons, than it does a real reason for rejecting dualism. Nonetheless, he takes this step and concludes that there are only two possibilities, one of which can be ignored, leaving us with physicalism as the only remaining option. That this type of idea is so pervasively held, and rarely even questioned, shows just how firmly ingrained naturalistic presuppositions have become in the past century. Even many people who affirm some spiritual reality in addition to the material reality often view the spiritual reality as somehow *less* real because it is not physical.

But why do we make this assumption? Might it not be the case that the spiritual reality is *at least* as real, *at least* as substantive, *at least* as potent as what we call the physical? This suggestion is in some ways on dangerous ground, for it may seem to be leading toward gnosticism or Platonism or forms of dualism that emphasize the spirit or soul or mind and deny the importance of the body. And these are precisely some of the forms of dualism from which I want to distinguish integrative dualism. As we saw in chapter 6, and will see again later in this chapter, the dualism consistent with Judeo-Christian theism fully affirms the body and the physical cosmos. Of course no such denial is really necessary. One can fully affirm both the body and the spirit, which is what integrative dualism does.

And yet, even as we affirm the appropriateness of the physical body as the dwelling place of the spirit—perhaps even viewing the embodied state as the *highest* state, or even the *only* meaningful state, to which the spirit might attain, rather than a lower state to be escaped—and as we affirm the goodness of physical creation, might it still not be true that somehow spirit is as real and potent as flesh? Why couldn't it be the case that, while the spiritual world may *seem* ephemeral because we cannot control it with our bodies, or see it with our eyes, in fact it is our flesh that is more fleeting?

Consider, for starters, just one simple observation: if a spiritual being (God or a god) created the material universe, then spirit must be, and indeed is, able to bring forth matter—potently so, we might add, given the magnitude of mass and energy in the cosmos. Indeed, any *cosmogony*[2] that affirms the material universe as having a moment of beginning—a "big bang," as it were—with no existing material universe before that moment of beginning, affirms at some level the concept of materiality rising from the immaterial. (This is such an important concept that we will return to it in the next section, contrasting naturalism and theism with respect to the origin of the universe.) If we accept just this one act of creation, or this one instance of the spiritual or immaterial *causing* the material, then it should not be any more surprising or difficult to accept the idea of an immaterial human mind or soul or spirit bringing about changes in a material brain, which in turn brings about our bodily movements. Indeed, I would argue that there is no particular reason to doubt, as an a priori assumption, the ability of a spirit to "press buttons" in a material world. But if one accepts even a single instance of something immaterial having an impact on the material world (by bringing it into existence), then we can make an even stronger statement: the possibility has become an actuality, and there are positive reasons to assume it might happen again, that the immaterial would effect causes in the material universe.

Perhaps one more analogy will help to envision this or change our limited understandings in this regard. Consider a two-dimensional world: a single flat *XY*-plane, with width and length, but no height, like the surface of an infinite sheet of paper.[3] Consider also that this world is inhabited by two-dimensional creatures, each with some two-dimensional shape that has *area*, but no *volume*. Now imagine that this two-dimensional world actually sits inside a three-dimensional world like our own: a world of *XYZ*-coordinates, of width, length, and height, where objects (including creatures) have volume. The two-dimensional world is just a single plane of the three-dimensional world: a single infinite (but infinitely thin) two-dimensional sheet of paper stretching across three-dimensional space. But the two-dimensional creatures cannot leave their planar two-dimensional world. They cannot see or experience *anything* of the three-dimensional world except for instances when three-dimensional objects may be intersecting or passing through their planar world. And even then, they see the three-dimensional objects only as two-dimensional shapes.

Indeed, creatures in the two-dimensional world don't even see each other as two-dimensional creatures, but as one-dimensional beings. Sitting on the plane looking at a circle on that same plane, we would see the circle only as a fixed-length line segment, no matter what side we were looking from. We would have to infer two-dimensional shape from other clues, such as color, or perhaps "facial features" particular to one side of the circle. Looking at a triangle, as opposed to a circle, we might notice that the line segment—remember that a triangle, just like a circle or any other shape would appear only as a line segment to another two-dimensional creature on the same plane—would change length as we moved around it; how much it would change would depend on whether the triangle was long and skinny or close to equilateral.

Meanwhile, there are also three-dimensional creatures living in the three-dimensional world. They are not subject to the physical laws of two-dimensional creatures; they are free to move about in space. Thus, they can look through three dimensions and see the two-dimensional creatures moving about their two-dimensional world. (The three-dimensional creatures could see the two-dimensional ones more completely and clearly than their two-dimensional kin could see each other, for the three-dimensional creatures could see the full two-dimensional shapes, "from above" as it were, and know more fully their nature.) At times, the three-dimensional creatures might even cross into and inhabit the two-dimensional world, and in those moments they could interact with the two-dimensional creatures. They (or that part of them intersecting the two-dimensional world) could temporarily be seen, felt, touched, or heard by creatures in that flat world (though only as two-dimensional shadows of their three-dimensional forms). However, as soon as they moved above or below the planar world, the three-dimensional creatures would no longer be visible to the two-dimensional creatures.

So what would this be like for those living in and bound by the laws of two dimensions? Though on rare occasions the two-dimensional creatures might have contact with their three-dimensional cousins passing through their world, they would have no ability to do experiments on them. They have no eyes that can see in three dimensions, and only limited ability to understand three-dimensional concepts. (As noted, even their understanding of their own two-dimensional reality would be limited to one-dimensional views). They couldn't summon a three-dimensional creature at will. Most of the time they would not even see such creatures or be aware of them. And so, to many creatures living in the two-dimensional subworld, the creatures of three dimensions would *seem* unreal. They would be ephemeral: coming and going for fleeting moments, disappearing into nothingness.[4]

Might not the spiritual reality be something like that? If so, it is not any *less* real than the physical. Of course, it isn't any *more* real either, but it might be more dimensional, or other dimensional, and certainly it is not subject to the laws of the physical world we know. And yet, though it is just as real, the spiritual might seem *ephemeral* to physical beings, just as a three-dimensional creature would seem so to a two-dimensional one.

Like all analogies, this one eventually falls short. Our spiritual reality may be utterly unlike an extension of the physical reality to additional dimensions. Yet it does at least suggest that there is no reason we should limit dualism to a ghost in a machine and then presuppose that the ghost is somehow less real than the machine.

Spirituality, Physicality, and Creation

So let us return to the possibility that prompted this analogy: *if* a spiritual being created the material universe, then right away we know that spirit is able to bring forth matter, and there is no reason to rule out by necessity any later instance of spiritual nature impacting material nature. Of course, naturalists such as Richard Dawkins not only deny that the universe was created but often ridicule the very notion of creation as nonsensical or unreasonable, claiming it is not even an answer. "As ever," Dawkins argues in *The God Delusion*, "the theist's answer is deeply unsatisfying, because it leaves the existence of God unexplained."[5] In one way, this comment is not surprising. As we already noted, if one accepts even the one act of the "big bang" as creation, then the door is open for spiritual creative energies in the material world. So naturalists like Dawkins need to deny a priori even the possibility of creation.

Nonetheless, the phrasing of this claim by Dawkins—and his corresponding explaining away of the cosmological argument for the existence of God—seems to miss the point. At the least, it shows failure to understand the philosophical gist of the argument. *Both* the naturalist *and* the theist must explain the existence of the physical universe. In that regard, they are in the same boat. The question comes particularly to the forefront if one accepts the universe as having a finite age, and thus also having had a particular moment of beginning: a moment of *creation* in the view of theists, or some other *impersonal* beginning event (often described as a "big bang") in the view of most naturalists. The question could be phrased, "What *caused* the beginning?" Now some naturalists—perhaps in a desire to evade this question—claim that material existence is infinitely old, and that there was no *beginning*. This claim can be made either by denying the big bang altogether and arguing that our current universe is infinitely old or by positing an infinite sequence of expanding and collapsing universes and hence an infinite series of big bangs.[6] But the basic question of the existence of matter remains, whether the universe had a beginning or not. Why is there matter? What is the *cause* of the physical universe?

As has often been pointed out, an infinite regress of causes will not do. It is not an explanation to say that the current existence of the universe—the current state of all its matter and energy—owes itself to the state of the universe an instant before, which owes itself to the state of the universe an instant before that, which owes itself to its prior state, etc. At some point there must be some *uncaused* cause. For the naturalist or materialist, matter itself is the uncaused cause. For the theists, the uncaused cause is God. Though both theists and materialists have mistakenly argued that *their* philosophy explains things, and the *other* one doesn't, both leave something unexplained. So Dawkins is correct when he says of the theists' answer, "it leaves the existence of God unexplained." But naturalism also leaves something unexplained. Naturalism leaves matter itself unexplained. *Why is there matter? We don't know*. Theism explains matter in terms of God, but then leaves God unexplained. *Why is there matter? Because of God. Why is there God? We don't know.*

What theists simply point out—often in a form known as the cosmological argument for God's existence—is that it makes *less* sense to see matter as the uncaused cause than it does to see God as the uncaused cause. Why? Everything we know about nature, or the physical cosmos, says that it follows laws of cause and effect. *Inside* the material world, under strict naturalism, we have no examples of uncaused causes. Everything in the material world that exists owes it existence to some prior conditions of matter and energy. So the claim that matter itself is an uncaused cause may be true, but it would be the one glaring contradiction to all that we know about matter. There is no such contradiction if we point to something *outside* of matter as the uncaused cause: the one thing that is not explained. This, it seems, is the point that Dawkins misses. At the very least, it makes no sense to me to argue against God (as a designer or creator of matter) based on statistical probability, as Dawkins does: "However statistically improbable the entity you seek to explain by invoking a designer, the designer himself has got to be at least as improbable."[7] How can we reason about the character of a singular and unique entity based on statistics? If we are to apply statistics and probability, it seems that they would apply in the other direction. Through the known history of the universe, 100 percent of everything *material* has had a cause, and so to claim something *material* (the universe itself) as *uncaused* would have to be statistically unlikely.

The theists might phrase this argument as follows. Matter exists. There *must*, ultimately, be an uncaused and unexplained cause for the existence of matter. Either matter itself is the uncaused cause, or something other than matter is. Both answers are possible. However, the study of matter through human history—especially the work of the natural sciences over the past few centuries—*suggests* through induction that there are *not* any uncaused causes in the material world. Let us then assume some other uncaused cause that is not material, and let us call that cause *God*.

Now perhaps Dawkins does understand this argument well enough to see the suggestion of God's existence in it, because a little later he gives a slightly different argument against God as creator based on how he imagines the capacities—or, rather, the *limit* of the capacities—of such an uncaused cause as a God.

> To suggest that the first cause, the great unknown which is responsible for something existing rather than nothing, is a being capable of designing the universe and of talking to a million people simultaneously, is a total abdication of the responsibility to find an explanation. It is a dreadful exhibition of self-indulgent, thought-denying skyhookery.

> I am not advocating some sort of narrowly scientific way of thinking. But the very least that any honest quest for truth must have in setting out to explain such monstrosities of improbability as a rainforest, a coral reef, or a universe is a crane and not a skyhook.[8]

As noted earlier, both a naturalist and a theist metaphysics ultimately point to some uncaused and unexplained cause. The only way that one could avoid "abdication of the responsibility" of looking for an explanation, as Dawkins puts it, would be to continue to explain everything in terms of something else—that is, to work toward an infinite regress of causes. And that, it seems, is a greater abdication of responsibility. As Goetz and Taliaferro observe: "Philosophical theism takes its key line of reasoning not from . . . items in the cosmos, but from the cosmos as a whole. Why is there a cosmos of gravity, electromagnetism, and so on? Merely explaining parts of the cosmos in terms of other factors within the cosmos will not do, for so long as all these elements are contingent, we will not have a reply for why there is a cosmos at all."[9]

The rest of Dawkins's argument makes even less sense. He seems to be imagining some very limited, impersonal self-existent entity, or uncaused cause, and claiming that, since the being (or impersonal force) that *he* (Dawkins) is able to imagine wouldn't have the ability to design a universe, there cannot exist *any* sort of God such as has been posited by theists. The theist's rejoinder might be that it is difficult to imagine that *any* being capable of bringing into being all the complex matter of the universe, or creating the sort of energy present in the big bang, would *not* be extremely powerful, creative, capable, and knowledgeable. More to the point, to use one of Dawkins's favorite metaphors, to point to physical matter itself as being self-existent and the uncaused cause is every bit as much of a skyhook as to point to God, and indeed more so since it denies what we have observed to be true of matter.

Wind in the Trees and the Integration of Body and Spirit

Let us return, then, from the general notion of material and nonmaterial reality to the more specific notion of body and spirit. Just as a belief that the cosmos was created affirms both the material universe and something else that is not material (but gave rise to the material), integrative dualism affirms both body and spirit. It affirms that they are distinct, but also intimately related. Which is to say, human persons are simultaneously bodily and spiritual beings, and we would be incomplete persons if we lacked either body or spirit. Indeed, we might argue, we would not be *persons* at all if we lacked either.

Charles Taliaferro phrases this idea as follows, distinguishing this form of dualism from Gilbert Ryle's "ghost in the machine."

> As embodied beings, however, persons are not ghosts or mere accessories to their bodies. Persons are integrally related to their bodies so that the person and his or her body function as a singular unit mentally and physically. The person and body are not, strictly speaking, metaphysically identical. They are separable individuals, but all this is in keeping with the proximate, materially conditioned, embodied nature of personal life.[10]

What is central here is the affirmation of both body and spirit, as intimately related, but metaphysically distinct. This is not a new view, suddenly invented by Taliaferro, but a historic one common to major forms of theism. Earlier in his book, Taliaferro also notes:

> Integrative dualism is in accord with theological accounts that insist upon the interwoven nature of the mental and physical, God and the world. Such an integrated viewpoint is in keeping with many of the Church's early theologians. . . . Following them, I want to acknowledge the interrelated but distinct realities of both the material and the immaterial.[11]

Let us then turn, for a moment, and consider this from a standpoint of Christian theology. The Christian Bible certainly affirms that humans are spiritual beings. It repeatedly affirms that humans have the capacity not only for spiritual life, but for *eternal* life—life that does not end when our current mortal bodies die. Jesus himself speaks often about such things as *spiritual* birth (John 3:6–7). The apostle Paul (a central leader of the first-century church) writes about the *spiritual* man (1 Cor. 2:15), *spiritual* fruit (Gal. 5:22), and *spiritual* gifts (1 Cor. 12). We could go on. The Bible even contains frequent suggestions that we would be better off dying a bodily death than a spiritual one. Jesus asks, "What good will it be for a man if he gains the whole world, yet forfeits his soul? Or what can a man give in exchange for his soul?" (Matt. 16:26). And at another time, he says, "Do not be afraid of those who kill the body but cannot kill the soul. Rather, be afraid of the One who can destroy both soul and body in hell" (Matt. 10:28). These passages, when viewed alone, could easily lead one to the conclusion that the spirit only, and not the body, is important to Christianity.

The point here, however, is not that we should despise the body. Later in the same letter in which he refers to the "spiritual man," Paul also notes, "Do you not know that your *body* is a temple of the Holy Spirit, who is in you, whom you have received from God?" (1 Cor. 6:19, emphasis added). The Bible makes it clear that the body is the very thing with which we are supposed to live out our spiritual lives. It is with our *bodies* that we are supposed to obey God.

And it is not just our *own* bodies that matter. According to Christian teaching, we are supposed to take care of the bodies of others as well as our own. Numerous sermons and parables of Jesus, as well as most of the New Testament book of James, all make it clear that the way to be *religious* or *spiritual* is to feed, clothe, and take care of bodies that are hungry, naked, or sick. As for the promise of *salvation*, or *eternal life*, so often associated with Christianity, the Bible also affirms that the eternal spirit is intended to be reembodied, and not to remain *dis*embodied. I noted this earlier and cited C. S. Lewis's comment (in his book *Miracles*) that the early church was little interested in Platonic ideas of immortal soul, but very interested in the resurrected body. And, as noted in chapter 6, with our bodies we are to take care of the physical world (God's creation).

While integrative dualism might describe the human person as a *spirit embodied* (which for some readers seems to place emphasis on the spirit, with the body seen only as habitation), it could equally describe the human person as a *body inbreathed with spirit*. The later phrasing is actually closer to the biblical account of the first humans (Gen. 2:7), which speaks of God forming the first human, Adam, from the stuff of this earth—that is, starting with a physical body—and then breathing life into that body, giving him spirit. The name *Adam* is related to the word for soil or earth. In both ancient

Hebrew and Greek, the primary languages of the Bible, the word for spirit shares the same root as the word for breath or wind.

In fact, wind is an apt analogy in many ways for an integrative dualist's understanding of spirit. Consider wind blowing through the trees. The wind, though it is invisible, has an unmistakable impact on the trees. Using the language of Kurzweil cited in the previous section, the wind "operates" in the world of trees. It "affects" them and "interacts" with them. But it is not part of them. You cannot understand the motion of trees without reference to the wind; all the study about botany, without some study also of wind, will not help you understand a tree's gentle (or perhaps not-so-gentle) swaying and blowing on a breezy day. On the flip side, trees cannot control the wind. They cannot cause the wind to blow. Wind can snap and break a tree, or force it to bend, but a tree cannot break the wind or force it to stop. Though the wind impacts the trees, it would be a mistake to try to reduce the wind to simply an effect of trees, or to try to understand the wind by understanding tree biology.[12]

Returning, then, to the biblical teaching about the importance of saving the spiritual life over saving the bodily life, the central point is simply that the physical body, while not unimportant, can (and will) be replaced—and replaced, moreover, by an even better one that is not subject to the same illness and decay as our current ones. Plato seemed to desire a soul free from the body. Kurzweil wants the conscious mind to be free from failing physical bodies by escaping to virtual ones. Christianity, by contrast, promises resurrected *bodies*—better bodies that won't fail, but bodies nonetheless, with our spirits not left forever *un*housed. With that promise in mind, it is better to do what is morally (or spiritually) good and right, even if our mortal bodies suffer, than to try to bring pleasure to our bodies by doing what is morally wrong. But both our body and our spirit are important, and both are important to who we are.

Science, Ecology, and Ethics

And this brings us to the final point of this book. Integrative dualism, in seeing the human as having a spiritual dimension and thus also having free will, also affirms some moral dimension of the human person. If dualism is correct, then we are not automata. We make choices, and these choices may have spiritual ramifications that are best described in terms such as "good" and "evil." Yet because we are also bodily creatures, and the body is important, these moral choices are not played out only on some immaterial spiritual plane, but also in the physical bodily world. The Christian version of integrative dualism affirms that the most important *spiritual* actions we take relate to what we do with *bodies*: our own, those of fellow human persons, and the bodies of other creatures with whom we share the cosmos.

Of course, this relates directly to ecology, as I argued in chapter 6. Indeed, we might define one's philosophy of ecology—or, to use a phrase from the title of two other books, one's "environmental vision"—as their *principles for* and *approach to* interacting with the physical or natural world. And, according to integrative dualism, the free-will moral choices of what we do with our bodies also make heroism possible, as I argued in chapter 5. What I did not explicitly argue earlier is that there may also be moral implications to how we practice science. If integrative dualism is correct, however, then the moral implications for science and ecology may be tightly interwoven. How we practice science has ecological consequences, and thus if there is a moral dimension to ecology and to our treatment of nonhuman bodies—the physical bodies of plants as well as animals, and even the physical *body* of the earth itself in the form of soil, and water, and air—then there is a moral dimension to how we practice science. To phrase this simply, moral questions about our ecological practices may at times have strong implications for our scientific practices. And in bringing together morality, ecology, and science, this subject ties together the final four chapters of this book.

There are two aspects of this. One has to do with how we *apply* scientific knowledge in the form of technology (or applied science). The other is how we *gain* scientific knowledge. In the first category we might include the scientific knowledge that makes possible nuclear energy, mountaintop removal for coal extraction, genetic engineering, and advanced weapons for warfare. In the second category, the ongoing pursuit of scientific knowledge through the scientific method also includes research on laboratory animals (including vivisection), research on humans (including experimental drugs), stem cell research, and continued research in genetics and gene splicing (that will presumably later be applied to future advances in genetic engineering), as well as research in advanced biological and chemical weapons.

Now in all cases except possibly the development of weapons,[13] there are benefits (or potential benefits) to be had from both the increase of scientific knowledge and from the use of scientific knowledge. But it is also true that in every case, except possibly laboratory experiments on animals, there are practical risks involved for humans or negative consequences (potential or real). That is, there are drawbacks (in many cases unarguable ones) to be weighed against the benefits. Nuclear energy is relatively cheap, it is arguably less disruptive of landscapes than large-scale hydroelectric or wind-energy projects, and it does not emit the sorts of greenhouse gases as does fossil fuel–based energy production. Yet it leaves open not only the possibility of another Chernobyl incident, but the ongoing problem of nuclear waste disposal and contamination of soil, water, and air in and around the energy plant as well as the disposal site. Genetic engineering has resulted in the development of many new useful varieties of food plants resistant to droughts, insects, or diseases. But the cost of introducing new genes into the environment is still unknown; there is a potential for engineered genes to "escape" as invasive species with unknown (and almost certainly irreversible) consequences to native plants. Mountaintop removal may be a comparatively economical way of extracting coal, but it is inarguably devastating to the earth—to soil, water, and every single species that depended on that land and on the water downstream, including human life and culture. At one level, these are practical concerns. The risks versus the rewards can be measured by scientists, or argued by politicians or economists. These are important consequences, and hence important discussions, whether one is a naturalist or a supernaturalist, a physicalist or a dualist.

But what if the world has a spiritual nature as well as a physical one? More specifically, what if nature has a *telos*—a purpose? And what if we, as humans, are moral creatures accountable for real choices? Then we may need to ask moral as well as practical questions about our ecological and scientific practices, and about the ecological consequences of our scientific and technological practices. For example, even if somebody could inarguably prove that mountaintop removal for coal extraction had economic and social benefits that clearly outweighed all the drawbacks, it still might be the case that it was simply wrong—*morally* wrong: wrong because it harmed human beings, or wrong because it harmed trees and other plants, native fish, and birds, and insects, and countless other animals, or wrong because the mountains being "removed" existed for, or were created for, some purpose other than to be destroyed for the sake of coal. And now the question of whether to allow mountaintop removal has a moral dimension that cannot simply be reduced to economic or social utility.

We could raise similar questions about the whole list of modern technologies enabled by modern science, including genetic engineering. Are there certain types of genetic engineering projects that we *ought* not to do, not because of practical considerations or risks, but because of moral ones? Spirituality, ecology, and the practice of technology are all related.

Now the examples of the previous paragraph come from the technological *practice* enabled by modern science. But similar examples could be raised about the practice of scientific discovery—the use of the scientific method—for the pursuit of knowledge. As I argued in chapters 4 and 7, I believe that integrative dualism, especially in the form of Christian theism, provides a much stronger basis for faith in the validity of the scientific endeavor than does physicalism or strict naturalism. Indeed, metaphorically speaking, theistic philosophies may be the strongest allies of the presuppositions that make science possible. Thus, many of history's most important early scientists (as noted in chap. 7), as well as many respected scientists today, are theists and dualists of some form.[14] Their belief in spiritual reality enhances rather than detracts from their scientific study. As Taliaferro has noted, in exploring the implications of integrative dualism to the practice of science: "God has created and now sustains a causally complex, interconnected cosmos. Theism does not so much displace neurophysiology as provide it with an underlying metaphysical account within which to understand both the mental and the physical."[15]

Nonetheless, while I argued in chapter 7 that integrative dualism provides a very good reason to trust the scientific method for the pursuit of knowledge, I also argued that science is not the *only* means toward knowledge. The integrative dualist may look also to history, philosophy, theology, and even art and imagination as means by which we know the world. This goes against some strains of Enlightenment rationalism and scientism—including materialism and physicalism as defined at the start of this book—that view all knowledge ultimately as scientific. Now we argue something stronger that also ruffles the feathers of some scientists: if there is a spiritual reality, if integrative dualism (or even some other form of dualism) is correct, then there may be some scientific pursuits that should not be carried out because they are morally wrong. That is, the scientific pursuit may lead to some new knowledge, and it may even be a useful piece of knowledge, but perhaps the experiment should not be carried out because the very means of the experiment is immoral.

Or, if we are allowed to consider *telos* in our ecology—if we say that a tree or a forest, a single animal or a species, a mountain or even a small molehill, has some purpose that must be acknowledged, and that it cannot necessarily be considered as mere raw material resources for humans to use as we see fit—then perhaps some scientific experiments should not be carried out because of those ecological moral considerations.

C. S. Lewis made an argument of this sort about the practice of vivisection. While he allowed that vivisection might be justifiable as a means of gaining scientific knowledge, he at least raised the point that there was a moral issue involved and that we needed to consider experiments on (live) animals from that moral standpoint:

> If on grounds of our real, divinely ordained, superiority a Christian pathologist thinks it right to vivisect, and does so with scrupulous care to avoid the least dram or scruple of unnecessary pain, in a trembling awe at the responsibility which he assumes, and with a vivid sense of the high mode in which human life must be lived if it is to justify the sacrifices made for it, then (whether we agree with him or no) we can respect his point of view.[16]

Now Lewis, a Christian theist, seemed to hold a position that was against vivisection in all situations. Lewis scholar Clyde Kilby described him as "a strong anti-vivisectionist," though one who left "room for honest difference of opinion."[17] In fact, the quote above is from a tract he agreed to write for an antivivisection society. While he did acknowledge that there were multiple viewpoints that could be respected,[18] one thing he wanted to make clear was that there were moral and not merely scientific aspects to this question—that there were spiritual and moral aspects to how humans live on and take care of the earth and our fellow creatures. That is, since how we interact with the nonhuman world is at the core of our ecological practices, there are ecological implications of science. Under integrative dualism, science, ecology, and morality begin to meet in questions like this.

Unfortunately, the raising of ethical or moral questions with respect to the practice of science also often raises the hackles of some scientists who resist *anything* that may prohibit or restrict *any* scientific endeavor. This, indeed, may be at the root of some of the hostility expressed by scientists who are strict naturalists toward any philosophy other than naturalism and causal closure. It is not that theism or a denial of causal closure undermines the validity of science as a means to truth. They do not. Rather, they may suggest some ethical or moral restraint on the practice of science, including ecologically based restraints on both science and technology. Few of us willingly seek or accept restraints, and those who wield power are often able to avoid them.

Ultimately, however, whether we think moral restraints in general make sense—and specifically whether it *rings true* to us that there should be limits on the use of technology and the practice of science—leads us back to the start of this book. In the introduction, I did not claim to have a rational argument for or against naturalism, at least not in a Cartesian sense. I do not have, and did not seek to present, a deductive or analytic argument for integrative dualism. I certainly did not claim a scientific argument one way or the other, and I even argued that science could not answer such philosophical questions.

What I suggested was that *if* humans were spiritual beings, then we ought to have some spiritual compass. Just as we have physical senses, which enable the practice of science, if we are also spiritual beings, then we have spiritual senses. If we begin with the assumptions of strict naturalism and materialism and physicalism, and cannot step free of those for a moment, then what I have said cannot make sense. If the spirit *were* reducible to the body, then Dawkins would be right that we could discover it by science, but then also what we discovered would not be spirit, but simply more body.

But what if we seek to leave all our assumptions open for question? What I have asked from the beginning of the book is whether the assumptions of integrative dualism make sense of the world, and if so, whether they make more or less sense of the world than physicalism. Does some spiritual sense inside of us speak at all about whether humans are mere biochemical computers? About whether creativity and heroism are real, and whether reason is normative and the scientific method is trustworthy? Perhaps, especially, does our spiritual sense speak to the questions of ecology, and the final questions raised in this chapter—whether there is a moral or spiritual basis to our ecological practices, and whether these moral or spiritual bases for ecology in turn may have any implications to our scientific practices?

I would now end the book with one other question—or rather, proposal. I have raised the hypothetical possibility of the human person as a spiritual as well as an embodied being and suggested a way that possibility may be explored. Ultimately, that exploration involved not only asking philosophical questions, but also attempting to listen to a spiritual voice, to see if that voice might actually be present. We may also raise a similar question about the existence of a God—a divine spiritual person, or (as Lewis would say) the divine Reason. It is reasonable to approach this topic with philosophical questions. Indeed, since the questions of the existence of spiritual human persons and the existence of a divine spiritual being are related, we have also explored at times some specifics of theism as it relates to integrative dualism. But we might also explore this question simply by listening. *If* the divine Reason is personal, and if we try communicating with that being, especially listening to or for that being, then we might hear something. It is certainly not unreasonable to expect to.

Works Cited

Berry, Wendell. "The Body and the Earth." In *The Art of the Commonplace: The Agrarian Essays of Wendell Berry*, edited by Norman Wirzba, 93–134. Washington, DC: Counterpoint, 2002.

———. "Christianity and the Survival of Creation." In *The Art of the Commonplace: The Agrarian Essays of Wendell Berry*, edited by Norman Wirzba, 305–20. Washington, DC: Counterpoint, 2002.

Bradley, Walter, and Roger Olsen. "The Trustworthiness of Scripture in Areas Relating to Natural Science." In *Hermeneutics, Inerrancy, and the Bible*, edited by Earl D. Radmacher and Robert D. Preus, 285–317. Grand Rapids: Academie Books, 1984.

Bouma-Prediger, Stephen. *For the Beauty of the Earth*. Grand Rapids: Baker, 2001.

Dawkins, Richard. *The God Delusion*. Boston: Houghton Mifflin, 2006.

Dembski, William. "Kurzweil's Impoverished Spirituality." In *Are We Spiritual Machines? Ray Kurzweil vs. the Critics of Strong AI*, edited by Jay W. Richards, 98–115. Seattle: Discovery Institute, 2002.

Dennett, Daniel C. "Can Machines Think?" In *Alan Turing: Life and Legacy of a Great Thinker*, edited by Christof Teuscher, 295–316. Berlin: Springer, 2004.

———. *Consciousness Explained*. Boston: Little, Brown, 1991.

———. "In Darwin's Wake, Where Am I?" In *The Cambridge Companion to Darwin*, edited by Jonathan Hodge and Gregory Radick, 357–76. Cambridge: Cambridge University Press, 2003.

DeWitt, Calvin. "Seeking to Image the Order and Beauty of God's 'House': A Scriptural Foundation for Creation-Care." In *Creation-Care in Ministry: Down-to-Earth Christianity*, edited by W. Dayton Roberts and Paul E. Pretiz, 9–24. Wynnewood, PA: Aerdo, 2000.

Dickerson, Matthew. *Following Gandalf: Epic Battles and Moral Victory in The Lord of the Rings*. Grand Rapids: Brazos, 2004.

Dickerson, Matthew, and David O'Hara. *From Homer to Harry Potter: A Handbook of Myth and Fantasy*. Grand Rapids: Brazos, 2006.

———. *Narnia and the Fields of Arbol: The Environmental Vision of C. S. Lewis*. Lexington: University Press of Kentucky, 2009.

Dickerson, Matthew, and Jonathan Evans. *Ents, Elves, and Eriador: The Environmental Vision of J. R. R. Tolkien*. Lexington: University Press of Kentucky, 2006.

Goetz, Stewart, and Charles Taliaferro. *Naturalism*. Grand Rapids: Eerdmans, 2008.

Hobson, J. Allan. *The Chemistry of Conscious States: How the Brain Changes Its Mind*. Boston: Little, Brown, 1994.

Howard, Thomas. *An Antique Drum*. Philadelphia: Lippincott, 1969.

Hummel, Charles. *The Galileo Connection*. Downers Grove, IL: InterVarsity Press, 1986.

Keyes, Dick. *True Heroes in a World of Celebrity Counterfeits*. Colorado Springs: NavPress, 1995.

Kilby, Clyde S. *The Christian World of C. S. Lewis*. Grand Rapids: Eerdmans, 1964.

Kreeft, Peter. *The Philosophy of Tolkien*. San Francisco: Ignatius, 2005.

Kurzweil, Raymond. *The Age of Spiritual Machines*. New York: Penguin, 1999.

———. *Are We Spiritual Machines? Ray Kurzweil vs. the Critics of Strong AI*. Edited by Jay W. Richards. Seattle: Discovery Institute, 2002.

———. "Dembski's Outdated Understanding." In *Are We Spiritual Machines? Ray Kurzweil vs. the Critics of Strong AI*. Edited by Jay W. Richards. Seattle: Discovery Institute, 2002.

———. "The Material World: 'Is That All There Is?' Response to George Gilder and Jay Richards." In *Are We Spiritual Machines? Ray Kurzweil vs. the Critics of Strong AI*. Edited by Jay W. Richards. Seattle: Discovery Institute, 2002.

———. *The Singularity Is Near: When Humans Transcend Biology*. New York: Penguin, 2005.

Lewis, C. S. *The Abolition of Man*. New York: Touchstone, 1996.

———. "On Living in an Atomic Age." In *Present Concerns: Essays by C. S. Lewis*, edited by Walter Hooper, 73–80. San Diego: HBJ, 1986.

———. *Miracles*. New York: Macmillan, 1947.

Moreland, J. P. *Christianity and the Nature of Science*. Grand Rapids: Baker, 1989.

Moreland, J. P., and William Lane Craig. *Philosophical Foundations for a Christian Worldview*. Downers Grove, IL: InterVarsity Press, 2003.

O'Hara, David. "Daniel Dennett: Naturalism and Philosophical Theology." Lecture presented at the University of Sioux Falls Forum for Conversations in Theology and Science, February 23, 2009.

Roberts, W. Dayton. "Icons at the Gates of History." In *Creation-Care in Ministry: Down-To-Earth Christianity*, edited by W. Dayton Roberts and Paul E. Pretiz, 1–3. Wynnewood, PA: Aerdo, 2000.

Russell, Bertrand. "Has Religion Made Useful Contributions to Civilization?" In *Why I Am Not a Christian and Other Essays on Religion and Related Subjects*, 24–47. New York: Allen and Unwin, 1957.

———. "Why I Am Not a Christian." In *Why I Am Not a Christian and Other Essays on Religion and Related Subjects*, 3–23. New York: Allen and Unwin, 1957.

Russell, Stuart, and Peter Norvig. *Artificial Intelligence: A Modern Approach*. 2nd ed. Upper Saddle River, NJ: Prentice Hall, 2003.

Ryle, Gilbert. *The Concept of Mind*. London: Hutchinson's University Library, 1949.

Schaeffer, Francis. *Back to Freedom and Dignity* in *The Complete Works of Francis A. Schaeffer*. Vol. 1. Wheaton: Crossway, 1982.

Searle, John R. *Freedom and Neurobiology: Reflections on Free Will, Language, and Political Power*. New York: Columbia University Press, 2007.

———. "Minds, Brains, and Programs." *Behavioral and Brain Sciences* 3 (1980): 417–24.

———. *The Rediscovery of the Mind*. Cambridge, MA: MIT Press, 1992.

Shippey, T. A. *J. R. R. Tolkien: Author of the Century*. London: HarperCollins, 2000.

Skinner, B. F. *Beyond Freedom and Dignity*. New York: Alfred A. Knopf, 1971.

Snyder, Gary. "The Etiquette of Freedom." In *The Practice of the Wild*, 3–24. Berkeley: North Point Press, 1990.

Taliaferro, Charles. *Consciousness and the Mind of God*. Cambridge: Cambridge University Press, 1994.

———. "Lewis and Naturalism." In *The Cambridge Companion to C. S. Lewis*, edited by Michael Ward and Robert MacSwain. Cambridge: Cambridge University Press, forthcoming.

Tolkien, J. R. R. "On Fairy-Stories." In *Tree and Leaf*, 9–73. Boston: Houghton Mifflin, 1989.

———. *The Hobbit or There and Back Again*. Rev. ed. New York: Ballantine, 1982.

———. "Leaf by Niggle." In *Tree and Leaf*, 75–95. Boston: Houghton Mifflin, 1989.

———. *The Letters of J. R. R. Tolkien*. Edited by Humphrey Carpenter with the assistance of Christopher Tolkien. Boston: Houghton Mifflin, 1981.

———. *The Lord of the Rings*. Boston: Houghton Mifflin.

———. *Morgoth's Ring: The Later Silmarillion*. Edited by Christopher Tolkien. New York: Houghton Mifflin, 1993.

———. *The Silmarillion*. Edited by Christopher Tolkien. Boston: Houghton Mifflin, 1977.

Wirzba, Norman. "Placing the Soul: An Agrarian Philosophical Principle." In *The Essential Agrarian Reader: The Future of Culture, Community, and the Land*, edited by Norman Wirzba, 80–97. Lexington: University Press of Kentucky, 1993.

Recommended Further Reading

General Critiques of Naturalism: *The Abolition of Man* and *Miracles* by C. S. Lewis; *Naturalism* by Stewart Goetz and Charles Taliaferro; *Christianity and the Nature of Science* by J. P. Moreland.

Christianity and the Value of Creativity, Art, Story, and Imagination: *From Homer to Harry Potter* by Matthew Dickerson and David O'Hara; *Walking on Water* by Madeleine L'Engle; *Breath for the Bones* by Luci Shaw; *Tree and Leaf* by J. R. R. Tolkien.

Christianity and Ecology: *For the Beauty of the Earth* by Stephen Bouma-Prediger; *While Creation Waits* by Dale and Sandy Larsen; *Ents, Elves, and Eriador: The Environmental Vision of J. R. R. Tolkien* by Matthew Dickerson and Jonathan Evans; *Narnia and the Fields of Arbol: The Environmental Vision of C. S. Lewis* by Matthew Dickerson and David O'Hara; *The Agrarian Essays of Wendell Berry* (edited by Norman Wirzba) by Wendell Berry; *The Paradise of God: Renewing Religion in an Ecological Age* by Norman Wirzba.

Christianity and Reason: *Mere Christianity* by C. S. Lewis; *Scaling the Secular City* by J. P. Moreland; *Philosophical Foundations of a Christian Worldview* by J. P. Moreland and William Lane Craig; *Why Believe* by C. Stephen Evans; *Handbook of Christian Apologetics* by Peter Kreeft and Ronald K. Tacelli.

Notes

Introduction

1. Certainly this idea can be traced further back than two hundred years. Prior to the late nineteenth century, however, the idea was not yet prevalent among many prominent and influential thinkers, and it did not have the scientific language of the twentieth century to provide an alternate model.

2. Raymond Kurzweil, *The Singularity Is Near: When Humans Transcend Biology* (New York: Penguin, 2005), 7.

3. This philosophical idea (physicalism) has actually been held, suggested, or defended by at least a few persons for hundreds of years. Before the mid-twentieth-century invention of high-speed digital computers, it would have been phrased philosophically in terms of "machines" rather than "computers." Nonetheless, though computers are immeasurably more complex (and also faster) than even the most advanced machines of the eighteenth or nineteenth centuries, the underlying philosophical idea is essentially the same.

4. Keyes is by no means the first person to suggest three fundamental philosophical questions. Immanuel Kant, in his *Critique of Pure Reason* (1787), suggests three great existential questions: "What can I know? What ought I to do? What may I hope?" Though I don't attempt to directly address Kant's questions as they are phrased, they are all certainly relevant to the topic and are not unrelated to Keyes's questions. I am exploring what is true about the human person, and how one might attempt to know what is true. In doing so, I will also address the question of whether the word "ought" makes sense with respect to human actions and choices.

5. Certainly everybody can say, "I exist," without reservation. However, each individual who says this has a different subject—a different "I"—in mind, and perhaps even a different understanding of what "existence" is. Beyond that, there appears to be no universal agreement. It is possible to argue that everything else that *seems* to exist independently of my mind actually exists *only* in my own mind. Charles Taliaferro, in *Consciousness and the Mind of God* (Cambridge: Cambridge University Press, 1994), notes: "According to many idealists, the commonsense, ordinary notion of a material object is a theoretical construction of our own. We become accustomed to thinking of material objects existing independently of experience. This informal assumption becomes such an habitual, humdrum affair that it appears natural, almost instinctive, to believe that we live among experience-independent entities. We lose track of the fact that the belief in such material objects is a convenient hypothesis" (24). There are also religions that seem to

deny even *individual* existence, seeing the concept of the individual as illusory.

6. There are some philosophers of mind who hold a form of naturalism and yet still argue that mind is not reducible to brain. They deny the reality of *spirit*, affirming some form of naturalism, and yet argue that *mind* is still more than *body*. John Searle is a notable example. See, for example, John R. Searle, *The Rediscovery of the Mind* (Cambridge, MA: MIT Press, 1992), a careful and thoughtful contribution to the topic. While I believe this a difficult position to hold consistently, my argument as well as this particular argument of Searle's are beyond the scope of this book.

7. Bertrand Russell, "Has Religion Made Useful Contributions to Civilization?" in *Why I Am Not a Christian and Other Essays on Religion and Related Subjects* (New York: Allen and Unwin, 1957), 38–39.

8. J. R. R. Tolkien, *The Lord of the Rings* (Boston: Houghton Mifflin). Quotation is from vol. 3, *The Return of the King*, book 5, chap. 1. Because of the many editions of this work, quotations from the three volumes of *The Lord of the Rings* are cited by volume name, book number, and chapter number.

9. William Dembski, "Kurzweil's Impoverished Spirituality," in *Are We Spiritual Machines? Ray Kurzweil vs. the Critics of Strong AI*, ed. Jay W. Richards (Seattle: Discovery Institute, 2002), 108.

10. Mark Heard, "Orphans of God," album *Satellite Sky*, Fingerprint Records, 1992.

11. David O'Hara, "Daniel Dennett: Naturalism and Philosophical Theology," lecture presented at the University of Sioux Falls Forum for Conversations in Theology and Science, February 23, 2009.

Chapter 1 Ghosts, Machines, and the Nature of Light

1. Cited from the publicity of Raymond Kurzweil, *The Singularity Is Near*, in the front of the book and on http://singularity.com.

2. Kurzweil argues elsewhere for the existence of randomness in the universe, as a result of the effects of quantum physics. In that sense, he could be said *not* to hold to a philosophy of strict determinism. However, he denies the concept of human free will and argues that human minds are completely reducible to physical computational devices following physical laws, and in that sense humans are determined and deterministic devices. The existence of random quantum effects, in Kurzweil's philosophical system, does not make humans less computational but simply makes us like computers whose behavior is controlled by a program that also makes use of random numbers to determine their behavior. I will briefly explore the impact of accepting randomness in addition to physicalism.

3. Regarding how widespread Kurzweil's beliefs are, I am referring here only to his underlying assumption of physicalism and the reducibility of human thought to a purely computational model. I am not referring to his writings as a futurist and his numerous predictions for computers and humans, about which many naturalists and determinists who may share his underlying philosophical assumptions may still remain skeptical simply because of the complexity of the human brain.

4. William Dembski, in "Kurzweil's Impoverished Spirituality," also argues that Kurzweil's use of the word *spiritual* is "impoverished" to the point of being meaningless. Dembski explains several things that a real spiritual being would be capable of, but that are not capabilities of a computer or of a machine of any type. One of the most important aspects of a spiritual being is the ability to be aware of God's presence or to commune with God. "But how can a machine be aware of God's presence?" Dembski asks. "Recall that machines are entirely defined by the constitution, dynamics, and interrelationships among their physical parts. It follows that God cannot make his presence known to a machine by acting upon it and thereby changing its state. Indeed, the moment God acts upon a machine

to change its state, it no longer properly is a machine, for an aspect of the machine now transcends its physical constituents" (106). For a naturalist, an inability to commune with a hypothetical but nonexistent God is not a limitation of machines; if there is no God, an inability to commune with God is irrelevant. Nonetheless, it does suggest that the use of the word *spiritual* is problematic.

5. J. Allan Hobson, *The Chemistry of Conscious States: How the Brain Changes Its Mind* (Boston: Little, Brown, 1994), 5.

6. Stewart Goetz and Charles Taliaferro, *Naturalism* (Grand Rapids: Eerdmans, 2008), 7.

7. Taliaferro, *Consciousness and the Mind of God*, 121.

8. Peter Kreeft, *The Philosophy of Tolkien* (San Francisco: Ignatius, 2005), 86. Note that in the paragraph cited, Kreeft is describing the impact of Descartes on the Western mind. Speaking of the complete body–soul or physical–spiritual distinction made by Descartes, he adds, "But before Descartes it was not so. The distinction was there, but not total. There was an in-between category, *life*, which Descartes eliminated. (He thought of even an animal as a complicated machine.)"

9. Gilbert Ryle, *The Concept of Mind* (London: Hutchinson's University Library, 1949), 22.

10. To accept a belief or proposition *a priori* means to accept it as, or based on, a previously held principle or conviction rather than as the result of observation or experimentation. We often refer to our central a priori beliefs as *assumptions* or *presuppositions* for our other beliefs or conclusions.

11. John R. Searle, "Minds, Brains, and Programs," in *Behavioral and Brain Sciences* 3 (1980): 417–24. See also Searle, *Rediscovery of the Mind*, 45.

12. Searle, *Rediscovery of the Mind*, 204.

13. John R. Searle, *Freedom and Neurobiology: Reflections on Free Will, Language, and Political Power* (New York: Columbia University Press, 2007), 49.

14. For a brief summary, see Stuart Russell and Peter Norvig, *Artificial Intelligence: A Modern Approach*, 2nd ed. (Upper Saddle River, NJ: Prentice Hall, 2003), 956–58.

15. Searle, *Rediscovery of the Mind*, cited in ibid., 957.

16. Taliaferro, *Consciousness and the Mind of God*, 134.

17. Daniel Dennett, "Can Machines Think?" in *Alan Turing: Life and Legacy of a Great Thinker*, ed. Christof Teuscher (Berlin: Springer, 2004), 296.

18. Ibid., 297.

19. Ibid., 310.

20. Ibid., 300, emphasis added.

21. Daniel C. Dennett, *Consciousness Explained* (Boston: Little, Brown, 1991), 431.

22. Credit should be given here to John Searle. Though he is a naturalist, his thought experiment, in some ways, does not presuppose a materialistic universe. At least for some readers, part of the strength of Searle's argument is based on an *intuitive* understanding of what the conscious mind is. In particular, the experiment appeals to that intuition of the relationship between the mind and understanding. This is at least one reason why those who start with a materialist understanding of the mind don't accept the argument; they don't accept Searle's intuitive definition.

23. We are really speaking here of what is sometimes called "natural science" as opposed to "social science." Natural science would include, for example, physics, chemistry, biology, geology. Of course, if the naturalists are correct and all that exists is the material world, then all sciences ultimately can be reduced to the natural sciences, because all phenomena ultimately have purely material causes.

24. Dennett, "Can Machines Think?" 313.

25. Richard Dawkins, *The God Delusion* (Boston: Houghton Mifflin, 2006), 2.

26. Ibid., 50.

27. Ibid., 71.

28. Ibid., 59.

29. John Searle, cited in Goetz and Taliaferro, *Naturalism*, 9.

30. Dawkins, *God Delusion*, 31.

31. Daniel C. Dennett, "In Darwin's Wake, Where Am I?" in *The Cambridge Companion to Darwin*, ed. Jonathan Hodge and Gregory Radick (Cambridge: Cambridge University Press, 2003).

32. Ibid., 368.

33. Dennett, *Consciousness Explained*, 37.

34. Dennett, "In Darwin's Wake," 361.

35. Ibid., 370.

36. Taliaferro, *Consciousness and the Mind of God*, 49.

37. The song "Spirits in the Material World" was first released on the Police album titled *Ghosts in the Machine* (A&M, 1990). The point of this reference is not to defend ghost-in-the-machine dualism suggested by the title of the album, but to point out the innate sense of human spirituality suggested by the passionately sung lyrics.

38. Dawkins, *God Delusion*, 11.

39. Ibid., 61.

Chapter 2 Physicalism, Creativity, and Heroism

1. Dick Keyes, *True Heroes in a World of Celebrity Counterfeits* (Colorado Springs: NavPress, 1995), 16.

2. Ibid., 16–17.

3. Tolkien, *Lord of the Rings, The Fellowship of the Ring*, book 2, chap. 2, emphasis added.

4. Tolkien, *Lord of the Rings, The Two Towers*, book 4, chap. 8. Though Sam does not use explicitly use the word *hero* in this sentence, he does a few sentences later. The reference to Beren, considered by Tolkien to be the greatest hero in all his tales, also puts Sam's comments into context.

5. Dawkins, *God Delusion*, 164, emphasis added.

6. Chris Frith, "Neuroscience enters the debate on free will," *Boston Globe*, October 15, 2002, C3.

7. Raymond Kurzweil, *The Age of Spiritual Machines* (New York: Penguin, 1999), 6.

8. Ibid., 57.

9. Ibid., 58.

10. Ibid., 302.

11. Earlier in his book, Kurzweil does acknowledge that the free-will question is a philosophically complex one. But what he seems to mean is that if one accepts the notion of a soul, then the only possibility is a sort of Cartesian dualism, and we are faced with a problem of deciding whether to root our free will in our brain or in our soul as two utterly distinct possibilities. He argues that either answer is troublesome. Since he can't figure out how free will would work with a soul, and he understands that with only a material body there is no possible source for free will, he takes the easier route and just ignores the possibility of soul and returns to a materialist presupposition that we have no free will.

12. Kurzweil, *Age of Spiritual Machines*, 60.

13. Russell, "Has Religion Made Useful Contributions to Civilization?" 37–39.

14. Ibid., 40, emphasis added.

15. Ibid.

16. B. F. Skinner, *Beyond Freedom and Dignity* (New York: Alfred A. Knopf, 1971), 21.

17. B. F. Skinner, cited in Francis Shaeffer, *Back to Freedom and Dignity*, in *The Complete Works of Francis A. Schaeffer* (Wheaton: Crossway, 1982), 1:375.

18. Skinner, *Beyond Freedom and Dignity*, 200–201.

19. Kurzweil, *Age of Spiritual Machines*, 159, emphasis added.

20. Ibid., 167.

21. Dennett, "In Darwin's Wake," 368–69.

22. Raymond Kurzweil, "Dembski's Outdated Understanding," in *Are We Spiritual Machines?* 185.

23. Kurzweil, *Age of Spiritual Machines*, 159.

24. There are nine squares in a board, and so there are nine possible first moves, eight possible second moves given the first move, seven possible third moves given the first two, etc, for a total of 9×8×7×6×5×4×3×2×1=362,880 possible sequences of moves. But many of these games end in victory for either "X" or "O" before the full sequence

of moves has been completed, reducing that number somewhat. More importantly, the board is symmetric, and so, for example, an opening move in any of the four corners is equivalent. So there are really only three distinct choices for the first move: a corner, a side, or the center. If the first move is in the center, there are only two distinct second moves: a side square or a corner square. Etc. If the "X" player takes the opening move in a corner, and the "O" player moves anywhere other than the center, then "X" can move to guarantee a victory.

25. "Estimates of the matter content of the observable universe indicate that it contains on the order of 10^{80} atoms." http://en.wikipedia.org/wiki/Observable_universe.

26. Kurzweil, "Dembski's Outdated Understanding," 187.

27. Kurzweil, *Age of Spiritual Machines*, 302.

28. Dennett, "In Darwin's Wake," 372.

29. Skinner, *Beyond Freedom and Dignity*, 67.

30. Ibid., 74.

31. B. F. Skinner, British Broadcasting Corporation, *The Listener* (September 30, 1971), cited in *The Complete Works of Francis A. Schaeffer*, 1:378.

32. Dawkins, *God Delusion*, 5.

Chapter 3 Naturalism and Nature

1. Kurzweil, *Age of Spiritual Machines*, 142.

2. Ibid., 141–42.

3. Ibid., 128–29, emphasis original. Kurzweil is quoting from W. B. Yeats's poem "Sailing to Byzantium."

4. Ibid., 129.

5. Ibid., 138.

6. Ibid., 148.

7. Ibid.

8. As noted earlier, Kurzweil's use of the word *spiritual*, here, is a clever though misleading ploy. Kurzweil denies any objective spiritual reality—that is, any reality beyond the physical/material reality testable by science. Specifically, he denies the existence of spirit or soul in any dualistic sense. Whereas we suggest that our sense of our own spirituality, which seems to be a universal human experience, is a pointer to something real in the world, Kurzweil claims that the human sense of spirituality is simply part of our computational process, and will be controllable.

9. Kurzweil, *Age of Spiritual Machines*, 151.

10. Norman Wirzba, "Placing the Soul: An Agrarian Philosophical Principle," in *The Essential Agrarian Reader: The Future of Culture, Community, and the Land*, ed. Norman Wirzba (Lexington: University Press of Kentucky, 1993), 86.

11. Kurzweil, *Age of Spiritual Machines*, 140.

12. Ibid., 142.

13. Ken Myers, *2008 Summer Letter* (to Mars Hill Audio subscribers), June 2008.

14. Ibid.

15. It is interesting to note that Miley Cyrus also provides the voice-over for the character Penny in the 2008 animated film *Bolt*. Penny is a child actor with a regular television show. So Cyrus is once again an actress providing the voice of an actress playing a part. Except now the actress Penny, voiced by Miley, is entirely virtual, the figment of computer animation. And her television character is even more virtual: a science-fiction action television series starring a dog with superhuman powers.

16. Wendell Berry, "The Body and the Earth," in *The Art of the Commonplace: The Agrarian Essays of Wendell Berry*, ed. Norman Wirzba (Washington, DC: Counterpoint, 2002), 103.

17. As noted in chap. 1, science does not propose that everything is natural. The statement "Everything is natural" is a philosophical statement and not a scientific one. It is completely possible—and history has numerous examples—to be a scientist and to do science, exploring cause-and-effect relationships *within* the natural world, without holding to this naturalistic presupposition that these are the *only* sorts of causal relationships. If one does hold to this philosophy,

however, then one can subsequently claim that science is sufficient to explain everything. Again, however, this is a philosophical assertion, and not a scientific one.

18. Gary Snyder, "The Etiquette of Freedom," in *The Practice of the Wild* (Berkeley: North Point Press, 1990), 8.

19. The term *ecology* refers either to the actual relationships and interactions between *individual* organisms, and between individual organisms and their environment, or to the *study* of these relationships and interactions. In either case, if there are no *individual* organisms to interact and interrelate, then there is no ecology.

20. Skinner, *Beyond Freedom and Dignity*, 9.

21. Ibid., 14.

22. Ibid., 18.

23. Matthew Dickerson and David O'Hara, *Narnia and the Fields of Arbol: The Environmental Vision of C. S. Lewis* (Lexington: University Press of Kentucky, 2009), 192.

24. C. S. Lewis, "On Living in an Atomic Age," in *Present Concerns: Essays by C. S. Lewis*, ed. Walter Hooper (San Diego: HBJ, 1986), 76–77.

Chapter 4 Reason, Science, and the Mind as a Physical Brain

1. The term *normative*, in this context, refers to an objective standard for how we *ought* to think if we want our thoughts to correlate with truth, as opposed to the term *descriptive*, which refers to how we *do* think *in practice*. The question is whether human reason has any normative value or only a descriptive value. We might ask this in another, more circular way: do we have any good reason to trust reason?

2. Of course, declaratives and interrogatives often get at the same underlying proposition. Just as we could reason about the truth of the proposition "All birds have wings," we could also reason about the answer to the question "Do all birds have wings?" It would be the same discussion. In both cases, the underlying issue is determining what is true. But since declaratives (propositions) must be true or false, while questions cannot be either, it is more natural to define reason in terms of the former.

3. Note that if there is an objective morality in the universe—if there is some definition of right and wrong, or good and evil, that transcends personal preference or even cultural practices; if morality is normative and not merely descriptive—then this purpose (or definition) of reason includes a broader and older understanding that sees a purpose (or even the *primary* purpose) of reason as determining what are morally right and wrong actions. In other words, one of the types of propositions that one could reason about are propositions about morality: "It is morally right for me to do this thing."

4. Technically speaking, a proposition involving a variable such as X is actually called a *propositional function*. A propositional function does not become a proposition until the variable is given a specific value. In this example, the propositional function becomes a proposition when X ceases to represent some animal *in general* and becomes associated with *a particular animal*—say, the sparrow that just flew past my window (which has wings and feathers, and appeared to be on its way to a nest where it likely had eggs).

5. Dennett, "In Darwin's Wake," 362.

6. Russell, "Why I Am Not a Christian," in *Why I Am Not a Christian*, 19.

7. C. S. Lewis, *Miracles* (New York: Macmillan, 1947), 16, emphasis original.

8. Ibid., 15.

9. See Charles Taliaferro, "Lewis and Naturalism," in *The Cambridge Companion to C. S. Lewis*, ed. Michael Ward and Robert MacSwain (Cambridge: Cambridge University Press, forthcoming).

10. Dawkins, *God Delusion*, 176.

11. Dennett, "Can Machines Think?" 313.

12. Lewis, *Miracles*, 15–16.

13. Dawkins, *God Delusion*, 5.

14. Skinner, *Beyond Freedom and Dignity*, 30.

15. Ibid., 24.

16. Russell, "Has Religion Made Useful Contributions to Civilization?" in *Why I Am Not a Christian,* 37–38.

17. Goetz and Taliaferro, *Naturalism*, 118–19.

18. Lewis, *Miracles*, 18.

19. "Science," *The Oxford Dictionary of English* (2nd edition revised), accessed via *Oxford Reference Online*, August 23, 2010, www.oxfordreference.com.

20. "Science," Encyclopedia Britannica, 2010, Encyclopedia Britannica Online, accessed August 23, 2010, www.britannica.com/EBchecked/topic/528756/science.

21. "Science," *The New Zealand Oxford Dictionary in English*, accessed via *Oxford Reference Online*, August 23, 2010, www.oxfordreference.com.

22. Percy W. Bridgman and Gerald Holton, "Science," in AccessScience, McGraw-Hill Companies, 2008, www.accessscience.com.

23. Ibid.

24. Taliaferro, *Consciousness and the Mind of God*, 30.

25. Ibid., 24.

26. J. P. Moreland, *Christianity and the Nature of Science* (Grand Rapids: Baker, 1989), 121.

27. Ibid., 122.

28. Taliaferro, *Consciousness and the Mind of God*, 73.

29. Lewis, *Miracles*, 14.

30. Moreland, *Christianity and the Nature of Science*, 121.

31. J. P. Moreland and William Lane Craig do a good job listing some of these, and readers are referred to part IV of their collaborative book *Philosophical Foundations for a Christian Worldview* (Downers Grove, IL: InterVarsity Press, 2003) and to chap. 3 of Moreland's earlier work *Christianity and the Nature of Science.*

32. Lewis, *Miracles*, 56.

33. Dawkins, *God Delusion*, 89.

34. Ibid., 90.

35. Taliaferro, *Consciousness and the Mind of God*, 165.

Part 2 The Spiritual Human

1. As noted earlier, we are speaking of *dualism* with respect to human nature: a belief that humans are both physical and spiritual beings. We are not trying to defend a Manichaean dualism or any metaphysical system that explains the nature of the universe in terms of opposed but equally balanced powers of "Good" and "Evil." We also acknowledge that there are both Jewish and Christian theists who deny dualism and are physicalist with respect to human nature, and possibly even divine nature.

Chapter 5 Affirming the Creative and the Heroic

1. T. A. Shippey argues that both "Leaf by Niggle" and *Smith of Wootton Major* (another of J. R. R. Tolkien's short fairy tales) are best understood as "autobiographical allegory." See T. A. Shippey, *J. R. R. Tolkien: Author of the Century* (London: HarperCollins, 2000), 265–77, 297–98. While this characterization of *Smith of Wootton* has been challenged by other scholars, it is a widely accepted reading of "Leaf by Niggle." See, for example, Matthew Dickerson, *Following Gandalf: Epic Battles and Moral Victory in The Lord of the Rings* (Grand Rapids: Brazos, 2004), 234; and Matthew Dickerson and Jonathan Evans, *Ents, Elves, and Eriador: The Environmental Vision of J. R. R. Tolkien* (Lexington: University Press of Kentucky, 2006), 163, 170–82.

2. Interestingly, B. F. Skinner does just that: he dismisses the ideas of the ancient Greeks in general, and Plato in particular, arguing that they provide no shred of valuable insight into what it means to be human. He writes, in *Beyond Freedom and Dignity*, "Greek physics and biology are now of historical interest only (no modern physicist or biologist would turn to Aristotle for help), but the dialogues of Plato are still assigned to students and cited *as if* they threw light on human behavior" (5–6, emphasis added). Skinner is explicitly referring to, and dismissing, the dialogues of Plato, at least with re-

spect to any insight into human behavior. A few sentences later he makes this even clearer. "Whereas Greek physics and biology, no matter how crude, led eventually to modern science, Greek theories of human behavior led nowhere. If they are with us today, it is not because they possessed some kind of eternal verity, but because they did not contain the seeds of anything better" (6). We note, however, that even Skinner must agree that mythic dialogues at least contain "theories" or ideas—ones with which we might agree or, in his case, disagree. And so we argue also that the mythic dialogues of J. R. R. Tolkien must also be taken seriously in terms of their content, ideas, and theories.

3. Christopher Tolkien, in J. R. R. Tolkien, *Morgoth's Ring: The Later Silmarillion*, ed. Christopher Tolkien (New York: Houghton Mifflin, 1993), 303.

4. Tolkien, *Morgoth's Ring*, 329.

5. Ibid., 329–30.

6. Literally, the making of myth.

7. Plato, *Phaedrus*, 246c. Jowett translation.

8. Tolkien, *Morgoth's Ring*, 330–31.

9. Readers are referred to J. R. R. Tolkien's work *The Silmarillion*. The entire tragedy of that story, and especially of the life of Fëanor, can be seen to have roots in the decision of Miriel. Readers are also referred to the draft of an unsent letter on page 286 of Tolkien, *The Letters of J. R. R. Tolkien*, ed. Humphrey Carpenter, with the assistance of Christopher Tolkien (Boston: Houghton Mifflin, 1981).

10. Tolkien, *Morgoth's Ring*, 308.

11. Tolkien's Middle-earth mythology is fundamentally theistic, and by intention is compatible with Judeo-Christian monotheism. There is one eternal creative being, known as Eru ("The One") and Ilúvatar ("Father of all"). Among Eru's first created beings are angelic beings known as the *Valar*. Though neither omnipotent nor omniscient, nor even capable of creating free-willed beings, they are essentially spiritual (rather than physical) beings who appear from time to time in physical form as great, majestic beings among Elves and Men of Middle-earth. Thus, they play a *literary* (though not theological) role not unlike that of the gods of various polytheistic mythologies such as those of the Greeks or Norse tribes. Aulë, Yavanna, and Manwë are among these *gods*, or *Valar*, and so conversations among them may be viewed much like mythic conversations among the gods of Olympus in Greek mythology, or the gods of Asgard in Norse mythology. But it is clearly understood that the Valar are not divine or eternal; rather, they owe their existence to the divine, eternal creator Eru.

12. J. R. R. Tolkien, *The Silmarillion*, ed. Christopher Tolkien (Boston: Houghton Mifflin, 1977), 43.

13. Ibid.

14. Ibid.

15. Ibid., 44.

16. J. R. R. Tolkien, "On Fairy-Stories," in *Tree and Leaf* (Boston: Houghton Mifflin, 1989), 52.

17. Kurzweil, *Age of Spiritual Machines*, 58.

18. J. R. R.Tolkien, "Leaf by Niggle," in *Tree and Leaf*, 75.

19. Ibid., 85. Note that this also suggests value in the leaves themselves, as objects of nature worthy of being painted; this is an important observation to keep in mind for the next chapter of this book.

20. Ibid., 78.

21. Ibid., 93.

22. Tolkien, "On Fairy-Stories," 66.

23. J. R. R. Tolkien, *The Hobbit or There and Back Again*, rev. ed. (New York: Ballantine, 1982), 62.

24. T. A. Shippey argues persuasively in his book *J. R. R. Tolkien* that goblins (also known as orcs) have some ethical or moral framework for viewing the world, and despite their cruel and immoral behavior would prefer to think of themselves as ethical creatures. Shippey writes, "Orcs . . . have a clear idea of what is admirable and what is contemptible behavior, which is exactly the same as ours. . . . They are moral beings, who talk freely and repeatedly of what is 'good,' meaning by that more or less what we do. The puzzle

is that this has no effect at all on their actual behaviour, and they seem . . . to have no self-awareness or capacity for self-criticism. But these are human qualities too" (133).

25. Tolkien, "Leaf by Niggle," 94.

26. Ibid.

27. Ibid., 95.

28. Tolkien, "On Fairy-Stories," 64.

29. Tolkien, *The Lord of the Rings*, *The Fellowship of the Ring*, book 2, chap. 8, emphasis added.

30. Tolkien, *The Lord of the Rings*, *The Two Towers*, book 3, chap. 2.

31. Tolkien, *The Lord of the Rings*, *The Fellowship of the Ring*, book 2, chap. 7.

32. Tolkien, *The Lord of the Rings*, *The Two Towers*, book 4, chap. 5.

Chapter 6 Body, Spirit, and the Value of Creation

1. Wendell Berry, "Christianity and the Survival of Creation," in *The Art of the Commonplace*, 305–6.

2. Ibid., 307–8.

3. Ibid., 308.

4. Calvin DeWitt, "Seeking to Image the Order and Beauty of God's 'House': A Scriptural Foundation for Creation-Care," in *Creation-Care in Ministry: Down-To-Earth Christianity*, ed. W. Dayton Roberts and Paul E. Pretiz (Wynnewood, PA: Aerdo, 2000), 20.

5. W. Dayton Roberts, "Icons at the Gates of History," in *Creation-Care in Ministry*, 1.

6. DeWitt, "Seeking to Image the Order and Beauty of God's 'House,'" 19.

7. Stephen Bouma-Prediger, *For the Beauty of the Earth* (Grand Rapids: Baker, 2001), 74.

8. Tolkien, *The Lord of the Rings*, *The Fellowship of the Ring*, book 1, chap. 2.

9. Tolkien, *The Lord of the Rings*, *The Return of the King*, book 6, chap. 9.

10. For further reading on J. R. R. Tolkien's environmental vision and the worldview on which it is based, see Dickerson and Evans, *Ents, Elves and Eriador*.

11. Consider the scene in Plato's *The Phaedo* when Socrates is preparing to drink poison to complete his death sentence. He says, "When I have drunk the poison I shall leave you and go to the joys of the blessed. . . . I may and must ask the gods to prosper my journey from this to the other world—even so—and so be it according to my prayer." After this, Plato's narrator says, "Then raising the cup to his lips, quite readily and cheerfully he drank off the poison" (Jowett translation). For Socrates, the joys of the blessed means an eternal soul free from bodily existence.

12. Lewis, *Miracles*, 29.

13. Wirzba, "Placing the Soul," 86.

Chapter 7 A Biblical Defense of Reason and Science

1. Lewis, *Miracles*, 22.

2. Ibid., 28.

3. Taliaferro, *Consciousness and the Mind of God*, 273.

4. AΩ: *The Online Greek Bible*, www.greekbible.com.

5. See, for example, the reasoning of the philosopher C. Stephen Evans in chap. 8 of his book *Why Believe: Reason and Mystery as Pointers to God* (Grand Rapids: Eerdmans, 1996), especially 76–77. See also the work of philosophers Peter Kreeft and Ronald K. Tacelli in chap. 8 of their book *Handbook of Christian Apologetics* (Downers Grove, IL: InterVarsity Press, 1994), especially 184–86.

6. The Greek verb *dialegomai* is defined by W. E. Vine as follows: "To think different things with oneself, to ponder, then, to dispute with others." W. E. Vine, *Vine's Expository Dictionary of New Testament Words.* (Iowa Falls, IA: Riverside Book and Bible House), 934.

7. The Greek verbs used here are *dianoigo* and *paratithémi*. Vine translates this phrase as "opening [of the mind] and alleging," and explains that it connotes "setting subjects before one's hearers by way of argument and proof" (ibid., 49, 823).

8. The Greek verb here is peitho, used in the passive voice. Vine explains the meaning of this verb as "bringing about a change of mind by the influence of reason or moral consideration" (ibid., 861).

9. Walter Bradley and Roger Olsen, "The Trustworthiness of Scripture in Areas Relating to Natural Science," in *Hermeneutics, Inerrancy, and the Bible*, ed. Earl D. Radmacher and Robert D. Preus (Grand Rapids: Academie Books, 1984), 285–317. Also available at www.origins.org/articles/bradley_trustworthiness.html.

10. Ibid.

11. Ibid.

12. Lewis, *Miracles*, 47.

13. Taliaferro, *Consciousness and the Mind of God*, 86.

14. Charles Hummel, *The Galileo Connection* (Downers Grove, IL: InterVarsity Press, 1986), 39, 55, quoting from Copernicus, "On the Revolutions of the Heavenly Spheres," Charles Glen Wallis translation.

15. Newton, *Principle*, in Hutchins, *Great Books*, 34:369–70, cited in Hummel, *The Galileo Connection*, 144.

16. In Greek, *logos*.

17. The basic idea of this metaphor is borrowed from the writings of Francis Schaeffer.

18. Thomas Howard, *An Antique Drum* (Philadelphia: Lippincott, 1969), 25.

Chapter 8 The Integrated Person

1. Raymond Kurzweil, "The Material World: 'Is That All There Is?' Response to George Gilder and Jay Richards," in *Are We Spiritual Machines*, 218.

2. Cosmogony is a study of, or philosophical theory of, the origins (genesis) of the cosmos and its existence.

3. Edwin Abbott, in his 1884 novel *Flatland: A Romance of Many Dimensions*, invites his readers to a similar sort of thought experiment, though his goal was apparently social criticism and not philosophical metaphor. Abbott's novel has remained popular and has spawned numerous other books, short stories, and films primarily because of its insights into the mathematics of geometric dimensionality.

4. We could extend this metaphor into four dimensions or—perhaps more appropriately—five. Remember that a two-dimensional creature in a planar world sees in only one dimension; if you are sitting on a two-dimensional plane with a circle, then the circle looks like a stick (a line segment) from no matter what angle you look at it. Suppose this generalizes to higher dimensions: that a creature can always see with one less dimension than the dimensionality of the world in which it dwells. Suppose humans were four-dimensional creatures, and thus we could see ourselves in only three dimensions. We would need other clues to guess at our four-dimensional nature. But what if there were five-dimensional beings, which could pass into our four-dimensional world. They would be able to see our full nature, and while in our world they would be able to communicate with us, though they could also pass out of our four dimensions and leave us wondering about their very existence.

5. Dawkins, *God Delusion*, 143.

6. Scientific evidence for the big bang, as well as the Second Law of Thermodynamics, provides rather potent evidence that our universe is finitely old. Thus, most scientists who believe that matter has always existed adhere to the second of these theories: an infinite series of big bangs, followed by an expanding and then collapsing universe.

7. Dawkins, *God Delusion*, 114.

8. Ibid., 155.

9. Goetz and Taliaferro, *Naturalism*, 104.

10. Taliaferro, *Consciousness and the Mind of God*, 114–15.

11. Ibid., 16.

12. It is worth noting that trees can, in fact, have some effect on the wind. That is the purpose of using a line of trees as a windbreak. The worlds of trees and wind are interrelated. Integrative dualists believe the same thing about body and spirit. They affect each other. They are interrelated. But neither is reducible to the other. A person studying a tree swaying in the wind would want to make reference not only to the wind, but also to the biology and structure of trees.

13. This remains a hotly debated issue. Some would argue that there is no good use of weapons. Others have argued that one

good use of the scientific *development* of weapons is the deterrence of others' use of weapons. This topic is well beyond the scope of this book.

14. Richard Dawkins repeatedly disputes the idea that anybody who does not share his philosophy of naturalism could be respected as a top scientist. (He makes the argument, for example, starting on p. 99 of *The God Delusion*.) But his reasoning here, as elsewhere, is circular. Consider that in support of his claim that theists or nonnaturalists are not good scientists, his central piece of evidence seems to be that few religious people are in prestigious positions of science. But elsewhere he argues that anybody who does not hold to a philosophy of strict naturalism—that is, anybody who does not hold to his metaphysical presuppositions—should be removed from positions of responsibility because they can't possibly be good scientists. And that is precisely what has happened repeatedly in modern scientific establishments. As of December 2009, Dawkins boasted on his own website, richarddawkins.net, of his role in preventing Ben Stein from speaking at the 2009 University of Vermont commencement because Stein does not affirm causal closure with regard to the origins of life. In short, then, Dawkins claims philosophically that a nonnaturalist cannot be a good scientist, but then (using that definition of a good scientist) points out that there are no good scientists who are not naturalists.

15. Taliaferro, *Consciousness and the Mind of God*, 87.

16. C. S. Lewis, quoted by Clyde S. Kilby in *The Christian World of C. S. Lewis* (Grand Rapids: Eerdmans, 1964), 91.

17. Kilby, *The Christian World of C. S. Lewis*, 91.

18. While I share Lewis's form of integrative dualism, I disagree in part with what I understand to be his stance on this issue. Unlike Lewis, I would acknowledge that there is a place for experimentation on animals, including even vivisection. If an experiment on a laboratory rat, even cutting into a living one, would provide the knowledge necessary to save a human life, or even save a human from great suffering, I would permit that experiment. Indeed, as a member for several years of an Institutional Animal Care and Use Committee (IACUC), I helped approve many scientific experiments on animals at Middlebury College. Though, agreeing with Lewis, I (and our committee) also took great care to ensure that the approved experiments made every effort to eliminate or minimize suffering of the animals involved.

Index